The Republican Dilemma

The Republican Dilemma

Promoting Freedom in a Modern Society

LARS J. K. MOEN

OXFORD
UNIVERSITY PRESS

Oxford University Press is a department of the University of Oxford. It furthers the University's objective of excellence in research, scholarship, and education by publishing worldwide. Oxford is a registered trade mark of Oxford University Press in the UK and certain other countries.

Published in the United States of America by Oxford University Press
198 Madison Avenue, New York, NY 10016, United States of America.

© Oxford University Press 2024

All rights reserved. No part of this publication may be reproduced, stored in a retrieval system, or transmitted, in any form or by any means, without the prior permission in writing of Oxford University Press, or as expressly permitted by law, by license, or under terms agreed with the appropriate reproduction rights organization. Inquiries concerning reproduction outside the scope of the above should be sent to the Rights Department, Oxford University Press, at the address above.

You must not circulate this work in any other form
and you must impose this same condition on any acquirer.

Library of Congress Cataloging-in-Publication Data
Names: Moen, Lars J. K., author.
Title: The republican dilemma : promoting freedom in a modern society / by Lars J. K. Moen.
Description: New York : Oxford University Press, [2024] |
Includes bibliographical references and index.
Identifiers: LCCN 2023057104 (print) | LCCN 2023057105 (ebook) |
ISBN 9780197757024 (hardback) | ISBN 9780197757048 (epub)
Subjects: LCSH: Liberty—United States. | Republicanism—United States. |
Dominance (Psychology)—Political aspects. | Liberalism—United States. |
Interference (Perception)—Political aspects.
Classification: LCC JC599.U5 M64 2024 (print) | LCC JC599.U5 (ebook) |
DDC 323.0973—dc23/eng/20240203
LC record available at https://lccn.loc.gov/2023057104
LC ebook record available at https://lccn.loc.gov/2023057105

DOI: 10.1093/oso/9780197757024.001.0001

Printed by Integrated Books International, United States of America

To the cockatoos of Lake Ginninderra

Contents

Preface   xi

1. Introduction   1
   1.1 The dispute   1
   1.2 Two concepts of liberty   2
   1.3 The dimensions of freedom   5
   1.4 The republican dilemma   7
   1.5 History   10
   1.6 The road ahead   12

2. Scope   15
   2.1 Introduction   15
   2.2 Sources of unfreedom   16
       2.2.1 Freedom as non-frustration   16
       2.2.2 Freedom as non-interference   17
       2.2.3 Freedom as non-domination   20
   2.3 Freedom as an empirical concept   22
   2.4 Freedom as a moralized concept   24
       2.4.1 Political decision-making   25
       2.4.2 Priority to instruction   31
   2.5 The problems of moralizing   33
   2.6 Conclusion   35

3. Robustness   37
   3.1 Introduction   37
   3.2 Robustness   37
   3.3 Pure negative freedom   41
   3.4 Republican freedom   43
       3.4.1 Accessibility, not probability   43
       3.4.2 The impossibility objection   45
       3.4.3 The eyeball test   46
   3.5 Domination as interference   48
       3.5.1 Subjunctive prevention   49
       3.5.2 Threats   50
   3.6 "Liberation by ingratiation"   52
   3.7 The benevolent master   55
   3.8 Reducing scope   57
   3.9 Conclusion   58

viii CONTENTS

4. Public reason 61
   4.1 Introduction 61
   4.2 Political constructivism 62
   4.3 Republican reasonableness 65
   4.4 Popular control 66
   4.5 A consensus model of public justification 70
   4.6 Context-sensitivity 73
   4.7 The basic liberties 75
   4.8 A republican political conception 79
   4.9 Overall freedom and the basic liberties 82
   4.10 Conclusion 85

5. Ethos 87
   5.1 Introduction 87
   5.2 Institutional protection 88
   5.3 The formal interpretation 91
   5.4 The gentle giant 95
   5.5 Protection and common interests 96
   5.6 The insufficiency of legal protection 98
   5.7 The comprehensive interpretation 99
   5.8 Norms of virtue 101
   5.9 Two kinds of constraint 103
   5.10 Are good norms sufficient? 106
   5.11 Ethos and pure negative freedom 108
   5.12 Conclusion 110

6. Pluralism 112
   6.1 Introduction 112
   6.2 Strong and moderate interpretations 113
   6.3 Rawls and republican protection 115
   6.4 Specifying republican preferences 117
   6.5 Republicanism and neutrality 120
   6.6 Liberal constraints on virtue 124
   6.7 Pettit's rejection of active control 127
   6.8 Motivating active control 129
   6.9 Freedom and efficiency 131
   6.10 Conclusion 132

7. Ideal 135
   7.1 Introduction 135
   7.2 The two approaches 136
   7.3 Constraints 140
      7.3.1 Personal prerogative 141
      7.3.2 Publicity 144
   7.4 Consequentialism 146

7.5	In defense of evaluative claims	149
7.6	Critical republicanism	153
7.7	Conclusion	157

8.	Conclusion	158
8.1	Republican trade-offs	158
8.2	Political liberal republicanism	159
8.3	Rhetoric	161
8.4	Analyzing moralized concepts	162

Notes	165
Bibliography	195
Index	203

Preface

This book is my attempt to provide a much-needed critical assessment of republicanism in contemporary political philosophy. There are several books defending and formulating the republican theory and its central concept of freedom as non-domination. Many have also written critically about the theory, its freedom concept, and its alleged distinction from liberalism. But this book offers the first book-length critical treatment of these issues. The aim is to position contemporary republicanism in political philosophy—to show what it is, what it is not, and what it can be.

Republicanism is presented by its defenders as a superior alternative to liberal theories with a prominent standing in the academic discipline. We are told this is especially due to the republican concept of freedom as non-domination, which is said to give us a more attractive basis for a normative political theory than does the liberal concept of freedom as non-interference. This claim is widely accepted, but this book demonstrates how it is a result of inaccurate conceptual analysis. The two freedom concepts are no doubt different, as the absence of interference does not mean absence of domination. But we shall see that regardless of which concept we apply, we can make the same judgments regarding how to promote freedom in a society. The institutions we take to promote non-interference will then equally promote non-domination. This result questions the status of republicanism as a distinct contribution to contemporary political philosophy, and I show how the institutional arrangement of Philip Pettit's republicanism turns out to fit well within the framework of John Rawls's liberalism.

A distinct republican position remains possible, however. Republicans consider people to be free insofar as they live under institutions constrained so as to reliably promote the common good. The book shows how a liberal understanding of the common good leads republicans to a liberal theory promoting freedom as non-interference. But with a more restrictive conception of the common good, one that puts more emphasis on citizens' political participation, republicans can break from liberalism and freedom as non-interference. On this view, republicans regard only highly virtuous citizens as truly free. The price to pay for this distinctly republican view of

xii PREFACE

freedom, however, is that it becomes too restrictive as an ideal to pursue in a large modern society where citizens hold a wide variety of conceptions of the good.

This is the republican dilemma: republicans can present freedom as non-domination as an ideal well suited for modern society, but then they end up with a liberal theory promoting freedom as non-interference. Or they can reject liberalism and freedom as non-interference, but then their freedom ideal becomes unsuited for modern conditions. Taking the latter horn of the dilemma, gives republicans a critical perspective that can give insight into the dangers of a liberal acceptance of politically inactive citizens.

I was first introduced to republicanism as a student in Martin Wilkinson's excellent undergraduate class on freedom at the University of Auckland. Martin was critical of the republican theory and especially its freedom concept. I was unsure, but Martin had made me interested, and I wanted to explore the matter further. I therefore went to the Australian National University to work on a PhD thesis with Keith Dowding, who is a critic of republicanism, and with Philip Pettit, who is undoubtedly the most prominent republican in contemporary political philosophy. I was extremely fortunate with my choice of supervisors. Keith, my main supervisor, read and commented on all my papers and chapter drafts, and he did an outstanding job helping me see where improvements were needed and which ideas to keep and which to discard. Philip also offered important feedback, especially by making sure I did not misrepresent his views. Much due to his help, I believe I have formulated a critical but fair treatment of republicanism.

The book is in large part a result of the work I did in a highly stimulating research environment in Canberra. But I have continued to develop my assessment of republicanism also after I completed my doctoral thesis. In this more recent work, I have especially benefited from sharp, insightful comments from Ian Carter, a first-rate philosopher of freedom. Ian examined my thesis and gave me several pages of detailed comments in addition to the report he was required to write. Thanks to his written feedback and the conversations we have had, I am convinced I have made significant improvements since I completed my PhD project.

I am also grateful to several other friends and colleagues for helpful discussions. They include Nick Barry, Matteo Boccacci, Will Bosworth, Geoff Brennan, Justin Bruner, Devon Cass, Annalisa Costella, Simon Cotton, Michael Garnett, Jessica Genauer, Niels de Haan, Ed Handby, Ilkin Huseynli, Elena Icardi, Matthew Kramer, Henrik Kugelberg, Leonie Möck, Alex

Oprea, Tom Parr, Céline Pieters, Stan Richard, Hallvard Sandven, Ronen Shnayderman, Michael Smith, Zofia Stemplowska, Zach Storms, and John Uhr. I also thank the two reviewers for Oxford University Press for their helpful reports. Last but not least, I thank my parents and two sisters for the interest they have taken in my research over the years I have attempted to do political philosophy.

1

Introduction

1.1 The dispute

The revival of the ancient ideal of republican freedom as non-domination has been widely celebrated as an important contribution to political philosophy in recent decades.[1] Its proponents understand it to possess the unique quality of illuminating a highly important problem in any society, namely the constraining effect of living under the oppressive power of agents capable of punishing you for not behaving in accordance with their desires. This is the problem of domination, which we find in relationships such as that between an employee and an employer in the absence of labor regulations, a wife and her husband where there are no laws against spousal abuse, and a slave and his master in a society where one person can legally be another's property.[2] The problem of such relationships is not just the powerful party's actually interfering with the unprotected party, but also the unrestricted capacity to interfere. This capacity means the weaker, vulnerable party will be constantly aware of what might happen should he act contrary to the wishes of his more powerful counterpart.[3]

Virtually everyone finds such domination morally appalling and will argue for institutions protecting individuals against ending up in a position of such vulnerability. Most of us will also think being subject to domination involves a loss of freedom. Yet, republicans argue, mainstream liberalism is based on a freedom ideal that fails to capture this widely held intuition. Liberalism is founded on the idea that individuals are separate persons that should not be interfered with, and liberals commonly understand freedom as the absence of interference. This is where liberals get it all wrong, according to the republicans. By taking the source of unfreedom to be interference, not domination, liberals' freedom concept fails to capture the constraining effect of being subjected to someone's uncontrolled power. Social institutions promoting liberal freedom therefore protect individuals against interference, but they do nothing to protect individuals against the vulnerability they experience in relationships of domination.

The Republican Dilemma. Lars J. K. Moen, Oxford University Press. © Oxford University Press 2024.
DOI: 10.1093/oso/9780197757024.003.0001

2 THE REPUBLICAN DILEMMA

This crude sketch of republican and liberal freedom is the story republicans tell to show how their freedom concept is the more attractive of the two.[4] Domination is clearly a source of unfreedom, and freedom is therefore better understood as the absence of domination rather than the absence of interference. Failing to recognize this important republican insight has led liberals to endorse what some republicans consider an "impoverished"[5] and "absurd"[6] concept of liberty.[7] Liberalism is said to be better served by adopting the richer concept of freedom as non-domination.

But many liberals remain hesitant. While sharing the intuition that the employee, spouse, and slave in the relationships just mentioned have less freedom by virtue of their status, they think a conception of freedom as interference can capture this intuition. We can regard domination as freedom-reducing without defining freedom as non-domination. Ian Carter and Matthew Kramer defend purely negative accounts of freedom that count physical prevention as the only source of an agent's unfreedom. And they argue that pure negative freedom can give us all we want in the measurement of freedom.[8] Republicans can set up institutions to protect individuals against domination, but the resulting gains of freedom can be captured in terms of pure negative freedom. Without claiming that republican and pure negative freedom are one and the same concept—they are clearly different— Carter and Kramer argue that these differences are irrelevant when it comes to judging how free a given person or society is, or how we ought to set up our political and social institutions to promote freedom. Freedom as non-domination, therefore, gives us nothing of importance we do not get from a liberal concept of freedom as non-interference.

1.2 Two concepts of liberty

I shall explore this debate in order to clarify whether or not reviving freedom as non-domination really does provide an important normative consideration not captured in freedom as non-interference. I shall focus on the most thoroughly defined versions of each of these freedom concepts, which I take to be Philip Pettit's conception of republican freedom and Carter, Kramer, and Hillel Steiner's pure negative freedom.[9] I explore each of these concepts in depth especially in Chapters 2 and 3. Here I shall only provide crude sketches of the two.

First, on Pettit's republican account, you are free to the extent that you can make choices knowing, with sufficiently high probability, that you could have pursued any of your other available options without having been interfered with in a way you have not yourself instructed.[10] You can choose any available option without fear of the consequences of not satisfying the wishes of some more powerful agent.[11] In this position, you can go about leading your life without feeling anxious about the prospect of suffering interference that is not under your own control. Pettit previously referred to such interference as "arbitrary interference," but in later works, he uses the term "uncontrolled interference."[12] He now also refers to the power possessed by an agent capable of uncontrolled interference as "uncontrolled" rather than "arbitrary." I shall use this the more recent terminology and distinguish between controlled and uncontrolled power or interference.

According to the concept of pure negative freedom, on the other hand, you are free to perform an action if and only if no other agent makes it physically impossible for you to do so. It is important to note that prevention need not be actual; it can also be subjunctive.[13] That is, while you are made unfree to perform an action, x, whenever an agent actually prevents you from doing so, you are also unfree to do x when someone will prevent you from doing x if you try to do x. I make you just as unfree to leave the room by locking the door only if you attempt to leave as if I have already locked the door.

I shall focus only on preventions by other agents as a source of unfreedom.[14] I thereby ignore accounts of negative freedom treating any hindrance of ability as a source of unfreedom.[15] I consequently treat pure negative freedom as a social relation: you can only be made unfree by other agents' prevention, not by your mere inability.[16] Like republican freedom, then, pure negative freedom, as I shall understand it, is a social, or political, concept.

A crucial distinction in the pure negative account of freedom is between specific and overall freedom. When no one prevents you from performing a particular action, you have a *specific* freedom to perform that action. You are therefore either free or unfree in this specific sense.[17] Freedom in this sense, then, is a count-noun, as you can count the number of specific freedoms a person has. *Overall* freedom, on the other hand, comes in degrees, as it indicates the number of combinations of specific freedoms you can exercise conjunctively. Thus understood, freedom is a mass-noun. When pure negative freedom theorists ask *how free* people are, they refer to this notion of overall freedom. To illustrate the difference between specific and overall

4 THE REPUBLICAN DILEMMA

freedom, suppose I credibly threaten you at time t by saying that if you do x rather than y, I shall force you to do z instead of w in your subsequent choice situation. In that case, you remain free at t to perform any of these actions, but not to do both x at t and w at $t + 1$. By accounting for the probability of the threat being enforced were you to do x, pure negative freedom theorists measure the loss of your overall freedom due to my interference.

Pettit identifies two main differences between republican and pure negative freedom. First, while pure negative freedom theorists think any prevention makes you unfree, republicans say you are made unfree only by interference you do not control. Pettit calls this first distinguishing feature "interference without domination."[18] The second feature is "domination without interference," which occurs when you are vulnerable to uncontrolled interference but the interference never materializes.[19] While republicans take such domination to make you unfree, they believe pure negative freedom theorists fail to do so, since no prevention has actually taken place.

We shall see that this attempt to distinguish republican freedom from pure negative freedom is problematic. First, while it is true that interference always makes you unfree to perform the action you are prevented from doing, it might enhance your overall freedom by giving you opportunities you otherwise would not have had. We shall indeed see how the kind of interference that is not treated as a source of unfreedom on the republican account can enhance pure negative overall freedom. This issue is central especially in Chapters 2 and 4.

Second, while your non-interfering dominator does not actually interfere with you, she can still do so subjunctively—that is, she will prevent you from performing the action were you to try. The threat of her interference might also reduce your overall freedom, as it restricts your set of combinations of actions you can perform in conjunction with not pleasing your dominator. I go deeper into this issue in Chapters 3 and 5.

These are, at any rate, crudely Carter and Kramer's responses to Pettit's arguments for the distinctiveness of republican freedom on the basis of interference without domination and domination without interference. They go on to conclude that we can make the same judgments about the extent to which people are free whether we define freedom in the republican or the pure negative way.[20] As Carter says, the pure negative view of freedom "implies comparative judgments about people's freedom that are, to all intents and purposes, equivalent to those comparative judgments implied by [Pettit's] republican view of freedom."[21]

This is Carter's "equivalent-judgments thesis." We can disagree about the definition of freedom, Carter says, but nonetheless "give very similar answers to questions like 'Who is freer than whom?,' 'Has this person's freedom been reduced?,' and 'How is freedom distributed in society?.'"[22] If the equivalent-judgments thesis is sound, any loss or gain in republican freedom will be a loss or a gain in pure negative freedom, and vice versa. Republicans would consequently be mistaken to think promoting republican freedom differs from promoting pure negative freedom. The equivalent-judgments thesis will remain at the core of my comparison of republican and pure negative freedom that runs throughout the book. I shall return to the questions just mentioned to test whether republicans have found, or can point toward, a measurement of freedom that differs from that of the pure negative freedom theorists.

If Carter's equivalent-judgments thesis holds, then republicans have failed in their attempt to reveal significant shortcomings in pure negative freedom as an important political ideal. Republicanism and its ideal of non-domination will then offer us nothing we do not get from a liberal theory based on freedom from interference.[23]

1.3 The dimensions of freedom

Throughout the book, I shall search for differences in the two freedom concepts with practical implications that can falsify the equivalent-judgments thesis. This process starts with an analysis and comparison of the two concepts in which I place them along two dimensions of freedom. By drawing on work by Pettit and Christian List, I identify scope and robustness dimensions, along each of which republican freedom and pure negative freedom occupy different positions.[24]

Scope refers to the extent to which freedom is defined to require the absence of interference. In a classic paper, Gerald MacCallum treats freedom as a triadic relation, where "x is (is not) free from y to do (not do, become, not become) z."[25] x here refers to an agent, y to a constraint, restriction, or interference, while z refers to an action. I associate scope with the y variable in MacCallum's formula because the literature on republican freedom focuses on the type of constraint with which freedom is compatible. Alternatively, scope could concern the actions an agent must be unprevented from performing. A reduction in scope, as I here understand it, means a narrower

6 THE REPUBLICAN DILEMMA

range of kinds of interference that count as constraints on freedom. By identifying some kinds of interference that do not make an agent unfree, we therefore reduce the scope of freedom. A definition of freedom has maximal scope if and only if it treats any interference as a source of unfreedom. Pure negative freedom is compromised by any kind of interference and therefore has maximal scope. Republican freedom, on the other hand, is not compromised by interference the agent interfered with controls and therefore has a lesser scope.

Robustness concerns how extensive protection against interference a definition of freedom requires. Protection against interference is measured in terms of the probability of an agent, A, succeeding in interfering with another agent, B, conditional on A trying to interfere. If we say that B's freedom to perform an action, x, depends on B to a certain extent being protected against A interfering with B doing x, then we make our definition of freedom robust to that extent. If we say that B is free to do x whenever she can do x, regardless of how well protected he is, we give freedom minimal robustness. If we say that B's freedom to do x depends on A having been made unable to interfere, then we give freedom maximal robustness. Pure negative freedom has minimal robustness, since it takes B to be free to do x whenever A does not prevent him from doing x.[26] To be free to do x in the republican sense, however, B must be protected against A's interference to a certain extent— that is, institutions must be in place to make it difficult for A to interfere, but not impossible. In Chapter 3, I explore in depth to what extent republican freedom requires institutional protection.

Crucially, scope and robustness are inversely related, so that by enhancing the robustness of our definition of freedom, we must reduce its scope, and vice versa. A trade-off between the two dimensions is therefore unavoidable in a definition of freedom.[27] Reducing scope for the sake of robustness means the interference with people that protects them against each other's interference does not make them unfree. Conversely, reducing robustness for the sake of scope means treating this interference as a source of unfreedom.

While any interference is a source of pure negative unfreedom, pure negative freedom theorists can justify interference if it enhances overall freedom—that is, if it enables individuals to pursue a wider range of different courses of action. While B is free to do x if he can do x, protecting him against A interfering with his doing x could nonetheless enhance B's overall freedom by enabling him to perform other actions in conjunction with x. Pure negative freedom and republican freedom's different positions along

INTRODUCTION   7

the two dimensions will have no practical implications if republican robustness mirrors the protective measures required for promoting pure negative overall freedom.

I shall eventually form the view that we avoid this conclusion—we separate the promotion of republican freedom from the promotion of pure negative freedom—by making the robustness of republican freedom sufficiently great, and its scope correspondingly small, to protect individuals against interference beyond what is required for maximizing their number of conjunctively exercisable actions. In return, the actions they can perform will be more robustly exercisable. Republicans can treat interference for the purpose of such protection as uncontrolled interference that does not compromise freedom. An individual with a small but well-protected opportunity set might therefore enjoy greater republican freedom, but less pure negative freedom, than an individual with a larger but less protected opportunity set. This is how republicans can falsify Carter's equivalent-judgments thesis.

We shall see, however, that this is not how Pettit defines republican freedom. On his account, the trade-off point lies at greater scope and less robustness than does a definition of republican freedom that enables a distinctly republican promotion of freedom. Carter is therefore right to say the equivalent-judgments thesis holds with respect to Pettit's freedom concept. He does not, however, consider whether it could be falsified by other conceptions of republican freedom.

1.4 The republican dilemma

Pettit has good reasons for making his scope–robustness trade-off. Enhancing the robustness and, correspondingly, reducing the scope of freedom is to make more interference compatible with freedom. Promoting a version of republican freedom with lesser scope would therefore involve making people commit to a narrower behavioral pattern than what they would be afforded under the promotion of pure negative freedom. Promoting republican freedom would consequently mean greater restrictions on the set of permissible ways of life.

Now, such restrictions for the sake of protection might gain support in societies where people would in any case voluntarily conform to a distinctly republican way of life. But in more pluralistic societies, such as our own, this interpretation of republican freedom looks rather unattractive. The first horn

8 THE REPUBLICAN DILEMMA

of the republican dilemma is therefore that we can distinguish the promotion of republican freedom from the promotion of pure negative freedom only by making the former an unappealing ideal for society as it is. The second horn, conversely, is that we can make republican freedom an attractive ideal, but we must then accept the equivalent-judgments thesis.

In arguing that republicans must face this dilemma, I reach a similar conclusion to Geoffrey Brennan and Loren Lomasky when they argue that "[e]ither republicanism is non-threatening [to liberalism] because it is little more than a somewhat archaic rhetorical skin for a body of modern liberalism or, if substantively distancing itself from liberal precepts, is overtly oppressive to a troubling degree."[28] Either republicanism is a liberal theory that respects the diverse interests of individual citizens, or it demands that people take part in public life as active citizens whether they want to or not.

By insisting on both republican freedom's compatibility with pluralism and its incompatibility with the promotion of pure negative freedom, Pettit and other republicans give no decisive response to the dilemma. However, Pettit accepts that his republicanism is a liberal theory and says it could be appropriately named "republican liberalism or liberal republicanism."[29] This view seems to obviously conflict with his early understanding of "republicanism" as an alternative to "liberalism."[30] But as he says in his more recent work, there is no conflict between his republicanism and "left-of-centre liberalism." The conflict is with "classical liberalism," he says.[31] This later formulation is sensible especially because of the central role the basic liberties play in Pettit's theory. A person robustly enjoying the capacity to exercise the basic liberties is paradigmatically free from domination. And as we shall see in Chapter 4, Pettit gives the basic liberties their special place on the same grounds as John Rawls, the most prominent liberal theorist of the twentieth century. There it will also become clear that Pettit's republicanism is very similar to Rawls's political liberalism.[32]

So, Pettit denies the existence of the dilemma by taking his freedom ideal not to call for the promotion of pure negative freedom, while at the same time incorporating a liberal neutrality between the various conceptions of the good life in a modern society. He indeed sees republican freedom as a more plausible basis for a liberal theory than pure negative freedom—or any other conception of freedom based on the idea of non-interference or non-prevention—which he thinks of as a basis for libertarianism, not liberalism.[33] Freedom as non-interference, he argues, is no basis for liberalism, at

INTRODUCTION   9

least not before it has been traded off against other values, especially equality. Freedom as non-domination, on the other hand, provides a complete basis for a liberal-republican theory by itself. But this view is highly problematic, especially, as we shall see in Chapter 2, because republican freedom, unlike pure negative freedom, is not basic but is instead based on a normative theory. We need the theory before we can say what republican freedom is, and the freedom concept therefore cannot be the fundamental building block Pettit takes it to be.

In correspondence with accepting that his theory is liberal, and with his view that freedom as non-interference is a libertarian rather than liberal ideal, Pettit has in his later work abandoned the term "liberal freedom" and instead named the freedom concept he opposes "neo-liberal or libertarian."[34] Promoting this kind of freedom, he says, means implementing a market economy within which the government is to only enforce contracts individuals enter into voluntarily.[35] Government interference necessarily takes away freedom on this libertarian account, and should therefore be limited to the minimal role of only protecting private property. On the republican account, however, government interference does not reduce citizens' freedom as long as it is forced to promote their common interests. With freedom as non-interference thus understood, the equivalent-judgments thesis is no doubt false.

It is equally clear, however, that what Pettit calls "neo-liberal or libertarian" freedom is not pure negative freedom. Enforcing private property rights might actually involve significant government interference, as G. A. Cohen shows in his critique of Robert Nozick's libertarianism.[36] Enforcing one person's private property right in a certain resource means preventing everyone else from using that resource.[37] To say that a libertarian minimal government promotes non-interference is therefore highly questionable. It certainly cannot be asserted without empirical evidence. The same holds for the claim that minimizing interference involves stimulating a market economy. An anarchic society with no state and no market economy might be where people enjoy maximal pure negative freedom. Collective ownership in a sharing economy might, under certain conditions, give people more unhindered opportunities than does an economy in which the enforcement of private property rights prevents everyone but the right holder from making use of the property. After all, if resources were held in common, no one would be prevented from using them (except when others are actually using them).

10 THE REPUBLICAN DILEMMA

Here republicans might respond that republican freedom necessarily requires a state that protects citizens from uncontrolled interference. However, as we shall see especially in Chapter 5, republican freedom must depend on informal institutions, such as social norms. To the extent that republicans categorically insist on the presence of institutional protection, even when its establishment and maintenance will reduce the number of actions people can perform, they impose restrictions on which ends people can pursue in the name of freedom. While such a demanding protection requirement conflicts with pure negative freedom, we shall see that it also conflicts with Pettit's republican freedom.

1.5 History

Contemporary republicans are keen to emphasize the differences between two traditions of political thought both commonly referred to as republican.[38] The first is associated with communitarianism and is built around the idea that being free is to be a citizen actively participating in her or his political community. By not participating in politics, one is not governing oneself, and is therefore under the control of others. Freedom, on this account, is therefore self-mastery or self-government. This idea conflicts with liberal neutrality toward the plurality of conceptions of the good life that characterizes modern society.[39] This theory is known by many names, including "civic humanism,"[40] as well as "neo-Athenian,"[41] "Franco-German,"[42] or "Continental"[43] republicanism. It is commonly associated with Aristotle and Jean-Jacques Rousseau, and more recently with Hannah Arendt, Charles Taylor, and Michael Sandel.

My focus is on the other republican tradition, which has received much attention in recent decades, especially due to Pettit and Quentin Skinner. This is the "neo-Roman"[44] or "Italian-Atlantic"[45] tradition. Its roots go back to Ancient Rome, and its ideas can be found in works of Italian Renaissance writers, such as Niccolò Machiavelli, British republicans of the seventeenth century, including James Harrington and John Milton, and proponents of American independence from Britain in the eighteenth century.[46] The core ideal here, Pettit explains, is the Ancient Roman legal status of a free person, who is living *sui juris*—that is, "under his own jurisdiction." The free person is not under *potestate domini* ("the power of a master") and does not make decisions *cum permissu* ("with permission").[47]

INTRODUCTION 11

This ideal is well suited for a modern society, in Pettit's view, because it promotes no particular conception of the good, but instead protects citizens' capacity to exercise the basic liberties. Political participation is instrumentally important to ensure this protection against groups or individuals that would otherwise come to dominate the rest, but it is not itself a part of the ideal. This makes republicanism look compatible with Rawlsian political liberalism, which is neutral between reasonable conceptions of the good. Rawls himself indeed notes that "[n]othing in classical republicanism is incompatible with political liberalism."[48]

Republicans have emphasized the important differences between the two republican traditions in response to critics they have accused of getting them mixed up. Responding to Brennan and Lomasky's arguments "against reviving republicanism," Pettit argues they fail to see republicanism's important contribution to contemporary liberalism because they focus on the version that idealizes a particular conception of the good, and not the one that is neutral between conceptions of the good.[49] Pettit therefore responds quickly and dismissively to their charge against republicanism: the kind of republicanism they see as "oppressive to a troubling degree" is not his kind of republicanism. I shall focus strictly on the tradition Pettit and Skinner take themselves to adhere to by giving active political participation no more than instrumental importance with respect to republican freedom. I nonetheless show that the problematic illiberal element that Brennan and Lomasky identify will persist insofar as republicans want to avoid the equivalent-judgments thesis.

I shall have very little to say about Roman law or how freedom has been understood in past centuries and millennia. The approach I take is philosophical rather than historical, as I consider the concept of republican freedom as it is defined in contemporary political philosophy and how it compares to the contemporary conception of pure negative freedom. I shall not discuss how true this definition, or my interpretation of it, is to the more than two-thousand-year-old republican tradition. I thereby treat republican freedom as Pettit intends it to be treated. His republicanism is not an exercise of intellectual history, he says. The normative claims he defends by appealing to republican freedom "should not be judged by historical criteria . . . but rather by philosophical."[50]

Nor shall I go into Pettit's criticism of the use of "libertarian," "liberal," or "neo-liberal" freedom in past centuries. He frequently points out that it has been used to defend mistreatment of both workers and women and to

12 THE REPUBLICAN DILEMMA

oppose American independence, thus serving a purpose freedom as non-domination never could have performed.[51] I shall have nothing to say about how figures of past centuries may have used the freedom term to serve their questionable political agendas. I focus on the contemporary conception of pure negative freedom, and I cannot see how it could serve such a purpose.

1.6 The road ahead

The book follows a series of steps toward the conclusion that we do indeed make equivalent judgments about freedom whether we define it as pure negative freedom or as Pettit's version of republican freedom, and that a distinctly republican freedom ideal is more restrictive and demanding than Pettit's formulation.

In Chapters 2 and 3, I clarify the conceptual differences between republican freedom and pure negative freedom by placing them along the scope and robustness dimensions. While it is easy to see that the two concepts are different, placing them along these dimensions will help us see how they might pick out different aspects of social relations as sources of unfreedom. Detecting such differences is the key to seeing how the equivalent-judgments thesis can be falsified.

In Chapter 2, I focus on the scope dimension. I show that pure negative freedom has maximal scope since it treats any prevention imposed by another agent as a source of unfreedom. Republican freedom, on the other hand, takes a more moderate position by treating interference as a source of unfreedom if and only if it has not been instructed by the agent interfered with. At the collective, or political, level, such instructions are expressed in the people's common interests. This reduction in scope need not, however, lead to a difference in freedom judgments, since the republican scope reduction moralizes the definition freedom, thus making it plausible that interference in accordance with common interests correlates with interference for the sake of pure negative overall freedom.

We get a better sense of how republicans can make distinct freedom judgments when we consider the protection against interference the two concepts require. In Chapter 3, I show how scope and robustness are inversely related. Pure negative freedom is minimally robust, since an agent is free to perform an action, x, on this account, as long as no one prevents him from doing x. The maximal scope of pure negative freedom makes it incompatible with no more than minimal robustness, since the protection against interference involved in enhancing robustness itself involves interference. Republican freedom, on the other hand, has a lesser scope and can therefore require more robust protection. It does so by treating the interference that contributes to the protection of actions remaining within the scope as compatible with freedom. However, pure negative freedom theorists can justify interference for the sake of protection against interference if and only if it enhances overall freedom. To falsify the equivalent-judgments thesis, republicans must therefore enhance freedom's robustness requirement, and reduce scope correspondingly, beyond the level compatible with maximizing pure negative overall freedom.

In Chapter 4, I enter a less abstract and more practical part of the book. This chapter makes sense of the scope of Pettit's freedom concept by exploring his idea of the common interests he treats as the people's instructions to their government. Insofar as the government acts on these instructions, its interference will not make any citizen unfree. I show how the procedure Pettit employs to identify common interests is indistinguishable from Rawls's political constructivism. By taking the citizens of a modern, pluralistic society as they are, this procedure constructs a liberal conception of the common good that is particularly concerned with ensuring everyone's capacity to exercise the basic liberties. This conception, I argue, is compatible with the promotion of pure negative freedom. Pettit consequently ties his freedom concept to Rawlsian political liberalism, which promotes pure negative freedom.

In Chapter 5, I consider the practical implications of different positions along the robustness dimension. Here we begin to see the problems of defining the scope of freedom in terms of common interests, as identified by Pettit. I distinguish between two understandings of institutional protection against interference: formal and comprehensive. Formal institutions include the legal and coercive bodies of political construction, such as courts, parliaments, and laws. Formal institutions are a subset of the set of all comprehensive institutions, which also includes informal institutions, most importantly social norms. I show that on either understanding of institutional protection, republican freedom with Pettit's scope requires no more robust protection than does pure negative freedom. Strengthening the protection beyond the optimal level with respect to the promotion of pure negative overall freedom would involve institutions that are more constraining on people's behavior than is compatible with their common interests, as Pettit understands them. The scope of Pettit's freedom concept consequently

14 THE REPUBLICAN DILEMMA

prevents the level of robust protection necessary for falsifying the equivalent-judgments thesis.

In Chapter 6, I make sense of what it would mean to enhance robustness so as to enable republicans to make freedom judgments that conflict with those of pure negative freedom theorists. It involves undermining the pluralism that characterizes modern society in order to make citizens devoted to a distinctly republican way of life. They must conform to a particular conception of the good that they make sure their government promotes by committing to a high level of vigilance. Should their government deviate from this task, the virtuous citizens will notice and contest it. These citizens will enjoy much freedom in what I shall call a "strong republican" sense because of their firm protection against uncontrolled use of government power.

Common interests in such a conformist society are, of course, very different from any tolerant view of common interests in a large and diverse modern society. And trying to shape people's preferences so as to move toward this ideal of "strong republicanism" seems unappealing. The means required for such a transition would probably conflict with most people's intuitive understanding of "freedom." This is nonetheless the freedom concept republicans must adopt to make freedom judgments that conflict with those of pure negative freedom theorists.

However, the strong republican freedom ideal need not be entirely useless in contemporary political theorizing. In Chapter 7, I show that an ideal need not be an attractive target under current circumstances to play a role in evaluating these circumstances. Strong republicans may accept that transitioning toward their ideal society would involve too much intrusion in the lives of ordinary citizens, but they can nonetheless use their freedom ideal to evaluate and criticize the non-republican preferences of their fellow citizens. More generally, taking this approach is to use political ideals to see not just what we ought to aim for, all things considered, but also what we do not have, and what we inevitably forgo in political decision-making. A republicanism that conflicts with the promotion of pure negative freedom might be unattractive because of the way modern society is constituted, but that does not mean we should forget about it.

2

Scope

2.1 Introduction

This chapter focuses on the scope of republican freedom and pure negative freedom. Scope refers to the extent to which freedom is defined so as to require that an agent experiences no interference. As I note in the introduction, I take scope to concern the y variable in MacCallum's triadic formula, as it expresses the extent to which interference is compatible with a particular conception of freedom. Scope is the measure of the number of kinds of interference freedom is compatible, or incompatible, with. By understanding any act of interference to make you unfree, we have given freedom maximal scope.[1] The fewer kinds of interference a conception of freedom is compatible with, the greater is the scope of that conception of freedom.[2]

I show how republican freedom and pure negative freedom take different positions along the scope dimension. I scrutinize Pettit's reasons for preferring the smaller scope of republican freedom to the larger one of pure negative freedom and argue that the republican scope restriction causes problems that do not occur with the maximal scope of pure negative freedom.

I further show why the difference in scope between the two freedom concepts need not falsify the equivalent-judgments thesis. The reason is that republicans may plausibly restrict the scope so as to make all interference necessary for promoting pure negative overall freedom compatible with their understanding of freedom. While pure negative freedom theorists see any act of interference as a loss of a specific freedom, they can understand such a loss to enhance overall freedom. They can therefore make the same judgments as republicans about comparisons of different agents' freedom, about the extent to which freedom has been reduced, and about how freedom is distributed.

The Republican Dilemma. Lars J. K. Moen, Oxford University Press. © Oxford University Press 2024.
DOI: 10.1093/oso/9780197757024.003.0002

16   THE REPUBLICAN DILEMMA

2.2 Sources of unfreedom

Different freedom concepts typically identify different sources of unfreedom. They conflict with respect to whether or not all constraints imposed by other agents make an agent unfree, and what type of constraint makes an agent unfree. The wider the range of constraints understood to make an agent unfree, the greater is the scope of freedom. By understanding all constraints as sources of unfreedom, we give our definition of freedom maximal scope.

In this section, I distinguish among three freedom concepts: freedom from frustration, from interference, and from domination. I show why Pettit thinks differences in scope make non-interference superior to non-frustration and non-domination superior to non-interference.[3] The process starts with what he calls freedom as non-frustration, whose problems are remedied in freedom as non-interference.[4] But Pettit finds problems also with freedom as non-interference. Solving these problems, he argues, takes us to freedom as non-domination.

2.2.1 Freedom as non-frustration

On the account of freedom as non-frustration, you are free in a choice as long as no external hindrance stops you from choosing your preferred option. In other words, freedom requires that you can do what you want to do. Removing other, less desirable options has no impact on your freedom as long as the option you prefer remains available. This account of freedom is associated with Stoicism and with Thomas Hobbes. In response to John Bramhall's view that a person is not free to choose whether or not to play tennis if the door to the tennis court is locked, Hobbes argues that "it is no impediment to him that the door is shut till he have a will to play."[5] Unless the person has formed the will to play tennis, the locked door does not make him unfree to do so. On this view, the scope of freedom is minimal, since only one type of interference can make you unfree: the interference preventing you from doing what you prefer to do.

The minimal scope of freedom as non-frustration is the reason why it is widely considered an implausible account of freedom. Isaiah Berlin rejects freedom as non-frustration by showing how it implies that you can liberate yourself by adapting your preferences so as to prefer whatever options you are left with after having been constrained.[6] Suppose a prisoner successfully makes himself prefer the external limitations the prison guard imposes on his opportunity set. The prisoner's choice is not frustrated if he prefers life behind bars to life outside of the prison. But to say the prisoner is therefore free seems implausible and gives us reason to think non-frustration is not the right way to conceptualize freedom. Such adaptation might be a good strategy for dealing with a difficult situation, and it might be sensible for policymakers under conditions of scarcity to give priority to protecting options citizens are more likely to prefer, but it is a mistake to understand these strategies as liberating.

Any attraction of freedom as non-frustration appears to be based on a failure to recognize J. P. Day's distinction between *being free* and *feeling free*.[7] You may feel free as long as your desires are not frustrated, but you will not actually be free if you have adapted your preferences to the options others have left you with.

2.2.2 Freedom as non-interference

Berlin proposes a conception of freedom that is insensitive to whether a person *feels* free or not and incompatible with the idea that you can liberate yourself by adapting your preferences in response to constraints. On Berlin's account, freedom "consists in the absence of obstacles not merely to my actual, but to my potential, choices." It is, he says, "the absence of obstacles to possible choices and activities."[8] For Berlin, you are made unfree by someone's interference to the extent that it makes it more difficult or costly for you to choose an option in your opportunity set.[9] Suppose B has three options, x, y, and z. If A makes it harder or more costly for B to choose any of these options, A makes B less free in that choice. Unlike on the Hobbesian account, it does not matter whether B adapts to A's constraint and comes to prefer it. For Berlin, freedom requires that your options remain unobstructed regardless of whether you want them or not. If an option is taken away from you, you are made unfree. It does not matter whether you prefer that option or not.

Berlin illustrates how interference affects your freedom in a choice where the options are doors. How many doors there are and how open they are determine how free you are to choose among them.[10] Which one you decide to enter does not matter; you are made just as unfree when a door you do not want to enter, as when a door you do want to enter, is locked. And you are less

18 THE REPUBLICAN DILEMMA

free if the door is made hard to open. So, how many doors are accessible and how accessible they are determine how free you are. Berlin would presumably consider it less desirable to find the door he wants to enter obstructed than one he would not have entered in any case, but that has no relevance in terms of his conception of freedom as non-interference.

By treating any kind of interference as a source of unfreedom, Berlin and others understanding freedom as non-interference give freedom maximal scope and avoid freedom as non-frustration's problem of being compatible with a free prisoner. It does not matter whether the prisoner prefers being imprisoned to not being imprisoned. What matters is that imprisonment necessarily comes with constraints on the prisoner's opportunity set, and these constraints make him unfree no matter how well he adapts to his circumstances.

While Berlin sees interference as the act of making an option less accessible, we can define interference differently and consequently get a different conception of freedom as non-interference. Pettit includes mental obstacles as well as physical ones in his definition of interference.[11] Since deception and manipulation negatively affect their target's cognitive ability to choose according to his own will, they count as interference, on Pettit's account. A manipulates B by perverting B's preferences, beliefs, or ability to act or decide, thus denying him options otherwise available to him.[12] Even if B ends up choosing the option he in any case would have chosen, the manipulation or deception nonetheless restricts his ability to choose. Successful manipulation or deception makes options appear to be different from what they in fact are and imposes cognitive restrictions on B's ability to choose. Pettit further defines interference as an *intentional* constraint on another's choice.[13] On this understanding, freedom as non-interference does not have maximal scope, since one kind of restriction would not count as a source of unfreedom.

I shall use neither Pettit nor Berlin's definition of interference, since the account of freedom as interference I focus on is pure negative freedom. I explore this position more in depth in Section 2.3. Here I merely note that it sees physical prevention as the only source of unfreedom. It therefore conflicts with Berlin's account, as it does not understand B to make A unfree merely by making it more difficult or costly for A to perform an action, x. What counts is whether B makes it physically impossible for A to do x. This view also conflicts with Pettit's definition, since neither manipulation nor deception is a source of unfreedom. That is, such psychological constraints do not make you unfree as long as they do not involve another agent controlling your mind to the extent that you cannot form the intention to perform a particular action.[14] And whether the interference is intentional or unintentional is irrelevant. But as on any view of freedom as non-interference, pure negative freedom theorists think interference makes you unfree regardless of what your preferences happen to be. When A prevents B from doing x, A makes B unfree to do x whether B would have liked to do x or not.

Pettit is unimpressed by how freedom as non-interference avoids the problems of freedom as non-frustration. While he acknowledges that freedom as non-interference solves the problem of "liberation by adaption," he thinks it does so only by causing a new problem.[15] On any account of freedom as non-interference, Pettit argues, you can liberate yourself by "toadying, kowtowing and cosying up to the powerful."[16] This strategy of "liberation by ingratiation" is in Pettit's view just as absurd as "liberation by adaption." By ingratiation, Pettit means "an intervention that wins the indulgence of the powerful without exposing them to any cost or penalty, not even the cost of disesteem."[17] It is "downright outrageous," he says, to think you can increase your freedom by keeping another agent sweet.[18] Ingratiating yourself so as to reduce the probability of some more powerful agent interfering with you is no plausible way of making yourself free.[19] Due to this implausible implication, Pettit concludes that the "supposition that non-interference is enough for freedom of choice must be false."[20] Both adaption and ingratiation may be beneficial responses to difficult situations, but neither can make you free, he argues.

Pettit illustrates his point with the example of the master who can interfere with her slave at any time as it pleases her.[21] The slave can try to avoid the interference by ingratiating himself to his master, thus achieving or maintaining her goodwill toward him. If he is successful, Pettit argues, the slave has avoided the master's interference, but the slave still lives at the mercy of his master. The master might even be benevolent and let her slave do whatever he wants, but being the master means she can change her treatment of her slave as she wishes. This ever-present possibility of interference makes the slave dominated, and therefore unfree, in Pettit's view, regardless of whether the master actually interferes with him or not. "You cannot make yourself free, so the idea goes, by cozying up to the powerful and keeping them sweet."[22]

Here Pettit's understanding of freedom as non-interference is mistaken. It makes no sense to say, on the non-interference account, that you can "make yourself free" in the way Pettit suggests. This will become evident when we

20 THE REPUBLICAN DILEMMA

start exploring pure negative freedom.[23] But I first turn to Pettit's favored concept of "freedom as non-domination."

2.2.3 Freedom as non-domination

Pettit sets out to remedy the problem he finds with freedom as non-interference. He does so by defining freedom as the status of being protected against someone else's uncontrolled power—that is, the power A has over B when A can interfere with B as it pleases A. "Freedom as non-domination" therefore requires institutions that make sure no one acquires uncontrolled power over others. This definition does not run into the problems with freedom as non-interference, Pettit argues, since the slave is subject to his master's uncontrolled power and is therefore necessarily unfree.

For republicans, Pettit explains, "the real enemy of freedom is the power that some people may have over others."[24] You are unfree when a powerful agent can impose her will on you, even when she does not actively do so. As Pettit puts it, you are free "to the extent that I have a power, uncontrolled by you, of interfering in your choices."[25] Any interference is then conditional only on the will of the controller.[26] To be free, B must have the power to control any way in which A might interfere with him. Only then is B free from A's domination. Under such circumstances, A's interference with B will not make B unfree, since it is under B's control.[27] *Controlled* interference is therefore not a source of unfreedom, whereas *uncontrolled* interference is. Unlike freedom as non-interference, Pettit argues, freedom as non-domination captures the common intuition that asymmetries in interpersonal power are antithetical to freedom.[28]

By thus identifying a kind of interference that does not make you unfree, Pettit limits the scope of freedom. If freedom is the state of being protected against others' use of uncontrolled power, then interference you have yourself instructed does not make you unfree.[29] Such controlled interferences are interferences without domination, and therefore not a source of unfreedom on the republican account. In one of Pettit's examples, you give me the key to the alcohol cupboard with the instruction of giving it back to me only on twenty-four hours' notice when I later ask for it.[30] When I then ask for the key and you act on my instruction by refusing to give me the key, you interfere with me, but your interference is no act of domination.

SCOPE   21

Freedom as non-domination thus differs from freedom as non-interference in that preferences matter for the former but not the latter. Because you prefer not to have access to the alcohol, you instruct me to deny you access, and my acting on this instruction therefore does not make you unfree in the republican sense. Freedom as non-interference, on the other hand, is unconcerned with your preferences, and therefore takes my interference to make you just as unfree whether you have instructed it or not.

It will later be important to recognize that the protection against uncontrolled interference that republican freedom requires necessarily involves interfering with the individuals responsible for upholding this protection. They must be made to maintain the institutional constraints that constitutes the protection. We can therefore add to Pettit's idea of "interference without domination" by saying "no non-domination without interference."

At the collective, or political, level, citizens are free from domination when they collectively control their government to act as they have collectively instructed it to. The government does not make citizens unfree when it interferes with them in accordance with collective instructions. Here the scope of republican freedom is defined by the people's collectively defined interests. So long as it allows, or enables, citizens to satisfy these interests, it does not make them unfree by preventing them from satisfying whatever other interests they may have. When institutions are in place to make sure the government interferes with citizens only in accordance with laws the citizens had an appropriate role in creating and enforcing, it does not make the citizens unfree. When citizens are adequately protected against interference that conflicts with their common interests, the government is under "popular control," as Pettit puts it.[31] Under such circumstances, no citizen can reasonably feel governed by an alien will. Instead, all citizens are subject to a will they have an equal share in controlling. Government actions will still go against the interests of some citizens, but that will not be a matter of disrespect, but rather one of "tough luck," as Pettit explains.[32]

We can now see how non-frustration, non-interference, and non-domination differ in scope. On the non-frustration view, the scope of freedom is the set of actions you prefer—that is, you are free as long as you can do what you want to do. For those understanding freedom as non-interference, the scope includes all actions you can perform without being interfered with. And for republicans, it contains the set of actions the prevention of which you have not instructed. We can therefore order the three

22 THE REPUBLICAN DILEMMA

concepts according to the size of their scope, from small to large: non-frustration, non-domination, and non-interference.

2.3 Freedom as an empirical concept

Carter, Kramer, and Steiner, in particular, have in recent decades reinterpreted freedom as non-interference in the form of pure negative freedom.[33] On this account, you are free to act in any way no one physically prevents you from acting. As Carter puts it, "being prevented physically by someone else from doing something is a sufficient condition for being unfree to do that thing."[34] Whether B is free or unfree to perform a particular action, x, depends exclusively on whether or not another agent, A, prevents B from doing x.

Pure negative freedom is purely negative because it is insensitive to what motivates the constraining action, and to whether it is intentional, significant, or permissible.[35] It is insensitive to the will of an agent accounted for on a positive account of freedom. A less negative conception might allow us to say that A's restriction does not make B unfree if the reasons for interfering, whatever they might be, are superior to B's reasons for performing the action. Republican freedom is therefore not purely negative, since it specifies a set of restrictions that do not make the person interfered with unfree.

The purity of pure negative freedom makes it a strictly empirical, or descriptive, conception, since it only considers *how* people behave, and not *why* they behave in the way they do. In the next section, I contrast empirical conceptions with moralized conceptions, which evaluate constraints and consider morally permissible constraints not as sources of unfreedom. Unlike moralized accounts, the pure negative account is insensitive to any judgment of whether restrictions on the agents' opportunities are controlled or uncontrolled. It simply says that the greater the number of unrestricted actions, the freer is the agent. It is defined independently of any evaluation of restrictions.[36] Any interference therefore makes an agent unfree in the pure negative sense.

On the pure negative account, then, I make you unfree to have a drink when I refuse, on your instruction, to give you the key to the alcohol cupboard. I remove your specific freedom of drinking the liquor in the alcohol cupboard. And the government under popular control makes citizens unfree to break the law—at least without being penalized. I add the clause "without being penalized," since the government usually does not make people unfree—that is, physically unable—to break the law. If it could, then no one

SCOPE 23

would ever break the law.[37] An exception is law enforcement by anticipatory preventive measures that close off any opportunity to break the law.[38] Pure negative freedom theorists might consider such government interference justified, but it nonetheless takes away specific freedoms from the citizens, since the intention behind the interference is irrelevant. In Kramer's example, Mark and Molly are in the same room when Simon shuts and locks the only exit door.[39] Simon only knows that Molly is in the room, and he intends to confine only her in there, not Mark. But since pure negative freedom is insensitive to intention, Simon's action makes both Mark and Molly unfree to leave the room.

It is important to note that prevention here need not mean *actual* prevention; it can also mean *subjunctive* prevention.[40] You are made unfree to do x if someone actually stops you from doing x, but also if someone, subjunctively, will stop you from doing x if you to try to do x. The latter is illustrated by the example where you are in a room with an unlocked exit door, but if you try to leave the room, I will lock the door, thus making it impossible for you to leave. You are therefore unfree—that is, I make you physically unable—to leave the room regardless of whether I actually lock the door or not.[41]

This distinction between actual and subjunctive prevention identifies two different ways in which you can lose a specific freedom—that is, a freedom to perform a specific action. But specific freedom is only one half of the whole idea of pure negative freedom. The other half is the measurement of overall freedom. A person's overall freedom is measured in terms of the number of combinations of actions he can perform without being physically obstructed by another agent. In Section 2.2.2, I said that pure negative freedom theorists do not consider A to make B unfree to do x by making it more costly for B to do x. But by introducing the measurable concept of overall freedom, pure negative freedom theorists can understand A to make B less free to the extent that rising the cost of doing x makes B unable to perform other actions conjunctively with doing x. Making an action more costly can thus reduce B's overall freedom.

The distinction between specific and overall freedom is crucial for understanding how pure negative freedom theorists can justify some acts of interference—and therefore loss of specific freedoms—by appealing to the value of freedom. Following Carter, we can distinguish between the specific and non-specific value of freedom.[42] On the former view, only freedoms to do certain specific things are considered valuable. On the latter view, however, a freedom is valuable regardless of its particular content—that is, regardless of what it allows you to do. Freedom as such is then considered valuable. But

24   THE REPUBLICAN DILEMMA

freedom is in either case separate from its value, as we can define it empirically and then say why the absence of prevention is valuable.[43] And with reference to this value, we can consider the government justified in taking away some of your freedoms by punishing you for breaking the law, at least if you are caught, either because it ensures you have certain valuable freedoms, or because it enhances your overall freedom. It therefore makes perfect sense to prefer not to have certain freedoms because of the value you put on other freedoms or on how much freedom you have overall.

2.4   Freedom as a moralized concept

We have seen that the difference in scope between pure negative freedom and republican freedom is due to the republican view that controlled interference is no source of unfreedom. I shall now explain this reduction in scope by showing how freedom as non-domination is moralized, not empirical.[44] This is an important part of the comparison between pure negative freedom and republican freedom, and therefore important for the whole book. Showing how republican freedom is moralized is a step toward confirming Carter's equivalent-judgments thesis, since the interference compatible with a moralized freedom concept could turn out to promote pure negative overall freedom. If this is so, it is a significant problem for republicans denying the equivalent-judgments thesis.

On a moralized definition, only unjustified interference makes us unfree; justified interference does not.[45] Freedom is therefore defined on the basis of a theory determining what is justified and what is not. So, if A is justified in preventing B from doing x but not y, then A makes B unfree by preventing B from doing x but not by preventing him from doing y. Strictly empirical freedom, on the other hand, is defined independently of any moral theory, and consequently understands A to make B unfree whether she prevents him from doing either x or y. Pure negative freedom, as we have seen, is insensitive to considerations such as whether a constraint is justified or permissible.

An obvious example of a moralized definition of freedom is Robert Nozick's definition, which equates freedom with private property rights.[46] On Nozick's account, no one is made unfree when the government enforces individuals' private property rights. Maintaining distributive patterns involves continual interference, as the government must prevent people from transferring resources as they wish to and take away some of their resources that others chose to transfer to them.[47] Such interference, for Nozick, is a source of unfreedom. Stopping A from using her private property as it pleases her is a kind of interference that makes A unfree. However, stopping B from using A's private property is not interference that makes B unfree. Nozick's basis for understanding prevention as a source of unfreedom in one case but not in the other is his moral evaluation of private property rights. The enforcement of a right to exclude others from the use of private property acquired in a manner Nozick considers just makes no one unfree.

Pettit frequently associates Nozick's definition of freedom with freedom as non-interference, and it is therefore no surprise that he understands this concept as libertarian, and that promoting it involves government interference strictly for the purpose of enforcing whatever contracts individuals have voluntarily entered into.[48] Pettit can then deny the equivalence between measuring freedom as non-domination and freedom as non-interference, as his republicanism takes a less restrictive view of permissible government interference than does Nozick's libertarianism. But pure negative freedom is significantly different from Nozick's definition of freedom. As G. A. Cohen shows, Nozick is clearly no pure negative freedom theorist, since enforcement of property rights makes everyone except the right holder, A, unfree, in the pure negative sense, to use A's property.[49] I can therefore safely ignore Pettit's link between freedom as non-interference, which I interpret as pure negative freedom, and Nozickean libertarianism.

In response to his critics, Pettit has repeatedly denied that his conception of freedom as non-domination is moralized.[50] In the next two subsections, however, I show how Pettit's republican freedom *is* moralized. It is, as is commonly recognized, moralized at the collective level, where interference in accordance with citizens' common interests is understood not to make the individual interfered with unfree. But we shall see that it is moralized also when applied at the individual level, as it is necessarily based on an evaluation of an individual's preferences when it says A does not make B unfree when she acts on a preference B expressed in his instruction at one point in time to prevent B from acting on a conflicting preference at a later time.[51]

2.4.1 Political decision-making

On the republican conception, a government under popular control does not make citizens unfree. Crudely, the idea is that when every citizen is

26 THE REPUBLICAN DILEMMA

equally capable of influencing political decision-making and the govern-ment promotes common interests, the citizens have collectively instructed how the government is to act toward them. Government interference is then considered acceptable to everyone and makes no one unfree. Pettit stresses that he means "acceptable" in a "non-normative sense, implying that the ob-ject or policy or whatever is such that people are disposed to accept it."[52] In other words, these are not interests people ought to have, but interests they in fact do have and are ready to avow. Political decision-making under pop-ular control is therefore considered analogous to the alcohol cupboard case, since it tracks the interests citizens are ready, or inclined, to avow, not the interests we might think they ought to avow. It tracks "avowal-ready," not "avowal-worthy," interests.[53] Pettit therefore denies any moral evaluation of the interests promoted by the government of a free people. And he therefore thinks he avoids moralizing his definition of republican freedom.

But at least in a modern, pluralistic society, the analogy between political decision-making and the alcohol cupboard case is invalid. This is why Carter and other critics argue that republican freedom is moralized.[54] Carter here refers to the case of Ulysses, who instructs the crew on board his ship to tie him to the mast so that he can listen to the alluring song of the sirens without steering the ship into rocky cliffs. Coercing an individual in the collective interest, Carter says, is not analogous to the Ulysses case, since "it is diffi-cult to imagine a justly convicted thief affirming an interest in being impris-oned (analogous to that of Ulysses in being bound to the mast) either before or during the term of imprisonment."[55] More broadly, while the protection of private property and enforcement of progressive taxation might be in the common interest, an individual will likely have a personal interest in being the only one exempted from the constraints of such regulations.

Pettit, on the other hand, says "[t]here will be systems of law available, at least in principle, which are entirely undominating and entirely consistent with freedom."[56] But he realizes that a government cannot always act so as to promote each individual citizen's interests. "Any system of law and govern-ment is bound to mean that certain options are no longer available to agents, or at least no longer available on the previous terms."[57] Like Carter, Pettit notes that it may be preferable to benefit from everyone else being forced to pay taxes while one is oneself allowed to free-ride. For that reason, everyone cannot enjoy personal control over the decision-making one is governed by. This is impossible, Pettit says, given the "historical necessity of living in political society."[58] We are bound to be a part of a society, and are therefore

SCOPE   27

necessarily subjected to certain constraints beyond our personal control. The aim should therefore be to make each citizen feel minimally constrained by the collectively binding decisions that make social life possible. That is achieved by giving each citizen an equal share in the popular control. No individual can reasonably disagree with a collective decision coming out a procedure she controls to the same extent as any other individual in her society.[59] No one will then be dominated, no one will be unfree.

This might be an attractive model of political legitimacy, but it does not show how constraints imposed under popular control do not make citizens unfree—unless, of course, we moralize freedom. People might prefer to live together in a way governed by laws restricting what they can and cannot do to each other, and they might be far better off with than without a state. But that just means the restrictions necessary for keeping law and order are morally permissible. Pettit also imposes a reasonableness restriction on what kind of interest people can avow and therefore count toward specifying the set of common interests. Roughly, these are interests compatible with treating and respecting everyone as one's equal. This point about reasonableness and Pettit's idea of "avowal-ready interests" will be further explored in Chapter 4.

It seems obviously clear, then, that only by moralizing our definition of freedom can we say that interference in the common interest does not make people unfree. On a non-moralized definition, on the other hand, any restriction makes citizens unfree to perform certain actions no matter how collectively acceptable these restrictions might be.

Pettit nonetheless maintains that "neither a tax levy, nor even a term of imprisonment, need take away someone's freedom."[60] He is aware, of course, that individuals might want to free-ride on others' tax-paying and have laws that constrain everyone except themselves. But such interests are "irrelevant," he says, with respect to the definition of the common interests that the government of free citizens promote.[61] Living in a society is a "historical necessity," and our dependence on our society means we cannot demand the satisfaction of interests that will undermine it.[62] We must accept that we are bound by the same laws as everyone else and that certain options therefore will not be available to us.[63]

Pettit may be right that people are better off with than without a state imposing certain restrictions on their behavior, but that just means these restrictions are justified for this reason. Only by moralizing our definition of freedom—by basing it on a theory of justice specifying how institutions ought to operate—can we therefore say that interference in accordance with

28   THE REPUBLICAN DILEMMA

common interests does not make people unfree.[64] On a non-moralized definition, by contrast, any restriction makes citizens unfree to perform certain actions independently of how collectively acceptable these restrictions might be. It makes no difference whether the interference is justified or not. A person in prison is made unfree to perform various actions regardless of *why* he is imprisoned.

As we have seen, Pettit thinks republican freedom is not moralized because it does not impose on people interests they do not already have. The common interests promoted by the government of a free people are acceptable to everyone, and republican freedom is therefore a neutral ideal in the sense that does not impose a particular conception of the good on people. It is consequently anti-paternalist.[65] It therefore cannot be moralized, in Pettit's view, since a moralized conception "might justify a paternalistic concern for people's good, regardless of their perception of the good."[66]

But this response tells us that Pettit is talking about a different kind of moralizing than his critics do. Republican freedom may be anti-paternalist and neutral between conceptions of the good, but it is nonetheless moralized in the way this term is commonly used in the freedom literature. The freedom concept is still based on a normative theory of justice whether the theory is neutral in this sense or not. It may not be "moralizing" in the sense Pettit here has in mind, but it is moralized in the sense that it is based on a theory of justice. We moralize freedom by saying justified interference is not a source of unfreedom, while unjustified interference is. Whether justified interference is, or can be, paternalistic is a separate issue dealt with in the theory. Pure negative freedom, in contrast, is empirical, as it, without reference to justified prevention, describes the social relation where A does not physically prevent B from doing x.

Pettit seems to suggest also republican freedom is empirical when he points out that people with conflicting views of whether an act of interference is justified or not might agree on whether it is controlled or uncontrolled. Whether an act of interference is controlled or uncontrolled is a factual question, not a normative one.[67] The interference is controlled if and only if it accords with the interests of the agent interfered with and the interferer was constrained from interfering contrary to these interests. If the interference did not have these properties, it was uncontrolled and consequently an act of domination. We can disagree about how institutions should operate, and whether an instance of controlled interference is legitimate, Pettit says.[68] But everyone, regardless of their views on this matter, can agree on whether an act of interference is controlled or uncontrolled, and whether a relationship is one of domination or not.[69]

But this is not the issue when we consider whether a freedom concept is moralized. When Pettit has explained what he means by controlled and uncontrolled interference, we might agree on how to fit acts of interference into one or the other category.[70] But this distinction is based on a theory of justice, and we can argue about the merits of this theory. The basis on which we consider whether an act of interference makes the agent interfered with unfree or not is therefore normatively controversial. Once the theory is explained, we might agree on whether the theory justifies the interference or not, and therefore whether the interference is a source of unfreedom. But the freedom concept is still moralized, since we need this normative theory to distinguish the type of interference that does make you unfree from the type that does not.

Let us imagine a case of two prisoners, A and B. A is correctly convicted under a law made and enforced under popular control. The law, enforced by an agent, C, thus closes off some of A's opportunities. On the republican account, then, A is not made unfree with respect to C, since C's legal interference is under popular control. B, on the other hand, is *not* imprisoned under a law made and enforced under popular control. B is therefore made unfree by the agent, D, who enforces the law, or the will of the ruler. So, although the same choice restrictions are imposed on A and B, only B is made unfree. As Pettit says, "one and the same act may count as free in relation to one contrast and unfree in relation to another. And so, as different contexts put different contrasts in play, we may find ourselves ascribing freedom in one case, unfreedom in the other."[71]

This distinction is based solely on the different evaluations of the intentions behind the acts of interference. C acts to promote the common good, while D does not (or is at least not appropriately constrained to do so). And we saw in the previous section that such sensitivity to intention is incompatible with an empirical definition of freedom. Like republicans, pure negative freedom theorists might find the imprisonment of B more morally problematic than the imprisonment of A. But unlike republicans, they do not distinguish the two cases in terms of A and B's freedom: they are both made unfree to perform whatever actions C and D, respectively, prevent them from doing.

And the difference in intention is relevant on the republican account simply because they reflect difference moral standards. A is constrained in the name of the common good, whereas B is not. A might object to his imprisonment,

30   THE REPUBLICAN DILEMMA

but that is "an irrelevant consideration" with respect to the definition of the common interests a legitimate government must promote, according to Pettit's republican theory.[72] A might be unreasonable and a danger to others in his society. But to avoid moralizing the definition of freedom, we cannot deny that putting A in prison makes him unfree because it promotes the common good. We must rather say that it benefits the common good that the government has restricted A's freedom. While promoting the common good might morally justify government interference, saying that such interference does not make citizens unfree requires a moralized definition of freedom.

Let us briefly also note a further problem with the analogy between the Ulysses, or alcohol cupboard, type of case and political decision-making. The latter is often binding for a longer period of time and might even be irreversible. Once one path is taken, it might be impossible, or at least costly and therefore unattractive, to shift to another path. A society might therefore be stuck on one path despite a significant number of protestors. In the alcohol cupboard example, Pettit specifies that the instruction you give me is valid just for twenty-four hours. This condition is introduced to avoid the parallel to a slave contract.[73] Does that mean every decision we cannot reverse, or reverse only after a much longer period of time, turns us into slaves? If so, then, virtually all political decisions turn citizens into slaves. In any case, it is certainly easier to accept that you remain continuously in control of how I behave toward you in the alcohol cupboard case than to see how a people can exercise such control over its government.

So, Pettit must accept that each citizen has significantly weaker control of political decision-making than Ulysses does of his ship crew.[74] However, granted these problems, he might argue in response that his model of legitimate governance is not based on consent but on contestation.[75] Citizens must have the continuous opportunity to influence their government by speaking out against its decisions via various institutionally entrenched channels. Some decisions may prove irreversible or too costly to alter, but people will have the opportunity to contest them even though some of their complaints cannot be remedied. Consent is, in Pettit's view, more problematic with respect to domination.[76] The populist idea of everyone having consented when the majority rules, for example, allows the majority to dominate minorities. And a relationship whose terms are specified in a contract entered into voluntarily may allow for domination, as is the case in worker–employer relations where there are no labor regulations.[77] Non-domination is therefore better served if citizens can continuously contest and influence power.

SCOPE   31

However, as John Ferejohn points out, giving everyone the right to contest majority decisions will not protect members of minorities from domination.[78] This is due to the problem of persistent majorities—that is, the problem of political decisions persistently going against the interests of members of certain minority groups in a society. Pettit is well aware of this problem and suggests weakening the power of the majority by introducing alternative procedures.[79] One is to refer disputed majority decisions to an umpire.[80] Another procedure Pettit suggests is a lottery, in which members of society are randomly selected for legislative or judicial bodies.[81] This procedure, however, is unlikely to always reach unanimous agreements and must therefore often depend on voting.[82] A more plausible lottery procedure is a referendum, or voting within an assembly selected either by popular votes or by lottery, and instead of counting up the votes, we give the votes equal odds and draw one to determine the issue.

But no matter how satisfied and free citizens might feel under such procedures, it remains the case that the constraints they justify make the citizens unfree on any non-moralized account of freedom. They can never enjoy the kind of control Ulysses has with respect to his crew, or the control you have over my interference with you when I, on your instruction, deny you the key to the alcohol cupboard.

2.4.2 Priority to instruction

But even if each individual could exercise such control of government interference, a non-moralized concept of freedom would still not allow us to say that government interference does not make an individual unfree. Explaining why is to explain why republican freedom is moralized also when applied at the individual level. Carter suggests that "no independent moral considerations come into play" when we say that Ulysses is not made unfree when his crew refuse to unbind him from the mast of the ship, since they act on Ulysses' avowed interests.[83] But this is incorrect, as this judgment entails a priority to the preference Ulysses expressed when he instructed his crew over the preference he expressed when the crew refused to untie him. And this priority is based on moral evaluation.

Let us return to Pettit's alcohol cupboard example. Let us say that at time t_1, you give me the key to your alcohol cupboard with the instruction of not giving it back when you later ask for it. At t_2, you ask for the key and I refuse

32 THE REPUBLICAN DILEMMA

to give it back to you. I interfere with you, but since you instructed the interference, it is under your control and therefore does not make you unfree, in the republican sense. Pettit sees no basis for moral controversy in a case of this structure.

But Pettit cannot explain without moral evaluation why his definition of freedom gives priority to the preference you express in the instruction at t_1, and not the preference you express at t_2 when you want a to have a drink. Why does freedom require that your t_1 preference be satisfied and that your t_2 preference not be satisfied? One possible explanation is that you are more yourself at t_1 than at t_2, and that the preference you express at t_1 is therefore more your own than is the preference you express at t_2. The interference at t_2 therefore protects you from alien control, the antithesis of republican freedom. This would be to discriminate between a higher self and a lower self.

Pettit seems to take this view when he says the will you express when you give me the first instruction is "stable or authoritative in comparison with the will that the instructions require me to frustrate."[84] But this is an evaluation of your mental states. It suggests that Keith Dowding could be right when he understands republicans to make a welfarist measure of freedom.[85] The republican distinction between arbitrary and non-arbitrary (or uncontrolled and controlled), he argues, is based on a welfarist evaluation between two different option sets, the one before and the one after the interference. If I do not make you unfree when I act under the control of your t_1 interests because we believe these interests to best promote your welfare, then Pettit offers a welfarist account of freedom, which means republican freedom is moralized.

But this is just one way of justifying the priority to t_1 preferences, and I do not think it is how Pettit would justify it.[86] As already noted, Pettit considers his freedom ideal neutral between different conceptions of the good and not paternalistic. This view need not be based on a concern with people's welfare, and Pettit appears to instead base it on the importance of treating each individual citizen with respect. But that does nothing to deny that the priority to t_1 preferences is based on a moral evaluation of how we ought to treat each other.

Perhaps we are misled to the connotation to welfarism and moral evaluation by the alcohol cupboard example. We might be inclined to think your interests in not drinking are your true interests because alcohol consumption is bad for you, and that my stopping you from drinking is therefore good for you. Pettit, however, says freedom requires that we give priority to interests expressed at t_1 "regardless of whether or not those interests are true or real or valid, by some independent moral criterion."[87] If so, he could make his point clearer by reversing the example so that you, at t_1, instruct me to make you keep drinking if you later want to stop. At t_2, then, I do not make you unfree when I, on your t_1 instruction, make you drink more despite your desire to stop. To avoid giving priority to t_1 interests on moral grounds, Pettit must see this as a case of freedom-compatible interference.

But he gives no reasons for why we should think my interference in this example does not make you unfree. It is indeed hard to think of any good non-moral reasons for thinking why we should respect each other's expressed interests at one point in time but not at a different point in time. Pettit says his freedom ideal is opposed to paternalism, but paternalism is typically opposed on moral grounds, and Pettit gives no non-moral reasons for his opposition to it. I therefore cannot see that Pettit has, or ever will have, the grounds he needs for concluding that "there is no substance to the claim that the republican theory of freedom I favor is moralized."[88]

2.5 The problems of moralizing

An important reason why Pettit considers freedom as non-domination superior to freedom as non-interference is that he thinks we can derive a theory of legitimate political decision-making from the former but not from the latter. The connection between freedom and controlled government interference, he says, "is exclusive to the republican way of thinking about freedom."[89] With republican freedom, we can therefore say that a legitimate government "can coerce citizens without depriving them of their freedom."[90] But we can say no such thing if we take freedom to mean non-interference. Endorsing republican freedom therefore "has serious payoffs in normative thought," in Pettit's view, since it serves as the basis for theories of social justice, democracy, and political legitimacy.[91]

Let us first note that what Pettit says about freedom as non-interference here is wrong given his understanding of this conception of freedom. If freedom as non-interference calls for a libertarian minimal government protecting private property, as he says, then it too appears to serve as the basis for a theory of justice and legitimacy. Libertarians might therefore prefer this definition to freedom as non-domination because of its "serious payoffs in normative thought."

34 THE REPUBLICAN DILEMMA

But we have seen that these republican and libertarian definitions of freedom are moralized, and it is therefore a mistake to think we can derive theories of justice and legitimacy from either of them. Believing in that possibility is to take things in the wrong order. It is rather the case that we define freedom on the basis of such theories. Moralized freedom is defined in terms of the theory and is therefore of no use in formulating the theory. The freedom concept is logically posterior to the theory it is based on. Republicans therefore cannot use freedom as a building block when they condemn uncontrolled power for producing unfreedom and then define unfreedom in terms of presence of uncontrolled power. Freedom is doing no justificatory work; the work is done by the moral evaluation of uncontrolled power.[92] As Carter says, "[a]ny defence of an ideal which involves *defining freedom in terms of that ideal* is not, whatever its other strengths, a defence by appeal to freedom."[93] Freedom does not function as an ideal independent of the moral reasons for why constraints are permissible or desirable. "Freedom falls out of the picture," as Cohen says.[94]

Pure negative freedom, on the other hand, is not based on a normative theory. It is therefore compatible with Berlin's view that "[f]reedom is not, at any rate logically, connected with democracy or self-government." Berlin rejects any "necessary connection between individual liberty and democratic rule."[95] Precisely for this reason, pure negative freedom can serve a purpose in the construction of a theory. By making freedom strictly a matter of human behavior, not of intention and moral evaluation, we can argue about which freedoms, and how much freedom, individuals ought to have. So, the two concepts appear at two different levels of theorizing: pure negative freedom in the formulation of the theory, and republican freedom only once the theory is formulated. We shall indeed see in later chapters how we can add clarity to Pettit's liberal republicanism by revealing the place of pure negative freedom within the theory. We forgo the opportunity to use freedom in this way by moralizing it, as it then becomes something we can extract from the theory once it is built, not something we can use in building it.

This suggests that if Pettit wants to defeat his libertarian opponents, he ought to "de-moralize" his freedom concept. Otherwise, libertarians will remain unmoved by Pettit's criticism of their freedom ideal. De-moralizing freedom is Cohen's strategy in his critique of libertarianism.[96] If we take any kind of constraint to make us unfree, then we can show how government interference to protect private property makes everyone except the right holder unfree to use the good. By tying unfreedom to an empirical fact about the world, we give libertarians no way of denying that enforcing property rights makes people unfree. If we define freedom in terms of justified constraint, however, they can just disagree with our notion of justified constraint. That strategy is almost certain to result in stalemate. When both republicans and libertarians define freedom on the basis of their moral theories, neither side's appeal to freedom will move the other side. We then understand what Steiner means when he says moralizing freedom makes us "linguistically disabled from urging our moral opponents to allow people to have certain freedoms."[97]

A critique of libertarianism by appeal to empirical, non-moralized freedom would force libertarians to show how property rights promote people's freedom. We can then discuss meaningfully how to best promote freedom. Libertarians might try to justify private property rights by saying that it enhances the level of overall freedom in society, but they cannot deny that it does so by taking away certain freedoms from the property-less. Perhaps they could do so by showing how private property rights tend to give everyone more freedom overall than she or he otherwise would have had. Alternatively, they can argue for the importance of certain freedoms, most plausibly by explaining how they contribute to some other, more fundamental value, like individual dignity or self-respect.

Republicans might argue, with a non-moralized definition of freedom, that taxing people and putting some behind bars in accordance with laws made and enforced under popular control will enhance overall freedom. But of course, that would mean showing how promoting republican freedom is to promote pure negative overall freedom. They would consequently confirm the equivalent-judgments thesis. To avoid this outcome, republicans must show how promoting their moralized freedom ideal conflicts with the promotion of overall freedom. Exploring how they can do so is a central issue in this book.

2.6 Conclusion

Republican and pure negative freedom clearly have different scope, since the former specifies one kind of interference as not a source of unfreedom, whereas the latter takes all interference to make the agent interfered with unfree. We make sense of this difference by seeing how republican freedom is moralized, while pure negative is strictly empirical. For republicans, justified

36 THE REPUBLICAN DILEMMA

constraints do not make citizens unfree, whereas all constraints make citizens unfree on the pure negative account.

The issue of whether republican freedom is moralized is more than a "strictly irrelevant quarrel" with Carter, as Pettit himself perceives it.[98] Observing that the restriction in the scope of republican freedom is based on moral evaluation is an important step toward determining whether the equivalent-judgments thesis holds or not. It might be the case that the republican scope reduction reflects the preventions necessary for promoting pure negative overall freedom. In other words, the preventions not making you unfree on the republican account might be the specific unfreedoms pure negative freedom theorists will justify for the sake of promoting overall freedom.

If that is the case, then the equivalent-judgments thesis holds. And we shall see in later chapters that this is the right understanding of Pettit's account of republican freedom. For now, however, the point is just that the difference in scope between the two freedom concepts does not falsify the equivalent-judgments thesis because the republican scope reduction is due to a moralization of freedom.

3

Robustness

3.1 Introduction

Pure negative freedom clearly has a larger scope than republican freedom. In this chapter, I consider the two concepts' differences in robustness—that is, differences in the extent to which they require robust protection against interference. Republican freedom requires more such robustness, since domination can occur where there is inadequate protection but no interference.[1] Enjoying non-domination is not just to experience no uncontrolled interference, but to enjoy a certain degree of protection against uncontrolled interference. So, B's freedom depends not just on A not interfering with him, in a way he has not instructed, in the actual world. Institutions must also be in place to protect B from A's interference. B's pure negative freedom to perform some action, on the other hand, depends simply on A not preventing him from doing x in the actual world. No robust protection is required.

It does not follow, however, that the equivalent-judgments thesis is false. While republicans, unlike pure negative freedom theorists, require that protective institutions be in place in order for an agent to be free in any action, such institutions could be shown to enhance pure negative overall freedom. In this chapter, I show how a republican conception of freedom can be made to require more robust protection than is compatible with the promotion of pure negative overall freedom. But we shall see that such a conception demands more robustness than does Pettit's conception of republican freedom.

3.2 Robustness

We saw in the previous chapter that scope refers to the kinds of interference a definition of freedom picks out as sources of unfreedom. It refers, in other words, to an agent's range of possible actions that are not obstructed by another agent. Robustness, on the other hand, refers to the extent to which

The Republican Dilemma. Lars J. K. Moen, Oxford University Press. © Oxford University Press 2024.
DOI: 10.1093/oso/9780197757024.003.0003

38 THE REPUBLICAN DILEMMA

actions are available in a range of socially possible worlds. A socially possible world is defined by the n-tuple preference orderings across the m individuals in the society. It is, in List's words, "a particular combination of preference orderings across agents in the society."[2] Robustness is a measure of the extent to which an agent is protected against interference across different socially possible worlds. Maximal robustness requires that interference occurs in no socially possible worlds. In other words, it does not occur regardless of what other individuals' preferences might be. Minimal robustness requires only that no interference occurs in the actual world.

We might say the scope of freedom refers only to the preference ordering of the individual herself, since it indicates the extent to which the agent is free to act regardless of her preferences. Robustness, on the other hand, is sensitive to the social context—that is, the preference orderings of other individuals—since it indicates the extent to which an agent can perform an action independently of other individuals' preferences.

To give an example, if B has the options x, y, and z, a definition of freedom with maximal scope will tell us that A made B unfree, simply because A interfered with B. It does not matter what A prevented B from doing or why. The robustness of freedom, on the other hand, is a measure of the number of socially possible worlds in which a choice is available to B. If freedom requires that A lets B choose an option in the actual world but in no other possible world, then freedom is minimally robust. If, on the other hand, freedom requires that B can choose an option in any socially possible world, it has maximal robustness. The degree of robustness a definition of freedom requires is therefore a measure of the number of socially possible worlds in which it requires that the agent not be prevented from performing an action.

List also discusses these two dimensions of freedom to show how any conception of freedom with maximal robustness conflicts with the Pareto principle.[3] This result follows from Amartya Sen's liberal paradox, according to which no social aggregation function can satisfy the conditions of universal domain, minimal liberalism, and the Pareto principle.[4] Briefly, suppose there are two or more individuals and three or more alternatives. The Pareto principle requires that if both, or all, individuals prefer one alternative, x, to another alternative, y, then society will prefer x to y. And minimal liberalism requires that the individuals be decisive over at least one pair of alternatives each. Given universal domain—that is, the individuals can order their preferences over the alternatives in any way possible—Sen proves that

ROBUSTNESS 39

no social aggregation function can satisfy both the Pareto principle and minimal liberalism.

In Sen's illustrative proof, two agents, Lewd and Prude, have three alternatives, x, y, and z.[5] Here x refers to "Lewd reads *Lady Chatterley's Lover*," y to "Prude reads *Lady Chatterley's Lover*," and z to "no one reads *Lady Chatterley's Lover*." Lewd[6] wants to read the novel, and therefore prefers x to z. But he most of all wants Prude to read it. Lewd's preference ordering is therefore $y > x > z$. Prude, on the other hand, does not want to read the book, and therefore prefers z to y. But his least preferred alternative is that Lewd reads the book. Prude's preference ordering is therefore $z > y > x$. To satisfy minimal liberalism, Lewd and Prude must both decide over at least one pair of alternatives each. The social preference ordering $x > z > y$ meets this condition, since Lewd is decisive between x and z and Prude is decisive between y and z. But this ordering violates the Pareto principle, since A and B both prefer y to x. If we combine individually decisive preferences for x to z and z to y with the Pareto principle's requirement that y be preferred to x, we get the cyclical social preference ordering $x > z > y > x \ldots$ Each alternative is then defeated by some other alternative, and we fail to make a collective choice.

As an implication of Sen's "liberal paradox," List shows that "republican paradox" is that a definition of freedom requiring that agents' preferences be decisive across all socially possible worlds conflicts with the Pareto principle. This result holds even with the minimal scope requirement that two or more agents' preferences be robustly decisive over just one pair of alternatives each. As we see in the example above, A and B cannot be decisive over a pair of alternatives each without the social preference ordering violating the Pareto principle. No social aggregation function can satisfy the Pareto principle and republican freedom even when its scope is reduced to just one pair of alternatives. To avoid this result, a definition of freedom must therefore occupy a less then maximal position on the robustness dimension. That is, the definition must allow that one's freedom to do something is to a certain extent dependent on other people's preferences.

But List's result is actually an understatement, as the problem of maximal robustness is not just that it makes freedom impossible to combine with some other value. It also makes freedom itself impossible. We cannot give freedom maximal robustness, even with minimal scope, since there is no way of protecting individuals to the extent that they become incapable of interfering with each other.[6] Maximal robustness—that is, requiring that interference occur in no socially possible world—is incompatible with any scope.

40 THE REPUBLICAN DILEMMA

This is a rather obvious point, given the observation that A's ability to satisfy a preference for x depends on no one else not satisfying a preference for preventing x. So, if we define freedom to require maximal robustness, no one will ever be free to do anything whatsoever.[7] Maximal scope, on the other hand, can be combined with minimal robustness, which we shall see is the trade-off of pure negative freedom.

Although maximal scope is possible and maximal robustness is not, we can say that the two dimensions are roughly inversely related, so that we can only enhance robustness by reducing scope and vice versa. We cannot give freedom both maximal scope and maximal robustness. Freedom with more than minimal robustness requires that individuals be protected against each other's interference, and this protection itself involves interference. To give our definition of freedom more than minimal robustness, we must therefore specify a class of interference we do not count as a source of unfreedom.

No definition of freedom can therefore require both maximal scope and maximal robustness, at least insofar as we want freedom to be possible for two or more individuals. What preferences A can satisfy depends on what preferences B can satisfy. This observation makes the impossibility of combining the two maximum positions, or of avoiding the trade-off, trivially true: For A to satisfy her preference for doing x, B cannot satisfy his preference for preventing A from doing x.[8]

Unlike Sen and List, I focus on freedom in action rather than in preference decisiveness, as this is in line with the literature on republican and pure negative freedom. The difference between action and preference is significant, since whether or not your preference is decisive depends not just on whether you are free to perform some action but also on the consequences of that action, as well as those of other people's actions.[9] The republican paradox can nonetheless easily be applied to the debate on freedom in action. On any account of freedom of action, your freedom to perform an action will depend on the behavior of other agents constituting your society. B's doing x will always depend on A not preventing B from doing x. B's freedom to do x is therefore dependent on his social context. For B to do x, A cannot prevent B from doing x.

The impossibility of combining maximal scope with maximal robustness means we must weaken one or the other when we define freedom. We shall see that Pettit's republican freedom takes a moderate position along either dimension, while pure negative freedom has minimal robustness and maximal scope. A key issue in this chapter is whether the two concepts'

3.3 Pure negative freedom

Pure negative freedom has maximal scope, as it treats any prevention as a source of unfreedom. You are free, on this account, to perform any action no one prevents you from performing. It consequently has minimal robustness—that is, you are free to do x as long as no one stops you from doing x in the actual world. However, pure negative freedom theorists have two reasons for caring about protection against interference.

First, while you have a specific freedom to perform an action when no one prevents you from performing that action, that does not mean your freedom to do x depends strictly on whether someone *actually* stops you from doing x. Steiner defines prevention as "a relation between the respective actions of two persons such that the occurrence of one of them rules out, or implies the impossibility of, the occurrence of the other."[10] If both actions can occur, they are "compossible" and neither action is prevented by the other. Conversely, if one action makes the other impossible, one action prevents the other from occurring, and the actions are "incompossible." On this definition, prevention need not refer to actual prevention. It can also refer to subjunctive prevention.[11] In the example I have referred to earlier, you are in a room with an open door, but if you try to leave, I will lock the door. I thus make it impossible for you to leave the room whether I actually prevent you from doing so or not. We see, then, what Kramer means when he says that "the existence of unfreedom does not necessarily involve any actual endeavour and thus does not necessarily involve any actual obstruction; the endeavour and the obstruction can remain hypothetical."[12]

That means your freedom to leave the room depends on whether I am disposed to lock the door or not if you were to try to leave. So, if you are protected against my prevention—that is, if I am prevented from preventing you from leaving the room—then you might gain a freedom you did not already possess, in addition to all the freedoms depending on that freedom. While not giving pure negative freedom robustness, since you can freely leave the room in the one world where I do not prevent you from doing so, we see that robust protection can give you specific freedoms you otherwise would not have possessed.

42 THE REPUBLICAN DILEMMA

A further reason for pure negative freedom theorists to care about protection against interference is that it can enhance overall freedom. We saw in the previous chapter that republican freedom has a reduced, moralized scope. Reducing the opportunity sets of individuals on the basis of legitimate political decision-making does not make them unfree, on the republican account. Republican freedom can therefore be defined so as to specify a desirable level of robust protection for one to be free to perform those actions at all. We shall see in the next section how republicans specify that level of protection. What matters now is that achieving that level of protection might mirror the loss of pure negative specific freedoms necessary for promoting pure negative overall freedom.

Overall freedom, recall, is measured in terms of the number of combinations of actions you can exercise conjunctively.[13] The greater your number of combinations of conjunctively exercisable actions, the greater is your overall freedom. Overall freedom enables pure negative freedom theorists to think of threats as a source of unfreedom. Suppose A credibly threatens B by telling B that if he does x rather than y, then A will prevent B from doing z. A then prevents B from doing neither x, y, or z, but she does prevent him from doing x and z conjunctively. The extent to which A's threat makes B unfree depends on the credibility of the threat—that is, the probability of A actually enforcing the threat if B were to do x. The higher the probability of A's prevention, the greater is the loss of B's overall freedom.

We therefore see that protecting B against A's interference will likely reduce the probability of A preventing B from doing x and z, and consequently enhance B's overall freedom. The government can reduce the probability of A preventing B from doing x and z by making it costly for A to do so—perhaps by making her pay a fine or spend time in prison. This government interference is, of course, itself a threat, which reduces A's overall freedom. Law enforcement usually takes away freedoms after the crime is committed, but it can also do so by anticipatory preventive measures that close off any opportunity to break the law.[14]

Promoting pure negative freedom will therefore likely involve robust protection against interference. List is therefore wrong when he says that "[p]erhaps [pure negative freedom theorists] are also concerned with robustness, but if they are, that concern stems not from their commitment to liberal [pure negative] freedom itself, but from their commitment to other desiderata beyond freedom."[15] We shall see later in the chapter that neglecting this aspect of pure negative freedom has caused confusion in the debate between republicans and pure negative freedom theorists.

3.4 Republican freedom

We saw in the previous chapter that republican freedom, unlike pure negative freedom, has a restricted scope, as it specifies a kind of interference—controlled interference—that does not make the agent interfered with unfree. When I now turn to the robustness of republican freedom, I therefore exclude all actions that are prevented by controlled interference. The question is how robustly protected republican freedom requires that the availability of all other actions must be. We shall see that the scope restriction enables republican freedom to require a higher level of robustness than does pure negative freedom.

3.4.1 Accessibility, not probability

Republican freedom, Pettit explains, requires that interference not instructed by the agent interfered with be made "inaccessible."[16] Inaccessible here does not mean sufficiently improbable; it means not within another agent's power.[17] We thus notice a difference from pure negative freedom, which we have seen focuses on the probability of constraint in its measure of overall freedom. Pettit considers low probability insufficient for the control republican freedom requires. A reduction in probability of interference, he says, can, after all, be achieved by ingratiation, which would be an "absurd" way of making oneself free.[18] While admitting that lower probability of uncontrolled interference implies a lower intensity of the uncontrolled power, Pettit sees the mere existence of such power as a source of unfreedom.[19]

Institutions must therefore be in place to protect B against A's uncontrolled interference. Such institutions must exist regardless of how improbable it might be that uncontrolled interference would happen in their absence. Suppose A is unlikely to interfere with B just because she happens to like B. A's goodwill toward B will not affect B's republican freedom. B's republican freedom with respect to A depends on institutions being in place to punish A for interfering with B. Only then will B be free from A's domination.[20] Goodwill is fragile and therefore irrelevant for the measure of freedom.

44 THE REPUBLICAN DILEMMA

A can change her attitude toward B as it pleases her. Social institutions, on the other hand, are more robust, and can protect B against A's interference whether A remains favorably inclined toward him or not. Institutions can force A not to interfere with B. Such institutions, Pettit explains, *constitute* republican freedom. Non-domination, he says, "comes into existence simultaneously with the appearance of the appropriate institutions."[21]

This means that in a case where B's ability to do x is not institutionally protected against A's preventing him from doing x, B is unfree to do x even if he actually does x. In fact, A might make B unfree without ever actually constraining B in any choice. Here we see a difference in robustness between republican freedom and pure negative freedom, since on the latter account, B is free to perform any action he actually does perform, in addition to any other action no other agent prevents him, actually or subjunctively, from doing.

This difference makes sense when we think of republican freedom as a status. It is the status you enjoy when no one is in a position to interfere with you as it pleases her.[22] You possess the "antipower" to protect yourself against uncontrolled interference.[23] B is free with respect to A insofar as A lacks the uncontrolled power to interfere with B—that is, the power to interfere with B as it pleases her.

Pettit explains that there are many ways in which an agent can possess uncontrolled power over another. They may include "physical strength, technical advantage, financial clout, political authority, social connections, communal standing, informational access, ideological position, cultural legitimation, and the like." They also include monopolistic power, such as being "someone—say, the only doctor or police officer around—whose help and goodwill the other may need in various possible emergencies."[24] The essence of this kind of power is that it is not kept in check by some sufficiently powerful institution under popular control.

Republicans frequently refer to the slave and his relation to his master as an example of someone not enjoying the status of a free person.[25] The master may interfere with her slave at any time. She may not actually do so, but the slave will in any case live at the mercy of his master and must act so as to maintain his master's goodwill toward him. The slave behaves in a slavish manner, which is characteristic of what republicans consider an unfree person. The master may be benevolent and let her slave do whatever he wants, but being the master means that she possesses the power to at any time change how she treats her slave. This ever-present threat of uncontrolled interference makes the slave dominated, and therefore unfree, regardless of whether the master will actually interfere or not.

3.4.2 The impossibility objection

An important question is what it means to make uninstructed interference "inaccessible." How effective must the institutional protection against interference be to constitute freedom as non-domination? Pettit says institutions must make sure that people enjoy non-interference in "a range of nearby possible worlds." Worlds in which they are interfered with, he says, cannot be "readily accessible."[26]

This might appear to mean that no one can interfere with another without first having to go through a series of improbable actions. But if this is the level of robustness republican freedom requires, then republican freedom is impossibly demanding. Anyone living in a society can at any time interfere with another in a way the party interfered with has not instructed. So, on this interpretation, virtually anyone possesses uncontrolled power with respect to anyone else, and no one can ever be free, in the republican sense, to do anything whatsoever. "Only in a utopian fantasy," Kramer writes, "can the emergence of domination and its effects be strictly ruled out."[27] The eventuality of A interfering with B can never be made impossible. Several critics have argued along these lines to conclude that republican freedom is impossibly demanding.[28] In terms of the two-dimensional picture, this criticism says that republican freedom requires a level of robustness that entails reducing the scope of freedom to zero. That is, one can never be free to do anything.

But this is not actually how Pettit thinks about republican freedom's robustness requirement. He agrees that requiring protection to this impossible extent would be "utterly irrational."[29] And he accepts that "few obstacles are absolute." Most of them, he says, "just raise the costs, and therefore the penalty, attaching to an attempt to act in the manner prohibited."[30] And this is what the institutions constituting non-domination do. Like Skinner, Pettit says republican freedom does not require that all uncontrolled interference be made inaccessible; it requires that uncontrolled interference *with impunity* be made inaccessible.[31] Uncontrolled interference should "incur such difficulty or such danger for the interferer that it is relatively unacceptable or ineligible."[32] What makes an agent unfree, Pettit says, is another agent's "power of relatively costless interference."[33]

46 THE REPUBLICAN DILEMMA

A dominates B to the extent that A can interfere with B in an uncontrolled manner without having to pay a high price for it. B's freedom from A's domination requires that A's option of interference be replaced "by an option that involves choice-inhibiting costs and penalties."[34] The idea is to eliminate the possibility of "interference-at-an-acceptable-cost."[35] A then cannot interfere with B simply as it pleases her.[36] As Pettit says, "if [individuals] are caught attempting interference, they will be opposed and pursued, and, if they are apprehended and convicted, they will be forced to try to rectify their offense, forced to make redress."[37] We thus see a connection between republican freedom and the rule of law: everyone is equally constrained by the law.[38] But Pettit notes that an alternative way of protecting B against uncontrolled interference is to provide him with the resources he needs to protect himself.[39]

The requirement therefore seems to be that A cannot access a possible world in which she interferes with B without being appropriately punished. This impunity condition reduces the scope of republican freedom by making it compatible with more interference than the set of all uncontrolled interference. If A prevents B from doing x and is then appropriately punished for her interference, then A does not make B unfree in the republican sense. The range of interference compatible with freedom is thus enhanced, which is the same as saying the scope of freedom is reduced.

While this move makes republican robustness appear more achievable, it is still extremely demanding. As Dowding points out, criminals often do get away with their crimes.[40] Even with extensive surveillance, a highly active police force, and citizens motivated to report every crime they observe, a monitoring problem seems likely to persist. So, perfect law enforcement may at least come very close to being impossible. Sean Ingham and Frank Lovett call this perfect-law-enforcement understanding of republican robustness "strong republicanism," which they consider to be "too strong."[41] List takes this strong view when he understands republican robustness to require that uninstructed interference with impunity occurs in no socially possible world.[42]

3.4.3 The eyeball test

But Pettit denies also this interpretation of the republican robustness condition. He instead prefers an understanding in line with what Ingham and Lovett call "moderate republicanism."[43] On this account, all that is required is that it be common knowledge in the society—that is, everyone knows that everyone else knows that everyone knows that everyone else knows and so on—that uncontrolled interference is generally penalized. Most people will therefore refrain from such interference and feel sufficiently protected against it not to worry about it. Ingham and Lovett then consider the danger of uncontrolled interference "ignorable."[44]

On this account, then, even if the interferer gets away with it, that need not mean her interference made the person she interfered with unfree. What matters, Pettit says, is that punishment is sufficiently likely, so that we can consider the unpenalized interference "a contingent occurrence, not an event that reveals a systematic vulnerability."[45] So, the state's failure to prevent the occasional act of uncontrolled interference with impunity does not make citizens unfree. What matters is that there is no room for systematic domination.

How probable must successful law enforcement be for it to be sufficiently probable? Pettit sees no way of giving a precise answer in the abstract. The range of possible worlds without interference with impunity, he says, "is discernible only on an intuitive, context-sensitive basis."[46] He admits that this reliance on contextual assumptions is "regrettable, but from the point of view of formalizing the theory of freedom it seems inevitable."[47] Institutions must be in place, but Pettit does not specify the probability of their being effective.[48] To do so, we must depend on intuition with respect to specific cases. This vagueness is akin, he says, to that we find in epistemology when we determine how many possible worlds in which a true belief must be present for something to deserve being called knowledge.[49]

Pettit employs the heuristic device of "the eyeball test" to produce the required intuition.[50] This test will be met when "you have no good reason to be anxious," he explains.[51] It requires "a degree of protection against others that makes the interference option ineligible, if not actually impossible, and that does this more and more effectively with progressively more serious forms of interference."[52] People who are "able to walk tall, live without shame or indignity, and look one another in the eye without any reason for fear or deference" pass this test and are sufficiently protected against interference.[53] A dominated person, such as a slave, on the other hand, cannot look his superior in the eye and talk straight to her as his equal. He must always watch his words and actions so as to remain on good terms with the more powerful person.[54] The level of protection people actually need to pass the eyeball test will vary from one society to another, Pettit explains, "since there is likely to

48 THE REPUBLICAN DILEMMA

be cultural variation in what counts as mere timidity rather than rational fear or deference."[55]

When the sufficient level of protection, by local standards, is achieved, any person can operate "under his own jurisdiction" and not under "the power of a master" to whom he must seek permission for his actions.[56] Pettit believes people are then unlikely to experience much uncertainty in their lives.[57] They can make decisions they are responsible for, and they can plan ahead without anxiety for the prospect of uncontrolled interference.[58] They can make decisions and express their opinions without having to satisfy some superior agent.[59] People living under domination, on the other hand, must keep their superiors sweet by ingratiation and self-censorship.[60]

We see, then, that republican freedom takes place some way out on the robustness dimension. But the vagueness of its robustness condition makes it unclear how far out. And given the sensitivity to social context, the robustness requirement will differ from society to society and from one time to another. But we can stipulate that republican freedom goes out to a point on the robustness dimension at which it realistically requires that actions be successfully protected in a certain range of possible worlds. At this vaguely determined point, freedom realistically requires institutions protecting individuals' unprevented ability to perform a certain set of actions across a certain range of possible worlds. This vagueness makes it unclear what republican freedom actually is, but I shall proceed on the assumption that Pettit's view is a moderate one requiring a level of robustness that is possible when combined with a necessary scope reduction.

3.5 Domination as interference

The preceding analysis of the robustness conditions of pure negative and republican freedom brings out that the former is an action concept, whereas the latter is a status concept. Maximizing people's pure negative overall freedom requires institutions that give them the highest possible number of combinations of conjunctively exercisable actions. Republican freedom, on the other hand, depends on institutions that give people a certain status—the status of being protected against uncontrolled interference under actually enforced rules.

For republicans, more precisely, status precedes action in the sense that an action is free only insofar as it is performed by a free person.[61] A person not enjoying the protection republican freedom requires cannot act freely. On the pure negative account, on the other hand, you are always free to perform any action you actually can perform. Republicans object by denying that an action can be free if it is performed by someone who chooses her actions in accordance with what some more powerful agent will approve of because doing otherwise will likely have bad consequences. Freedom therefore necessarily depends on a level of protection not implied in the pure negative measurement of freedom.

In this section, I consider two kinds of case in which B is vulnerable to A's uncontrolled interference and therefore dominated by A. Despite conceptual differences regarding robustness, I show how republicans and pure negative freedom theorists will make the same judgments about B's freedom in these cases.

3.5.1 Subjunctive prevention

In their assessment of pure negative freedom, republicans typically focus only on actual prevention and not on subjunctive prevention and the measurement of overall freedom. A's uncontrolled power over B does not mean that B is *actually* prevented from choosing any option in his opportunity set. Pettit understands interference as an act of "active control"—that is, A interferes with B when she actually prevents B from performing an action.[62] An account of freedom as interference therefore necessarily fails to capture B's loss of freedom due to A's "virtual control."[63] A virtually controls B's behavior by possessing the power to interfere at any time. This readiness to interfere will affect B's choice situation whether A actually interferes or not. A's virtual control therefore causes a loss in B's republican freedom but not in his pure negative freedom, Pettit argues.[64] B cannot make a free choice—that is, free from A's control—even though A does not actually prevent B from choosing any particular option. We thus see how the problem Pettit finds with pure negative freedom is that it only focuses on actions, and not on the person choosing between available actions.

This view is based on an understanding of pure negative freedom as the absence of *actual* prevention. We have seen that this is a mistake, however, since an agent's pure negative freedom is conditional both on other agents' actual and subjunctive prevention. A can therefore make B unfree to do x without actually preventing him from doing x—that is, actively controlling

50 THE REPUBLICAN DILEMMA

his behavior. A's preventing B from doing x only conditionally on B trying to do x means A's virtual control over B can cause a loss in B's pure negative freedom. Pettit would say that A's interference might never materialize in this case, while pure negative freedom theorists would say that A does interfere with B. These differences in terminology are irrelevant with respect to judging whether B is free, which is what we are interested in.

To illustrate this point, let us again consider the example where you are in a room with an open exit door I will lock if you try to leave. You are not actually prevented from leaving as long as you do not try, but if you try, you will fail because I will lock the door before you can reach it. I can therefore prevent you from leaving the room without *actually* stopping you from doing so. My virtual control over your behavior thus makes you unfree also on the pure negative account. Likewise, the master might not actually prevent her slave from doing x, but the master nonetheless makes the slave unfree, in the pure negative sense, to do x if she will prevent him from doing so were he to try. The master's virtual control can thus make the slave unfree also on the pure negative account. As Kramer points out, this captures one aspect of how the dominated person is made unfree in the pure negative sense.[65]

3.5.2 Threats

It is, of course, possible that the master does not prevent the slave from doing x in either the actual or the subjunctive sense. Pettit says, for example, that A's virtual control can make it probable that B chooses a particular option, x, rather than another option, y.[66] Virtual control therefore need not imply subjunctive prevention—that is, B need not lose the specific freedom to do x.

The relevant case here is where A holds uncontrolled power over B but does not prevent B from choosing any option in his opportunity set at time t. B will succeed in taking any option if he tries. However, if B chooses an option, x, that A does not approve of, then A will penalize B by making B unable to do y at $t + 1$. This case has the structure of a threat. A's threat does not restrict B's choice situation; only A's enforcing the threat can do so, and that occurs at $t + 1$, not at t.[67] Pure negative freedom theorists must therefore conclude that A does not make B unfree to perform any particular action at t.

This case illuminates Pettit's "main problem" with pure negative freedom. It is "downright bizarre," he says, to think A has not changed B's choice situation at t.[68] If B's doing x at t will make A subsequently punish B, then A's threat has changed the nature of x in B's opportunity set. It will change how B evaluates x, and has therefore changed x itself. B can no longer think of x as an option he can just do.

Saying that B is free to do x in this case might seem counterintuitive, but it also seems counterintuitive to say that B is unfree to do an action he will succeed in doing if he tries.[69] Fortunately, however, we need not be concerned with this clash of intuitions. The issue I am interested in is whether republicans and pure negative freedom theorists will make different judgments regarding how free B is in this case. Pettit thinks A's threat— or, perhaps more precisely, A's power to enforce the threat—has negatively affected B's freedom. Would a pure negative freedom theorist think differently?

We have seen that A takes away none of B's specific freedoms at t. But this tells us little about how free, or unfree, B is. Making that assessment is to consider B's overall freedom, and when we do that, we see that A's threat has a negative impact also on B's pure negative freedom. A makes B unfree to do x only by preventing him from doing x, but the threat of sanction for doing x restricts the number of B's combinations of conjunctively exercisable actions, and therefore reduces his overall freedom. The likely consequence of doing x is a punishment eliminating some of the opportunities B otherwise could have pursued conjunctively with doing x. So, while A does not make B unfree to do x, she is making B unfree to perform certain actions in combination with doing x.

Carter can therefore conclude that to the extent that B's x-ing makes A more likely to prevent some of his otherwise available actions in the future, B "clearly enjoys less freedom in the liberal [pure negative] sense."[70] When A has the power to impose a sanction on B and B anticipates that A will exercise this power, whether she actually does so or not, A will limit B's freedom to act. "Being subjected to these forms of power," Carter writes, "generally implies strong limits not just on the freedom with which one acts, but also on one's freedom-to-act."[71] The more severe and more probable is A's interference, the more conjunctively exercisable freedoms A will take away from B.[72]

Kramer notes, similarly, that A's "very readiness" to interfere with B "eliminates many combinations of conjunctively exercisable freedoms for [B]."[73] Republicans and pure negative freedom theorists will therefore make equivalent judgments regarding B's (overall) freedom in this case. The overall freedom of a person who is dominated and dependent on another's goodwill

52 THE REPUBLICAN DILEMMA

is "seriously constricted," in Kramer's view. "We can discern as much on the basis of my negative theory of liberty alone," he says, "without any need for the putatively supplementary theses of civic republicanism."[74]

Now, here we suppose the threat is credible, so that the probability of A preventing B from doing y if he does x is significantly high. If the threat is not credible, however, it will not significantly affect the pure negative measurement of freedom. Republicans might insist that their understanding of freedom is less focused on the probability of prevention, and say that they take B's freedom to be considerably compromised also when the probability of A's interference is very low. This will be a central issue in this book, since it illuminates a path republicans can take to distance themselves from pure negative freedom. Later in this chapter, I say more about how this point shapes the rest of the book. It will also become clear in later chapters that insisting that freedom requires protection even when the probability of interference is very low comes at a cost that Pettit and other contemporary republicans are unwilling to accept.

3.6 "Liberation by ingratiation"

There is also another type of case that Pettit has placed much emphasis on in his attempt to distinguish republican freedom from any conception of freedom as non-interference.[75] This is the case where A's virtual control means B cannot simply choose an option, but must curry favor with A so as to win her goodwill and then allow him to do either of his options, y and z. On the republican account, B is unfree to do either y or z because he can do so only in the narrow range of possible worlds in which A lets him do either y or z. B's ingratiation reduces the probability of A's prevention, but A can easily access a world in which she prevents B from performing either of the actions. A's being merciful in response to B's self-abasing behavior does not change the fact that B is in control of A. On the republican account, B therefore remains unfree in this choice.

As Pettit says, A changes B's options from simply y and z to "y-provided-[B]-keeps-[A]-sweet and z-provided-[B]-keeps-[A]-sweet."[76] He thinks pure negative freedom theorists fail to recognize this change in B's opportunity set, and that they are consequently committed to the implausible view that B can make himself free to do x or y by ingratiating himself with A.[77] After all, such ingratiation might make certain actions available that would otherwise be unavailable. So, while B remains unfree on the republican account, he gains pure negative freedom. Pettit dismissively calls this strategy "liberation by ingratiation."[78] This strategy cannot make B free in the republican sense, since "[y]ou cannot make yourself free . . . by cozying up to the powerful and keeping them sweet."[79] But if we understand freedom as the absence of interference, Pettit argues, the strategy would be perfectly sensible.

Pettit often illustrates this strategy with the example of the slave who curries favor with his master so as to win her goodwill and thus reduce the probability of being interfered with.[80] While the slave can thus free himself from his master's interference, he cannot look his master in the eye as his equal; he must always choose his words and actions with care so as to stay on his master's good side. Skinner, similarly, thinks the problem of being dominated is that it makes you inclined to adapt your behavior in a certain way to minimize the risk of uncontrolled interference.[81] Slaves' pattern of conduct, Skinner says, "is nothing other than a reflection of what their master is willing to tolerate."[82] But the master's control and the slave's fear of interference are not captured in pure negative freedom, Pettit and Skinner argue. If a slave manages to maintain his master's goodwill toward him, he will be allowed to choose whatever options he likes and will therefore be free from interference. Pure negative freedom, and any other conception of freedom as non-interference, is therefore compatible with what Pettit considers a "downright outrageous" liberation strategy.[83]

If this argument is sound—if pure negative freedom is compatible with "liberation by ingratiation"—then Pettit has falsified the equivalent-judgments thesis. The slave's pure negative freedom will then increase when he employs the ingratiation strategy, while his republican freedom, or unfreedom, remains unaffected. The idea of a slave making himself free is, as Pettit says, a conceptual impossibility on the republican account. Considering this argument requires a look back at earlier discussion of both specific and overall freedom. We shall then see that liberation by ingratiation is a conceptual impossibility also on the pure negative account, as it neither enhances the slave's overall freedom nor gives the slave a specific freedom he did not already possess.

It is true, of course, that by ingratiating himself with his master, the slave can become able to perform an action he otherwise could not perform. But it does not follow that the slave thereby gains a freedom. For pure negative

54 THE REPUBLICAN DILEMMA

freedom theorists, if ingratiation makes the slave able to do x at t, then he is always free to do x at t—he just has to curry favor with his master first. The ingratiation therefore gives the slave no specific freedom he did not already possess. This point is illustrated by Kramer's example where Barry the large Bully prevents Ernest from eating a russet apple at t_1. After a series of self-abasing actions, however, Barry finally lets Ernest eat the apple at t_6.[84] At t_1, Ernest is unfree to eat the apple at t_1, but he is free at t_1 to eat it at t_6. He is also free at t_2–t_6 to eat the apple at t_6 if he performs the required series of self-abasing actions.

We can use Carter's model of an "act-tree" to clarify this matter further.[85] We can often perform an action, x, only after performing other actions, "basic actions," that form the trunk of the act-tree out of which our ability to do x grows. It makes no difference what these basic actions are. I might be free to buy a house, although I have to work and save before I can do so. It is therefore a conceptual mistake to say that I "make myself free" to buy the house by working and saving. Likewise, ingratiation is no way for either Ernest or the slave to gain a new freedom.

Nor is it a way for them to increase their overall freedom. If the slave has to curry favor with his master before he can do x, then his overall freedom is reduced by the master. He has the freedom to do x, but if the master makes it the case that only a small number of conjunctively exercisable actions can be combined with doing x, then the master reduces the slave's overall freedom. In Kramer's words, the master reduces "the frequency of [x's] inclusion in the combinations of conjunctively exercisable liberties that are available to [the slave]."[86] The master's impact on the slave's overall freedom therefore remains the same whether the slave ingratiates himself with her or not. We thus make sense of Kramer's view that the interference in such cases of domination "does not come about through the actual application of violence (*ex hypothesi*), but it consists in the undoing of the conjunctive exercisability of many opportunities—opportunities that could have been exercised conjunctively in the absence of the dominant party's sway."[87]

Pettit believes this "observation may soften the difficulty of living with the conclusion of [the pure negative freedom] argument—that one can make oneself free in a given choice by adaption or ingratiation—but it does not remove it."[88] But since ingratiation can affect neither the specific nor the overall aspect of pure negative freedom, we see that this "observation" does not just soften the alleged problem with pure negative freedom, it eliminates it.

3.7 The benevolent master

However, if republicans see the slave as categorically unfree, their freedom judgments might come apart from those of pure negative freedom theorists in cases where the master lets the slave do whatever he wants whether he curries favor or not. This master has easy access to a world in which she interferes with her slave, she just never does so. Slaves typically have narrower opportunity sets than non-slaves have, but the slave in this particular set of cases has an extraordinarily benevolent, or perhaps just indifferent, master who lets her slave do whatever he wants regardless of the level of humility he shows toward her and how hard he works.

Now, there will always be certain types of action associated with citizenship that slaves cannot perform. "Slave" is a legal status that comes with legal constraints on the person who is a slave. The slave cannot vote in political elections or run for public office, for example. We might suppose that the master does nothing to stop him from voting or running for public office, perhaps because she is opposed to slavery and keeps her slave only because she believes he would otherwise become someone else's property and consequently be worse off. However, those enforcing the law that permits slavery will prevent the slave from performing these particular actions. They will also make sure the slave cannot enter into a contract without his master's approval. Given the benevolence of the master in this example, however, this constraint might not reduce the slave's overall freedom by much.

While the slave in this example necessarily lacks certain freedoms, he might nonetheless enjoy more overall freedom than certain non-slaves, such as poverty-stricken citizens.[89] For this reason, Fabian Wendt argues that we cannot find the intrinsic problem of slavery by looking at the slave's pure negative freedom.[90] What is problematic about the slave's inferior status, according to Wendt, is not that he is constrained, but that he is owned by another person. He is denied self-ownership, but if we define freedom in a non-moralized way, we cannot say that he is necessarily denied freedom. What is problematic about lack of self-ownership, in Wendt's view, cannot be explained empirically by pointing to what the slave can or cannot do; it must be explained by saying what is morally right about self-ownership and wrong about lacking it. Unless we moralize freedom, then, we cannot say that slavery itself necessarily makes the slave unfree. By sticking to a

56 THE REPUBLICAN DILEMMA

non-moralized definition of freedom, we can only say that slavery is unjust because it violates self-ownership.

This is only partly correct, however, since we have just seen that there are certain freedoms the slave necessarily lacks. But Wendt is right insofar as he means we must moralize freedom to say the slave is unfree to perform even the actions no one either does or will prevent him from doing. The master has the power to interfere with her slave as it pleases her, without regard for any interests the slave might avow. Republicans believe this power asymmetry makes the slave unfree to do anything, and we saw in Section 2.4 why that implies a moralized definition of freedom. We also saw in the previous chapter that we can make the same judgments regarding a person's freedom with a moralized freedom definition as with a non-moralized one.

The slave example nonetheless points toward a way in which republicans can define freedom so as to make judgments about a person's freedom that deviate from those of pure negative freedom theorists. If republicans consider a person to be unfree in any action as long as someone has the power to interfere with him, regardless of how likely she is to actually do so, then their judgments about this person's freedom will differ from those of pure negative freedom theorists. Lovett also suggests this possible distinction when he says the servant of a benevolent master might have more pure negative freedom than a servant of a mean master, while they are equally unfree on the republican account.[91]

This observation identifies a path toward falsifying the equivalent-judgments thesis and, consequently, finding a republican freedom ideal that conflicts with the promotion of pure negative freedom. This is the path I shall follow in what remains of the book. Republicans need to make sure the robustness of their freedom definition is sufficiently strong by requiring that institutions be in place to make it the case that no one can access a nearby possible world in which they interfere with another with impunity, even when such interference is highly unlikely. To distance their freedom concept from the promotion of pure negative freedom, republicans must take freedom to require a level of protection that implies a loss in the number of actions citizens can do either separately or conjunctively, but a gain in their robust ability to perform the remaining actions. That is, individuals will have smaller opportunity sets, but they will possess their smaller opportunity sets even under unlikely circumstances. Pure negative freedom theorists cannot justify the interference involved in such extensive protection as necessary for enhancing overall freedom.

3.8 Reducing scope

We saw in Section 3.2 that scope and robustness are inversely related. An increase in robustness therefore entails a reduction in scope. In more practical terms, making freedom require more robust protection means increasing the number of kinds of interference that do not make people unfree.

We have now seen how protection can enhance pure negative freedom by giving individuals freedoms they otherwise would not have had. This is so even though being free to act, on this account, requires only the absence of prevention and not protection against such prevention. A republican definition of freedom in conflict with the promotion of pure negative freedom would have to require robust protection to the extent that it causes no gain, and perhaps even a loss, of pure negative overall freedom. We find such strong priority to robustness at the expense of scope in List's understanding of republican freedom. As he says, "republicans may have to reduce the scope of freedom to such an extent that very little individual freedom can be preserved if maximal robustness is to be achieved."[92]

This way of balancing scope and robustness blocks an optimal trade-off between the two dimensions with respect to Pareto efficiency. To illustrate, List imagines two societies, one in which there is redistributive taxation and an extensive welfare state, and one with a minimal state and redistribution only by informal charity between citizens.[93] People enjoy greater opportunity sets in the latter society, and most of them therefore prefer to live in it rather than in the former, where their opportunity sets are smaller but more robustly protected. But pursuing republican freedom, as List understands it with a firm priority to robustness over scope, means opting for the society most people do not prefer to live in.

Another way of understanding a firm priority to robustness is to say that it expresses greater risk-aversion than does the pure negative view of promoting freedom.[94] Risk aversion involves willingness to forgo something valuable to insure yourself against losing something valuable. A risk-averse person is willing to pay, or forgo a benefit, to avoid a gamble between a good and a bad outcome even when she is more likely to gain than to lose from the gamble. People who are risk-averse about wealth, for example, are willing to trade some of their wealth, or some of their opportunities for more wealth, to gain greater protection of the wealth they have.

While promoting republican freedom, on this account, means ensuring a particularly strong protection of certain freedoms, promoting pure negative

58   THE REPUBLICAN DILEMMA

freedom is to aim for an optimal trade-off between what individuals can do here and now and what they will be able to do across a range of scenarios. We do so by weighting different scenarios according to their probability of being realized. When we promote pure negative freedom, we will often consider greater security to involve too great a loss of freedom.[95] We will restrict liberty only for the sake of greater liberty, and therefore only allow for security up to a certain level. Extensive surveillance and security checks at public spaces, for example, might enhance our security but not our overall freedom unless the security threat is sufficiently credible and severe. On the other hand, if we define republican freedom with a strong priority to robustness, promoting republican freedom will involve such surveillance and security checks even when the probability of interference is low.

Another implication of this strong priority to robustness is that citizens will have to be firmly committed to ensuring the robustness of the institutional protection of what remains of the scope of their freedom. This observation makes sense of the republican slogan "the price of liberty is eternal vigilance." And this understanding of republican freedom fits well with Kramer's observation that republicans have traditionally viewed the process of securing individuals' liberty as inevitably involving a cost to their freedom from interference.[96]

This demanding understanding of republican freedom is not Pettit's understanding. Requiring robust protection only up to the level at which the eyeball test is met seems to involve no protection that will reduce people's number of available courses of action. People pass the eyeball test when they are not subject to subjunctive prevention or credible threats. We have seen that protection to this extent is required also for promoting people's pure negative freedom. A strong interpretation of republican freedom, on the other hand, requires protection beyond the point at which people can look one another in the eye without feeling constrained. This point will be made clearer in subsequent chapters.

3.9 Conclusion

Republican freedom and pure negative freedom occupy different positions along both the scope and the robustness dimension. But that does not mean republican and pure negative freedom theorists must make different judgments about how free someone is, whether someone's freedom has increased or been reduced, or about how freedom is distributed across the members of a society. Republican freedom has greater robustness than pure negative freedom has, but the institutions that must be in place to realize the protection against interference that republican freedom requires, at least on a moderate account, will promote pure negative overall freedom. The equivalent-judgments thesis therefore holds with respect to at least moderate conceptions of republican freedom, including Pettit's.

I have considered four kinds of cases we might think of as "domination without interference," and whether republicans and pure negative freedom theorists will make different judgments about the freedom of the dominated person, B, in these cases. I first found no difference in judgments about B's freedom where A will prevent him from performing an action, x, were he to try to do x. Likewise, I found no difference in freedom judgments in cases where A threatens B by saying she will punish him for doing x by preventing him from doing y. And if B must ingratiate himself with A before he can do x, then B restricts A's freedom on the pure negative as well as the republican account. Pettit is therefore wrong to think pure negative freedom theorists cannot fully account for the dominated person's loss of freedom in these cases. And Carter and Kramer are right when they say we ought to deny people uncontrolled power whether we promote one or the other of the two freedom ideals.[97]

I have, however, detected a possible difference in republican and pure negative judgments of freedom in a fourth kind of case in which we might think A dominates B. Here A has the power to interfere with B as it pleases her, but she is so unlikely to do so that the power asymmetry has no impact on B's combinations of conjunctively exercisable actions. No difference in judgments is likely if republicans cling to Pettit's eyeball test to determine freedom's required level of protection. Passing this test will enhance pure negative freedom, since it means freeing up all actions conjunctively exercisable with looking anyone in the eye without reason for fear or deference. However, republicans can increase the robustness and, correspondingly, reduce the scope of their understanding of freedom by saying that B's freedom depends on A's power being further weakened when no such additional protection will increase the number of combinations of actions B can exercise conjunctively. Republican freedom will then require protection beyond what is compatible with the promotion of pure negative freedom, and republicans' judgment of B's freedom will differ from that of pure negative freedom theorists.

60 THE REPUBLICAN DILEMMA

Here lies the key to distinguishing republicanism from a theory promoting pure negative freedom. The catch is that this level of protection makes republican freedom compatible with more kinds of interference for the sake of protecting against the interference with which it is incompatible. We shall see how that makes the ideal less attractive, at least from a liberal point of view. This is the republican dilemma: equivalent freedom judgments or loss of attractiveness and applicability.

4

Public reason

4.1 Introduction

For republicans, people are free insofar as the power of government officials is constrained so that they reliably promote the people's common interests.[1] Under such conditions, government interference promoting these interests does not make citizens unfree. The definition of common interests, or the common good, therefore specifies the scope of republican freedom. In this chapter, I focus on Pettit's republican view of the common good to work out how he defines the scope of freedom. This is an important step toward understanding the republican position along the scope dimension, which in turn determines how robust republican freedom can be. In the next chapter, I consider what it means to constrain the government to make sure it reliably promotes common interests, as that concerns the robustness of republican freedom.

This chapter provides a more comprehensive account of the scope of republican freedom than Chapter 2 by examining the nature of, and grounds for, the constraints on individuals' opportunity sets understood not to contribute to republican unfreedom. These constraints are compatible with collectively defined, or common, interests that must be robustly promoted—that is, promoted across a range of possible worlds—for citizens to be free from domination.

The chapter first considers the procedure of identifying common interests. I show how Pettit understands citizens' common interests as the output of Rawlsian public reasoning. The idea of public reason, Rawls writes, "is a view about the kind of reasons on which citizens are to rest their political cases in making their political justifications to one another when they support laws and policies that invoke the coercive powers of government concerning fundamental political questions."[2] Political deliberation among reasonable persons appealing to public reason constructs principles that protect and promote everyone's opportunity to develop and pursue a wide range of conceptions of the good.[3] Pettit, likewise, says common interests are the

---

The Republican Dilemma. Lars J. K. Moen, Oxford University Press. © Oxford University Press 2024.
DOI: 10.1093/oso/9780197757024.003.0004

62 THE REPUBLICAN DILEMMA

interests people have in leading their lives as they prefer and can therefore be avowed publicly without shame because they are shared by everyone in the society.

Demonstrating Pettit's connection to Rawlsian political constructivism is important for understanding the scope of Pettit's republican freedom. In later chapters, it will become clear why this way of defining the scope of freedom is incompatible with the level of robustness required to falsify the equivalent-judgments thesis.

This chapter also shows how Rawls and Pettit's shared constructivist procedure takes them both to a special concern for the basic liberties. A crucial question will be whether promoting citizens' capacity to exercise these liberties is compatible with the promotion of pure negative freedom.

4.2 Political constructivism

Rawls formulates the basic principles on which a modern, pluralistic society ought to be governed in a procedure he calls "political constructivism."[4] Constructivism, more broadly, defines morality as what rational agents would agree to under specified conditions. These agents are motivated by a conception-dependent desire, which is the desire to act in ways they can justify to others.[5] They therefore propose principles of fair cooperation among equals.[6] Conception-dependent desires reflect what T. M. Scanlon calls "a conception of morally legitimate interests."[7] These are interests in proposing moral principles no person can reasonably reject.[8] An action is right if and only if it is compatible with such principles.[9] Constructivism thus offers an account of the standards of practical reason—that is, a way of resolving through rational deliberation what one ought to do. Individuals exercising such reasoning are reasonable persons proposing fair terms of social cooperation that they are themselves willing to abide by as long as they expect also others to do so.[10]

For Scanlon, conception-dependent desires are basic—that is, we have a desire to justify our actions to others that is not based on any other desire. I shall not consider the plausibility of this metaethical view. I instead, like Rawls, understand reasonable persons to be motivated by this conception-dependent desire without taking a stand on whether these desires are basic or not.[11] When we construct the principles of a political conception of justice, Rawls says, "we rely on the kind of motivation Scanlon takes as basic."[12]

Reasonable persons, Rawls explains, "desire for its own sake a social world in which they, as free and equal, can cooperate with others on terms all can accept."[13] As long as they expect others to reciprocate, they willingly "propose fair terms that others may reasonably be expected to accept, so that all may benefit and improve on what every one can do on their own."[14] Motivated by this desire, reasonable persons agree on principles that can be met without compromising anyone's reasonable comprehensive doctrine.[15] We have then achieved the ultimate goal of political liberalism, namely "full public justification" of the principles of the political conception of justice.[16]

A political conception, Rawls explains, has three defining features.[17] First, it applies to society's basic political and social institutions, or what Rawls calls "the basic structure." Rawls defines the basic structure as "the background social framework within which the activities of associations and individuals take place."[18] It consists of institutions that inevitably shape the lives of the individuals living in the society. Here it is important to note that these are institutions of a modern society, which is characterized by the fact of reasonable pluralism—that is, the fact that a "diversity of reasonable comprehensive religious, philosophical, and moral doctrines . . . is a permanent feature of the public culture of democracy."[19]

Second, a political conception is independent of any particular comprehensive doctrine. It is not a compromise between comprehensive doctrines for the sake of stability, but rather a set of principles that no reasonable citizen can reject. Here we see how Rawls accounts for the fact of pluralism. Making citizens of a pluralistic society comply with social institutions promoting a particular comprehensive doctrine would necessarily involve oppressive use of political power. Such use of power is illegitimate, in Rawls's view.

Third, the principles of a political conception reflect a public political culture formed around the view of society as what Rawls calls "a fair system of cooperation."[20] A basic structure operating in accordance with a political conception thus defined satisfies Rawls's liberal principle of legitimacy.[21] Later in this chapter, we shall see that Pettit also prescribes such a political conception, but he takes it to apply to more than just the basic structure.

For constructivists, justification is based on a conception of reason and reasonableness. Conception-dependent desires are reasonable desires. Specifying these desires is to specify a conception of reasonableness. And moral principles are then based on what is considered reasonable. For constructivists, there is no moral order prior to, and independent of, this procedure of construction. Instead, moral facts are expressed in the principles

64   THE REPUBLICAN DILEMMA

this procedure generates.[22] The procedure constructs these facts from non-constructed basic assumptions about people's reasonableness and how they interact in a society. In Rawls's political constructivism, the fact of pluralism is such a fact.

The conception-dependent desires defining reasonableness in Rawls's political constructivism is the desire to live in a society in which all citizens cooperate on fair terms as free and equal reasonable persons.[23] Further specification of these desires depends on the public political culture of the particular society in question.[24] Different sets of principles can pass the reasonableness test, and which one will actually do so in a given society depends on the particular features of that society. It follows that constructivism allows for a certain degree of cultural relativism.[25] What is considered reasonable will vary from one society to another, as well as from one time to another within the same society. Principles must be publicly justified to the individuals of the society to which they apply, and not to people outside of it. Universal principles would be inapplicable and therefore useless as principles of practical reason.[26] The "no reasonable rejection" criterion does, however, provide an objective standard of public justification and reasonableness.[27] In political constructivism, a conviction meets this standard of objectivity insofar as it is based on reasons sufficient for convincing all reasonable persons that it is reasonable.[28]

Rawls's political constructivism seeks agreement on a basis shared by a diverse group of citizens, and therefore does not deliver the principles of a comprehensive moral doctrine, as they would inevitably conflict with some reasonable doctrines in a pluralistic society. Instead, it constructs principles of justice to govern society's basic structure that are compatible with all reasonable comprehensive doctrines within a modern, pluralist society. The principles proposed by a reasonable person, then, are acceptable not just to people similar to the person herself or himself, but also to people of different cultural backgrounds. Rawls admits, however, that reasonable persons will not always reach an agreement. In cases of disagreement, they will agree on a procedure for making decisions despite their reasonable disagreement. And as part of their reasonableness, they will accept the outcome of this procedure.[29]

To act as a reasonable person, you must place yourself in another person's position. Whoever that person is, you must make sure she or he will have reasonable grounds for accepting the principle you propose, or no reasonable grounds for rejecting it.[30] Constructivism thus models impartiality. And when we employ this methodology, Scanlon explains, "our attention is naturally directed first to those who would do worst under [the principle]."[31] After all, if the worst-off can reasonably accept it, or if they have no reasonable grounds for rejecting it, then it seems likely that also other reasonable persons will be motivated to accept it, or not reject it. If the worst-off can accept the principle, it passes Rawls's requirement that we should, as a matter of mutual respect, be able to justify it to anyone affected by it.[32] We shall see in the next section that also Pettit has special concern for the worst-off.

In his political liberalism, Rawls's model of impartiality is the idea of public reason. Public reason defines the appropriate motivation for people making decisions concerning fundamental political issues. Reasonable persons motivated by public reason, Rawls explains, "are ready to propose principles and standards as fair terms of cooperation and to abide by them willingly, given the assurance that others will likewise do so."[33] They will accept principles emerging from public reasoning. Importantly, although a principle in a political conception of justice is acceptable to all reasonable persons, it is unlikely to be endorsed by everyone as the best or most just principle. It instead means that everyone appreciates the reasons supporting this principle and is willing to comply with it should it be democratically implemented.

4.3 Republican reasonableness

Pettit criticizes constructivism for its idealized reasonableness condition. He claims to be opposed to "any idealizing assumptions about human nature or compliance with the law that would render [an ideal] difficult to apply in the ordinary world."[34] A political ideal, he says, must be supported by people "as they are actually disposed." It cannot just "satisfy terms that they would endorse if they were properly rational or reasonable."[35] Constructivists, Pettit says, "tend to neglect the issue of legitimacy, ignoring the importance of how people actually relate to the regime under which they live."[36] He therefore rejects the version of legitimacy "now often invoked within contractualist circles, which equates legitimacy with civic justifiability" and mentions Rawls's liberal principle of legitimacy as an example of this approach.[37] He rejects the constructivist reasonableness condition and argues for institutions that enables citizens to contest political decisions. When such institutions are established, he says, "then of course everything is up for grabs."[38]

66   THE REPUBLICAN DILEMMA

However, Pettit cannot give citizens such free reins. His own approach, "legitimacy as popular control," must also rely on reasonableness.[39] Popular control, Pettit explains, requires that all citizens have an equal opportunity to influence their government by expressing their complaints in public. It further involves making sure the government remedies any complaint that is "publicly avowable in the context of reciprocal exchange"—that is, any complaint reflecting a willingness to live on equal terms with others.[40] These complaints must be widely accepted as relevant for society as a whole, and not just to certain individuals or groups.[41] Only those willing to live on equal terms with others can be influential. Pettit consequently supports a constructivist reasonableness condition. Everything is not up for grabs; contestation can influence political decision-making only if it is reasonable.

Pettit even endorses the constructivist reasonable rejection test explicitly when he says the government should be forced to promote the public interest, and "practices and policies will count as being in the public interest precisely so far as they are immune to reasonable objection, under a particular interpretation of what makes an objection reasonable." And he then says these "are practices and policies that might count, under a broadly contractualist approach, as arrangements required by justice."[42] This view is also shared by other republican theorists. Republicans, Maurizio Viroli writes, "understand that the common good is neither the good (or interest) of everyone nor a good (or interest) that transcends private interests; rather, it is the good of citizens who wish to live free and independent and as such is opposed to the good of those who wish to dominate."[43] Viroli finds in Machiavelli the idea that "the common good is the good of citizens who do not want to be oppressed and have no ambition to dominate."[44] Skinner also understands the idea of making decisions appealing to everyone's interests as central in the republican tradition.[45]

4.4 Popular control

To understand Pettit's account of legitimacy as popular control, let us consider the three features of his understanding of popular control: it is individualized, unconditioned, and efficacious. First, popular control is individualized because it gives each citizen a comparable role in the joint control of government.[46] All citizens have equal shares of the control, though they need not have the same influence on government, since they may choose to participate to varying degrees. The extent to which they participate does not make them more or less free, however, since freedom requires not equal influence, but equal access to influencing. We might think of a system where only one group of individuals—property-owning men, say—can vote and run for public office. Under such a system, fair treatment of individuals excluded from this privileged group is due only to the goodwill of the property-owning men. Avoiding such domination requires that all citizens have a status protecting their equal opportunity to influence their government.

Any demand for more than an equal share of the control of government can have no political influence. Only citizens who respect other citizens as their equals can influence political institutions. As Pettit writes, citizens must be "willing to live on equal terms with their fellow citizens" and not to "claim a special position for themselves."[47] In other words, the system of political decision-making cannot allow the citizens to undermine their individualized control. This is where a reasonableness condition enters into the republican theory. Republican freedom depends on what Pettit calls "patriotism," which is the commitment to establish a government that can accommodate everyone's shared interests, and not just the interests of oneself and one's own group.[48] The republic therefore cannot be based on any particular individual or group's conception of the good.

If some citizens have less than an equal share in influencing political decision-making, we risk making political decisions that express false negatives and false positives.[49] The former are oversights of concerns people have, and failures to act when necessary for promoting common interests. The latter are actions conflicting with popular opinion based on a misunderstanding of people's shared interests. To avoid these problems, citizens must have constitutionally protected rights to exercise the basic liberties, and especially the political liberties, in order to effectively influence political decision-making.[50] Unreasonable persons interfered with have no legitimate grounds for protesting against the interference necessary for this purpose.

The common interests promoted under individualized control can be satisfied without giving anyone exceptional treatment.[51] These interests can therefore be used as grounds acceptable to a broad range of the population in political deliberation. They can be avowed by "anyone in discourse with others about what they should jointly or collectively provide can adduce without embarrassment as relevant matters to take into account."[52] These avowal-ready interests are interests in goods "anyone who accepts the

68 THE REPUBLICAN DILEMMA

necessity of living on equal terms with others is likely to want to have collectively guaranteed or promoted."[53] Pettit has particularly in mind interests in exercising the basic liberties, which is a part of his theory I shall return to later in this chapter.

This demand for citizens to express avowal-ready interests looks much like the constructivist reasonableness condition outlined in the previous section. As Christine Korsgaard writes in her discussion of public reason in Rawls's theory, "[p]art of the appeal of the difference principle is that it is the source of justifications which you can offer to anyone without embarrassment."[54] Avowal-ready interests function in Pettit's theory as what Scanlon calls "morally legitimate interests."[55] They are legitimate because they have broad appeal in society and reflect citizens' willingness to live on fair and equal terms with others. Pettit indeed says his way of identifying common interests is "broadly contractualist in spirit; it owes much in particular to the interpretation of Rawlsian contractualism."[56]

The second feature of popular control is that it is unconditioned in the sense that people remain in control regardless of any change of will within the government.[57] As Pettit says, "[o]ne agent will count as controlling another only insofar as the influence exercised leads to the required result independently of the will of the controlled agent, or indeed of any third party."[58] Citizens do not control their government if government officials will act according to the people's interests only conditionally—that is, only if it suits them. People enjoy republican freedom only insofar as they possess the power to robustly make sure others will interfere with them only on their own terms. I shall say little about this feature of popular control in this chapter, as it concerns institutional protection against misrule and the robustness condition of republican freedom, which are issues I turn to in the next chapter.

The third and final feature of popular control, Pettit explains, is that it "must be effective or efficacious enough to impose a popular direction on government that nullifies the intrusion of alien will."[59] The government is not dominating, and government interference is controlled, if citizens can *effectively* contest any decision conflicting with their avowal-ready interests.[60] Pettit asks himself how effective the popular control must be in order for the citizens to enjoy republican freedom: "How far ought it to be able to impose a popular direction on government, removing opportunities for the intrusion of private interest and private will?"[61] His answer is that the people enjoy sufficient control if each citizen has good reason to believe that a decision going

PUBLIC REASON 69

against his interests was "just tough luck" and not some other agent's attempt to impose her will on him.

Here we see another feature of constructivism: its special concern for the worst-off. Those most disadvantaged by a political decision must be able to accept it as a matter of "tough luck." Of course, this group might not—indeed, should not—consistently contain the same individual citizens, as that would suggest systematic undermining of one group's interests rather than mere tough luck. But we here see in Pettit's theory, as in Rawls's, that legitimate political decision-making must be acceptable even to those benefiting the least from it.

No limitation on the effectiveness of popular control can be made "unnecessarily," Pettit says.[62] Accounting for local standards, he says "the state must secure people's equal, undominated status vis-à-vis one another to a suitably high level or degree."[63] Popular control is sufficiently efficacious when citizens "will not have a reason to feel resentment at how the state performs."[64] This sufficiency requirement, as opposed to an absoluteness demand, enables Pettit to say that people enjoy popular control also where conditions allow them less effective control over their government than people have elsewhere. After all, citizens will then have no good reason for complaining about unfair treatment. The same goes for complaints about the government when the citizens have not done enough, although they could have done more, to make effective use of their popular control. Then, Pettit says, "you and your fellows have only yourselves to blame. And if you don't blame yourself, you can only blame your fellows."[65] In other words, citizens cannot complain about their control not being efficacious if conditions do not allow for greater efficacy, or they choose not to exercise their control as effectively as they can.

This view of the efficacy condition for popular control suggests people can themselves decide for themselves how much it requires of them in terms of making the government serve their common interests. In the next chapter, I reject this view by arguing that popular control should be defined independently of human motivation, so that citizens decide how much popular control they will actually possess. By relaxing their level of vigilance, they might, as Pettit says, only have themselves to blame when their government does not effectively promote their common interests. But we should nonetheless interpret this decline in vigilance as a loss of popular control.

For now, however, I hope to have established that Pettit's notion of popular control fits squarely into the framework of political constructivism. Only

70 THE REPUBLICAN DILEMMA

reasonable citizens willing to live on equal terms with others can influence political decision-making. By letting people pursue a status elevated above their fellow citizens, individualized control is undermined. The control of government will then also be conditioned, as the satisfaction of avowal-ready interests becomes dependent on the will of particular agents with more power than others in the society.

4.5 A consensus model of public justification

Avowal-ready interests are the interests reasonable citizens share, which is why they can be avowed in public without embarrassment. Those lacking avowal-ready interests, or lacking a willingness to appeal to them when they seek political influence, cannot influence political decision-making. Pettit's idea of avowal-ready interests is thus based on what Rawls calls an "overlapping consensus," which is the set of values and convictions reasonable persons share and is therefore considered the appropriate basis for public reason and the principles of justice.[66] It is the basis for the public reasons supporting the principles of a fully legitimate political conception of justice. Reasonable persons accept these principles not merely for the sake of stability, but because they are based on values within their own comprehensive doctrines.

Rawls's political constructivism thus expresses what is often referred to as a consensus model of public justification. Consensus here refers to the restriction on what reasons people can appeal to in the political arena. For Rawls, political judgments must be based on reasons acceptable to all reasonable persons.[67] Each reasonable person can then see her or his personal convictions in the principles governing society's basic structure. No one can therefore reasonably feel that society's institutional structure suppresses her or his status as a separate individual. Political power based on a political conception is acceptable to all reasonable citizens, and therefore satisfies the liberal principle of legitimacy.[68]

Pettit's theory also requires that all citizens can see their will in their government. They cannot be governed by an alien will, as that would imply domination. Legitimate government interference accords with "multi-partisan terms," which "will lay down a foundation of common ground between [the involved parties]."[69] For both Rawls and Pettit, then, citizens must see their own reasonable convictions in the exercise of political power.

PUBLIC REASON 71

Other public-reason liberals reject consensus models of public justification and instead defend a convergence requirement.[70] Legitimate political decision-making, on their view, requires no firmer basis than convergence between people's comprehensive doctrines. Individuals must only have sufficient personal reasons for a collective decision on which their views converge.[71] People must be able to reach agreements but need not base these agreements on the part of their comprehensive doctrines that lies within an overlapping consensus. Their reasons should be intelligible—that is, understandable to others as reasons for their opinions—but they need not be widely accepted or shared. People may therefore appeal to their whole comprehensive doctrines and can bargain from different points of view and offer compromises instead of appealing to common ground. Without an overlapping consensus requirement, a convergence model can accept contributions from unreasonable persons. Even unreasonable persons might therefore accept its output. Convergence models consequently offer a broader, more inclusive approach to public justification than do consensus models. But while convergence ensures breadth, consensus goes deeper by requiring that all reasonable persons see their convictions in the whole political conception.

Rejecting the idealized reasonableness condition, as Pettit claims to do, means endorsing the convergence model.[72] But we have seen that Pettit is mistaken to claim he rejects reasonableness. This becomes even clearer when he discusses these two approaches to public justification and implicitly endorses the consensus model. Instead of using the terms "consensus" and "convergence," he contrasts "debate-based decision-making" to "bargain-based decision-making,"[73] respectively, or more recently as the "acceptability game" and the "acceptance game."[74] In the former, the players work toward consensus by shaping their preferences in response to what they learn about one another's concerns. They are rewarded for making proposals they believe everyone can accept. In the acceptance game, on the other hand, the players come to the table with predetermined interests and try to make agreements by trading concessions. They try to reach an agreement by announcing the minimal concessions they are willing to make.

Pettit favors the acceptability game because it fosters the norms of political argument required for popular control. "The only hope of getting individuals to share equally in a system of popular control," he says, "is to organize the influence they exercise under the protocols of an acceptability game."[75] Political decision, Pettit argues, should be based on avowal-ready interests identified

72 THE REPUBLICAN DILEMMA

in reasoned deliberation, not on personal interests.[76] "The guiding republican ideal," he says, "requires [citizens] to assume the role of democratically respectful interlocutors who aim at persuading others, not overwhelming them."[77] A system that rewards attempts to win a greater than equal share of popular control, however, conflicts with the republican freedom ideal. Nondomination therefore requires a system in which reasonableness is a requirement for influence. The players should be rewarded for taking a "group-level point of view," as they are in the acceptability game.[78] This game induces not norms of compromise, but norms of solidarity and reasonableness.

The acceptance game, on the other hand, does not require the players to take the perspective of society as a whole. Players are successful if they can reach an agreement with other players without having to (significantly) compromise their personal interests. In this game, as Pettit understands it, people will contest decisions simply because they do not serve their private interests, and not because they are considered bad for their society or because they undermine popular control.[79] In Rawlsian terms, the game induces no priority to the reasonable over the rational. The winner of this game is the player who gains most personal control over the government. State interference, then, will not be on the people's terms, but on the terms of those playing the acceptance game well. Successful players consequently end up dominating unsuccessful ones, as the latter's interests are significantly compromised and have no or little influence on political decision-making. "Nothing could be further from the republican ideal," Pettit says.[80]

Popular control requires that people take others' interests into consideration and reach political decisions everyone can accept, as opposed to trying to be more influential than others and having one's own private interests satisfied. It therefore depends on people's desire to be reasonable. People must be willing to take their group's point of view and accept concessions to their private interests willingly rather than resentfully.[81] Pettit therefore endorses the acceptability game and, implicitly, Rawls's consensus model of public justification.

But Pettit actually denies that his favored procedure is consensus-based. Controlled political decisions, he says, do not emerge from "some consensual process."[82] Popular control, in his view, is instead secured by the condition of contestation—that is, controlled decisions cannot be effectively contested as violations of avowal-ready interests. But we have now seen that contestation can only be influential if it expresses avowal-ready interests defined in a consensual procedure.

4.6 Context-sensitivity

We have seen that in constructivism, principles are constructed with sensitivity to facts about the particular society to which they apply. Pettit, however, argues that Rawls fails to fully appreciate how the common interests the government must strive to satisfy differ from one society to another.[83] Pettit sees his acceptability game as context-bound to a greater extent than is Rawls's idea of public reason. More specifically, considerations rewarded in the acceptability game, Pettit explains, are context-bound in three ways that Rawls's public reason is not.[84] First, considerations may be accepted only because of the society's history. Second, considerations must be widely acceptable only to society's current members. As the membership changes, the content of the acceptable might change with it. And third, the considerations endorsed in the acceptability game need not formulate basic principles; they may instead be applied directly to particular issues of policy or to how particular decisions are to be made.

First, then, Pettit notes that different societies might have different interpretations of the popular will, and therefore of alien will, due to events in their different histories. One example Pettit gives is that people in federal states will have reasonable considerations about equal representations of states that will not be considered reasonable among people in non-federal states.[85] While this seems plausible, I do not see why Rawls's idea of public reason cannot also be sensitive to such historical differences. Rawls even says that he is "not trying to find a conception of justice suitable for all societies regardless of their particular social or historical circumstances."[86] Public reason defines the framework of what a citizen sincerely believes to be the most reasonable political conception of justice for her or his particular society, and not just for any society.[87] This is an important reason for why there are many possible political conceptions of justice. Reasonable and rational persons, Rawls says, adjust their convictions in response to their environment.[88] A political conception reflects the political culture of the specific society to which it applies. Rawls emphasizes that "[a]n important feature of a conception of justice is that it should generate its own support."[89] Otherwise, it will not be stable, and political power will not satisfy the liberal principle of legitimacy. Rawls thus accommodates Pettit's concern about historical context-sensitivity. There is no reason why differences in political conceptions cannot reflect differences in societies' histories.

74   THE REPUBLICAN DILEMMA

Rawls's concern with stability is central also in responding to Pettit's second reason for thinking his theory is more context-sensitive. What is considered acceptable in a society, Pettit says, will vary over time as the society's membership changes. But since a Rawlsian political conception of justice reflects the political culture of the particular society to which it applies, it too must be responsive to changes in popular opinion. Indeed, this is why Rawls thinks "the content of public reason is . . . given by a family of political conceptions of justice, and not by a single one."[90] "Political liberalism," Rawls says, "does not try to fix public reason once and for all in the form of one favored political conception of justice."[91] New views of which reasons count as public will likely emerge over time.

Although Rawls expects people's comprehensive doctrines to be stable over time, he adds that they tend to evolve in response to good reasons.[92] The overlapping consensus will therefore also evolve, and so will the political conception. And the interpretation of the political conception, Rawls says, can change over time.[93] He considers it important to allow for this flexibility because "otherwise the claims of groups or interests arising from social change might be repressed and fail to gain their appropriate political voice."[94] Flexibility is therefore essential also for maintaining the stability of the political conception.[95] When the principles of justice begin, for whatever reason, to feel alien to the citizens, Rawls says they will not "acquire the corresponding sense of justice and develop a desire to act in accordance with its principles."[96] In other words, stability and legitimacy will start to wither.

However, Rawls's theory seems incapable of accommodating Pettit's third point given its focus on society's basic structure, and not on non-basic political decisions. In Pettit's acceptability game, the considerations accepted not only formulate fundamental principles for the governing of society, they also provide grounds for other political decisions. For Rawls, on the other hand, public reason produces the principles of a complete political conception of justice, which answers "all, or nearly all, questions involving constitutional essentials and matters of basic justice."[97] Constitutional essentials "specify the general structure of government and the political process" as well as the "equal basic rights and liberties of citizenship that legislative majorities are to respect."[98] They form "the general structure of government and the political process," and the "equal basic rights and liberties of citizens" that the basic structure and the political process specify.[99] Basic justice concerns distribution of goods and burdens, as well as ensuring everyone's fair opportunities.[100] Insofar as Rawls focuses only on these fundamental

PUBLIC REASON   75

political issues, Pettit has identified a genuine difference between his own theory and Rawls's.

However, this difference does not take Pettit's republicanism out of the Rawlsian framework. Rawls himself is actually not always clear on whether his public-reason requirement applies to only fundamental issues. Jonathan Quong understands Rawls to mean that public reason "*need not* apply beyond this domain."[101] At any rate, Pettit's third consideration is an internal critique of Rawls's theory along the lines of Quong's argument for a "broad view," in which public reason applies to all political decisions and not just to matters of constitutional essentials and basic justice, as on a "narrow view."[102] If we believe in the idea of public reason as an essential part of justifying political power, Quong argues, we should prefer a political decision grounded in public reason to one that is not, regardless of whether it concerns a fundamental political issue or not. For Quong, the neutrality of political liberalism—that is, its detachment from any particular comprehensive doctrine—is better served if all political decisions are grounded in public reason. So, when Pettit says that "unlike Rawls's reasons," the considerations accepted in the acceptability game "may be specifically tied to particular issues about whether to adopt this or that policy or to endorse this or that process of decision-making," he objects to the scope of Rawls's idea of public reason, not to the idea itself.[103] And by arguing for expanding the scope of public reason, Pettit actually goes further than Rawls in promoting political constructivism.

But perhaps Pettit means that the acceptability game could provide a basis *only* for dealing with particular issues, and not for formulating basic principles. This interpretation is implausible, however, since Pettit is especially concerned with ensuring everyone's capacity to exercise the basic liberties. This concern can only be understood as a fundamental principle in Pettit's theory, as it also is in Rawls's political liberalism.

4.7 The basic liberties

Rawls and Pettit's very similar procedures for determining what counts as common interests the government should promote lead them to a shared concern for the basic liberties. Rawls's concern with the basic liberties is made particularly evident in his understanding of the content of any political conception of justice. Irrespective of what society it applies to, a

76 THE REPUBLICAN DILEMMA

political conception has three defining features.[104] First, it contains a list of basic rights, liberties, and opportunities. Second, it assigns special priority to these rights, liberties, and opportunities. And third, it specifies measures for ensuring that all citizens have the means needed for effectively exercising these liberties. Reasonable persons in any modern, pluralistic society, then, will agree to fundamental principles to govern their society only if they give special priority to the basic liberties.

The basic liberties are important, in Rawls's view, because they are essential for anyone's ability to develop and exercise what Rawls calls the two "moral powers," which are the capacities for a sense of justice and a conception of the good.[105] Crudely, a conception of the good refers to whatever one considers worth pursuing over the course of one's life.[106] And a sense of justice refers to the willingness to see oneself and others as free and equal members of society, and to the desire for government based on fundamental principles acceptable to all reasonable persons despite their different conceptions of the good.[107] A sense of justice, Rawls says, is "the capacity to honor fair terms of cooperation and thus to be reasonable."[108] The sense of justice is superior to the capacity for a conception of the good, by which Rawls means that reasonable persons want nothing that conflicts with their sense of justice.[109] We see, then, that the two moral powers characterize the reasonable person. And since the capacity to exercise the basic liberties is necessary for developing the two moral powers, thereby becoming a reasonable person, they are also necessary for having political influence.

Pettit's reason for his special concern with the basic liberties is similar to Rawls's. Enjoying the capacity to exercise the basic liberties at one's own will is in Pettit's view an important part of being a free person. Citizens enjoying "sufficient power and protection in the sphere of the basic liberties," he says, can "walk tall amongst others and look any in the eye without reason for fear or deference."[110] The basic liberties enable each person to determine for herself how to act without restricting anyone else's capacity to choose for himself how to act.[111] The only restriction is on choices that can make one person superior to another.[112] Such choices would undermine an important purpose of the basic liberties, which is to ensure that all citizens are free persons with no good reason to fear the consequences others will inflict on them by expressing their sincere views.[113]

We see a similarity to Rawls here, as Pettit's emphasis on feeling free to make choices in accordance with one's own will is closely related to the ability to develop and pursue one's own conception of the good. As Pettit says, the

PUBLIC REASON 77

basic liberties enable people to determine for themselves how to behave without restricting anyone else's capacity to exercise such autonomy.[114] For this reason, as we shall see more clearly later in the chapter, Pettit and Rawls both identify the capacity to exercise the basic liberties as an interest everyone shares, and it therefore counts as a common interest.

However, Pettit thinks his account differs significantly from Rawls's with respect to which liberties should be considered basic. Pettit especially denies that Rawls sees sufficient importance in the political liberties. As Pettit writes, "as a matter of fact Rawls ... himself downplays the political liberties ... casting them as 'subordinate to the other freedoms,' and does not suggest that they ought to ensure control in that sense."[115] In Pettit's republican idea of popular control, on the other hand, the political liberties are crucial.

It is peculiar that Rawls would downplay the importance of the political liberties, since he considers the basic liberties essential for people to develop the capacities of reasonable persons, who are the main political actors in his theory. He also says the basic liberties give people an equal share in political decision-making, which is crucial for keeping the political procedure legitimate.[116] A constitution that protects the basic liberties, Rawls says, "establishes a secure common status of equal citizenship and realizes political justice."[117]

We straighten out this apparent contradiction if we put the passage Pettit quotes back into its context. Rawls does suggest that people might be wise to trust others of "superior wisdom and judgment" and to give greater weight to their opinions in political procedures. Similarly, he says, the passengers on board a ship will be wise to let the captain steer the course, "since they believe that he is more knowledgeable and wishes to arrive safely as much as they do."[118] To the extent that this analogy between the ship at sea and the ship of the state holds, Rawls thinks "the political liberties are indeed subordinate to the other freedoms that, so to say, define the intrinsic good of the passengers."[119]

But Rawls does not take this analogy as far as Pettit understands him to do. Pettit does not acknowledge that Rawls, after suggesting why the political liberties might be subordinate, adds that "[o]f course, the grounds for self-government are not solely instrumental. Equal political liberty when assured its fair value is bound to have a profound effect on the moral quality of civic life."[120] The political liberties, Rawls says, "strengthen men's sense of their own worth, enlarge their intellectual and moral sensibilities, and the basis for a sense of duty and obligation upon which the stability of just institutions depends." Without these liberties, people will become "estranged and

78 THE REPUBLICAN DILEMMA

isolated."[121] It is also important that the political liberties be of roughly equal value to the citizens, so that people will have about the same opportunities to influence political processes.[122] With the ability to exercise the political liberties, people can reflect on reasons everyone can accept and feel respected as full members of their society. The political liberties are thus essential for stimulating people's ties to their society and the reasonableness both Rawls and Pettit see as important. So, we see that Rawls does not downplay the significance of the political liberties in the way Pettit claims he does.

Furthermore, Pettit himself is not opposed to assigning greater weight to the opinion of some people in political decision-making. He rejects the Rousseauvian, or "Continental," view that political participation is necessary for the legitimate governance of free people.[123] What matters is that people have the capacity to contest political decisions, not that they necessarily take part in the decision-making. Political representatives and other public officials can therefore make decisions binding on the citizens without popular involvement. Rawls's ship analogy is therefore, to some extent, apt also in Pettit's theory, and there is no clear reason for thinking Rawls and Pettit's theories differ on this point.

Rawls is also particularly concerned with his observation that "our political liberties . . . [are particularly sensitive] to our social position and our place in the distribution of income and wealth."[124] Rawls says his first principle's "main requirements are that the fundamental liberties of the person and liberty of conscience and freedom of thought be protected and that the political process as a whole be a just procedure. Thus the constitution establishes a secure common status of equal citizenship and realizes political justice."[125] Rawls thus gives the political liberties the important place they have in Pettit's idea of popular control.

Pettit and Rawls's concern about private financial contributions in political campaigns further demonstrates their shared concern with giving people equal opportunities to exercising the political liberties. Rawls argues for restrictions on the "use of private means to enhance the value of some people's political liberties at the expense of others."[126] He refers to this problem as the "curse of money."[127] Pettit, similarly, sees measures to limit the influence of the wealthy in politics as necessary for achieving popular control.[128] He stresses the importance of constraining private groups and individuals' ability to gain political influence by making politicians dependent on their financial support in electoral campaigns, or on favorable treatment in the media these private actors control. Without such constraints, we can expect these actors

PUBLIC REASON 79

to possess a greater voice in government than others do. Protecting people's equal share in the control of government interference is incompatible with any inequality of income or wealth that leads to unequal opportunities for influencing government action.

Finally, also the list of basic liberties Rawls and Pettit identify are virtually indistinguishable. Pettit indeed admits his account "is deeply shaped" by Rawls's.[129] For Pettit, a freedom is a basic liberty if and only if it meets three conditions.[130] First, it must be exercisable without preventing any other number of people from exercising it simultaneously. This "equal co-enjoyment" condition means, for example, that rules might condition the basic liberty of expression so that it is a liberty for people to address the same assembly only one at a time, and not everyone simultaneously.[131] Second, a liberty is basic only if it is widely considered within a society to have an important role in the lives of normal people. This "personal significance" condition supports restrictions by rules, since addressing an assembly loses its significance if it is done by more than one at a time. And third, according to the "feasible extension" condition, the set of basic liberties are limited only by these first two conditions.

This definition leads Pettit to a list of basic liberties, which includes, at least, freedoms of thought, expression, religious practice, association, assembly, personal property, employment, and movement, as well as freedoms to take part in public life as a voter, candidate, or critic.[132] Additional liberties may be specified through a democratic procedure, Pettit says, and the list will therefore in part be context-sensitive.[133]

Rawls specifies a list of "important" basic liberties, without mentioning any other, less important basic liberties. The list includes "political liberty (the right to vote and to hold public office) and freedom of speech and assembly; liberty of conscience and freedom of thought; freedom of the person, which includes freedom from psychological oppression and physical assault and dismemberment (integrity of the person); the right to hold personal property and freedom from arbitrary arrest and seizure as defined by the concept of the rule of law."[134]

4.8 A republican political conception

Is the scope of republican freedom therefore defined by a political conception of justice? Despite Pettit's attempts to distance his republicanism from

80 THE REPUBLICAN DILEMMA

Rawlsian liberalism, we now see that the two share a politically constructivist basis for their shared concern with the basic liberties. The scope of republican freedom therefore mirrors the scope of legitimate state action that
Rawls's specifies in his political liberalism.

In one attempt to avoid this conclusion, Pettit argues that while Rawls is
concerned with the basic liberties, he fails to appreciate the importance of
making sure citizens can actually exercise these liberties. Rawls, in Pettit's
view, does not guarantee "resources required for exercising the relevant basic
liberties" and consequently "may leave some people in a position where they
are unable to exercise those choices."[135] But this is clearly not the case. We
have seen that Rawls requires that any political conception of justice gives
special priority to the basic liberties and requires that all citizens possess the
necessary means to effectively exercise these liberties.[136]

In another attempt to distance himself from Rawls, Pettit points out that
while Rawls's theory of justice has two principles, his own theory provides
the basis for just "a single principle that calls for giving people status freedom
in relation to one another."[137] The non-domination principle requires that
all citizens have the resources and protection they need to exercise the basic
liberties. This looks much like the first principle of Rawls's justice as fairness,
which says that "[e]ach person is to have an equal right to the most extensive
total system of equal basic liberties compatible with a similar system of liberty for all."[138] But Rawls's second principle, Pettit argues, conflicts with his
republicanism. This principle demands fair equality of opportunity, as well
as that the society's worst-off be made as well off as possible in terms of income and wealth and the social bases for self-respect.[139] The latter part of
the second principle is well known as the difference principle. Because Rawls
adds this second principle, Pettit thinks the two theories differ "in important
respects."[140]

It is especially the difference principle that Pettit takes to conflict with
republicanism. Pettit says he gets a theory of distributive justice from the
principle of non-domination alone, as it demands a distribution pattern
that "rules out domination." Protecting each citizen's capacity to exercise
the basic liberties, he says, requires "a high level of social insurance," as well
as "a firm basis for the insulation of people in vulnerable relationships."[141]
People need the guaranteed provision of resources and other protective
measures required to enjoy their basic liberties and thus be in a position of
equal standing with the other members of their society.[142] Pettit's republican

theory may therefore seem to have no room for a principle focused particularly on the worst-off.

Now, Rawls's first principle is lexically prior to the second principle, and we might therefore think the difference Pettit points out here is not all that important. But there are also reasons for thinking the difference might not even be there at all. First, as Rawls emphasizes in his later works, justice as fairness, which contains the two principles, is just one possible political conception of justice. As we saw in the previous section, Rawls's description of a minimal political conception includes a list of basic rights, liberties, and opportunities that have special priority. The conception must also specify measures for ensuring all citizens means to effectively use their liberties.[143] It need, in other words, not include the second principle of justice as fairness. This principle might apply only in certain societies.

Second, if justice as fairness is a plausible political conception of justice, then I cannot see why both of its principles could not fit into Pettit's republican theory.[144] For Pettit, republican freedom requires a redistribution of resources that keeps everyone above a threshold at which they are in a position they are not vulnerable to uncontrolled interference and can therefore make free choices.[145] Everyone must have "access to needed resources and protections in a range of choice where all can operate at once—perhaps with special assistance for some individuals—without getting in one another's way."[146] But Pettit gives no reason for thinking that satisfying people's avowalready interests will never go beyond just providing for the basic liberties. If the people demand, for example, that the worst-off be made materially as well off as possible, then they will be governed by an alien will, and therefore be dominated, unless the basic structure functions in accordance with such a redistribution principle. It seems arbitrary to think that republicanism will never demand redistribution beyond a sufficientarian threshold at which everyone can exercise the basic liberties.[147]

His reasons for rejecting the difference principle do not respond to this concern. Pettit lumps the difference principle together with luck egalitarianism and says that "those theories often seem like moral fantasies . . . rather than real-world manifestos for what the state should do in regulating the affairs of its citizens."[148] But it is unfair to suggest the difference principle is as fact-insensitive as luck egalitarianism, and it is imprecise to say, as Pettit does, that it implies "something close to material equality."[149] And there are grounds for thinking the difference principle could be included among

82 THE REPUBLICAN DILEMMA

the "quite extensive, even radical measures" Pettit considers necessary for protecting people against domination in real societies.[150] By saying citizens should be provided with "a certain threshold benefit in the currency of free or undominated choice, as required under the sufficientarian strategy," Pettit seems to reject an interpersonal principle, like the difference principle, taking what someone is due to depend on how much others have. But the difference principle appears to fit better than a sufficientarian principle with Pettit's central aim of ensuring that everyone enjoys the resources and protection they need to relate to one another as equals without feeling dependent on, or inferior to, others. After all, what is required for enjoying this status depends largely on how much others have to protect themselves against interference.[151]

Others also explicitly or implicitly suggest the difference principle is a plausible component of Pettit's republican theory. Alan Thomas considers the difference principle to be exactly the radical measure necessary "to make domination structurally impossible."[152] And Samuel Freeman notes that Rawls's second principle is meant to make sure that all citizens have what they need to effectively exercise their basic liberties and thus be "socially and economically independent, so that no one need be subservient to the will of another."[153] If Freeman is right, then what Rawls aims for is exactly Pettit's republican freedom as non-domination.

4.9 Overall freedom and the basic liberties

If republicans think people are free to the extent that their government protects their ability to exercise the basic liberties, the equivalent-judgments thesis depends on pure negative freedom theorists' making the same judgment. Maximizing pure negative freedom must be shown to require the institutional protection people need to enjoy the robust capacity to exercise the basic liberties.

But it is not obvious how promoting a particular set of freedoms will contribute to overall freedom.[154] We would achieve a higher level of overall freedom in a society if its inhabitants were not constrained by institutions securing everyone's capacity to exercise the basic liberties but nonetheless chose not to interfere. As Carter also notes, the highest level of overall freedom would be achieved in an anarchical community where citizens have the opportunity of anti-social behavior without the threat of legal punishment, but are nonetheless motivated to cooperate and thus create opportunities for everyone without taking any away.[155] If we introduce institutional constraints in this community so as to protect a certain domain of freedoms, we take away people's unused opportunity to violate these freedoms and thus reduce their overall freedom.[156] The key to demonstrating that such institutions will enhance overall freedom is to show that under the actual conditions of a real society, many freedoms would not be exercisable.

Carter distinguishes between two liberal approaches to the value of freedom: the "specific-freedom thesis" and the "overall-freedom thesis."[157] Liberals defending the specific-freedom thesis see value only in specific freedoms because they contribute to some more fundamental value, like dignity or respect.[158] Those holding the overall-freedom thesis, however, such as Carter, think of freedom (as the absence of prevention) as valuable as such. They are therefore not only concerned with particular freedoms but also with how much freedom people have, or ought to have. On this view, individuals' ends are better served not just by having certain important freedom but also by having more rather than less freedom overall. Rawls also appears to take this view when he says that "liberty can be restricted only for the sake of liberty."[159] Later, however, he denies the significance of "liberty as such" and endorses the specific-freedom thesis by finding value only in certain liberties because of their importance for developing the two moral powers.[160]

For Carter and other proponents of the overall-freedom thesis, the specific-freedom thesis is misguided, since it fails to recognize the importance of specific freedoms in promoting overall freedom. The basic liberties, for example, can be seen as especially important, at least in part, because they are the basis for many other freedoms. To again apply Carter's act-tree metaphor (Section 3.6), we might say that the basic liberties form the trunk out of which many other freedoms grow.

Pettit appears to accept the overall-freedom argument for providing for the basic liberties when he says promoting republican freedom requires institutions that provide the resources and protection required for everyone to enjoy "a generous set of compossible choices."[161] And as we saw in the last section, Pettit thinks each citizen is entitled to "a certain threshold benefit in the currency of free or undominated choice."[162] Enjoying the status of a free person, then, appears to mean having not just certain freedoms but also a certain level of freedom as such. And the inferiority one feels when one does not enjoy this standing is plausibly due to others having more

84 THE REPUBLICAN DILEMMA

freedom because they have more resources to spend on protection against interference.[163] Promoting republican freedom therefore appears to involve increasing individuals' sets of combinations of conjunctively exercisable actions, or compossible choices. That straightforwardly means promoting overall pure negative freedom.

However, Pettit seems to think republican freedom conflicts with the promotion of pure negative freedom because the former requires that these choices be more robustly protected than is compatible with the latter. Republican freedom always requires the existence of formal institutions (and, as we shall see in Chapters 5 and 6, informal institutions) that protect individuals against uncontrolled interference. Whether promoting pure negative freedom calls for such institutions, on the other hand, is conditional on whether they will actually enhance individuals' sets of conjunctively exercisable actions. As I have just noted, promoting overall freedom could, under certain ideal conditions, conflict with such institutional constraints.

However, the conflict between Pettit's institutionalist view of freedom and the promotion of overall pure negative freedom is weakened by the observation I made in the previous chapter of protection against interference in cases where interference is in any case highly unlikely. Now I can strengthen this argument by pointing to how individuals populating a community where they can reliably trust each other not to interfere with one another without the protection of formal institutions can reasonably reject such institutional protection. It does not seem reasonable to think they would accept institutions that would take away some of their freedoms without giving them new ones. If republicans would nonetheless insist on freedom depending on formal institutions, then their judgment about the freedom of people living in this community would differ from that of the pure negative freedom theorists. But republican freedom then cannot be based on political constructivism, as it is on Pettit's account. It must instead impose a particular comprehensive doctrine, according to which political engagement and protection against uncontrolled power is especially valued.

In the large, pluralistic society assumed in political liberalism, however, the level of society-wide trust we find in the anarchical utopia is extremely unlikely. People are less community-oriented and cooperative, perhaps primarily because they disagree about what they ought to cooperate to bring about. It is on the basis of this fact that Rawls thinks the citizens of a modern society will only agree on fundamental principles of governance if the principles ensure everyone the capacity to exercise the basic liberties. So, in a modern, pluralistic society, unlike in the conformist anarchical utopia, formal protection of the basic liberties will play a central role in promoting overall freedom. We can therefore expect the extent to which someone can exercise the basic liberties to be a good indication of how free that person is whether we take a republican or pure negative view of freedom.

This discovery supports the argument of the last chapter: republicans must reduce the scope of freedom at the expense of overall freedom in order to avoid making the same freedom judgments as pure negative freedom theorists. That means a more specific account of the common good than the one we get from political constructivism.

4.10 Conclusion

This chapter has analyzed Pettit's account of common interests and demonstrated how he identifies these interests within the framework of Rawlsian political constructivism. The chapter therefore supports Rawls's view of the exercise of public reason as "an aim . . . justice as fairness [as well as political liberalism generally] shares with civic republicanism."[164] Both accounts, Rawls says, call for stable institutions protecting freedom and equality in order to establish a broad basis for public reason and a political conception of justice.

Republican freedom is the status of being free from anyone's uncontrolled power to interfere with you contrary to your instruction. This is the status of people in popular control of their government. And they possess such control when the government is forced to promote their common interests. The scope of republican freedom is therefore defined so that government interference necessary for promoting the common good does not make citizens unfree. This specification of the scope of republican freedom will be important to keep in mind when we in the next chapter consider the extent to which republican freedom can require robust protection against uncontrolled interference. Republican freedom cannot demand more robustness than is compatible with its scope. On Pettit's account, that means the protection requirement cannot compromise citizens' capacity to exercise their basic liberties.

This account of the scope of republican freedom looks problematic with respect to falsifying the equivalent-judgments thesis. An account of republican freedom that achieves this falsification needs a scope–robustness trade-off

86 THE REPUBLICAN DILEMMA

that favors robustness to an extent that undermines pure negative freedom. By making this balance point between the two dimensions, republicans can identify a set of cases in which they think people's freedom increases while pure negative freedom theorists must say it decreases. However, this robustness-favored trade-off is beyond reach if we fix the scope to Pettit's understanding of common interests.

5

Ethos

5.1 Introduction

As we saw in Chapter 3, the robustness of a definition of freedom concerns the extent to which it requires protection against the kinds of interference specified by its scope. The less accessible is a possible world in which someone interferes with you, the more robustly protected are you against interference.

In this chapter and the next, I consider the institutional structure that must be in place to meet the robustness requirement of republican freedom. I compare this structure to the institutions pure negative freedom theorists would consider freedom-enhancing. I thus scrutinize Carter and Kramer's claim that the protection against interference required for republican freedom would also contribute to people's pure negative freedom. This view holds insofar as republican freedom is understood not to require protection beyond the level at which more protection would only reduce citizens' combinations of conjunctively exercisable actions. Protection beyond this point is possible, but we shall see that making it a requirement for freedom as non-domination would make the republican ideal highly demanding on the citizens. It would undermine the pluralism characterizing modern society and be unattractive from a liberal perspective.

I distinguish between formal and informal institutions. The former includes politically constructed legal and coercive bodies, such as courts, parliaments, and laws. The latter consist primarily of social norms. I show how the most plausible approach to institutional protection is the "comprehensive approach," which takes both kinds of institution into account. However, whether we take a strictly formal or a comprehensive approach, we can potentially find differences between the protection republicans and pure negative freedom theorists would see as freedom-enhancing. But republicans have good reasons for not taking a distinct approach, as it would involve significantly restricting the number of courses of action citizens can pursue. It would therefore conflict with common interests, at least as Pettit understands these interests.

The Republican Dilemma. Lars J. K. Moen, Oxford University Press. © Oxford University Press 2024.
DOI: 10.1093/oso/9780197757024.003.0005

88 THE REPUBLICAN DILEMMA

5.2 Institutional protection

Pettit identifies "three core ideas" in his own republican theory. The first idea is that republican freedom is the state's primary concern.[1] This idea is, of course, already familiar to us. Institutions should be set up to advance non-domination by making citizens and government officials disposed to letting the people control their government.

Here the second core idea—the mixed constitution—comes into play. Securing the citizens' republican freedom requires a mixed constitution that distributes political power evenly across society and prevents all power from ending up in one individual or group.[2] It is thus designed to consolidate popular control in equilibrium—what me might call the "power-sharing equilibrium." The different powerholders constrain one another, thus making sure no one can wield uncontrolled power. This idea expresses one aspect of the institutional protection of popular control that republican freedom requires. With political power distributed across the population, and each group interested in maintaining its share in this power, it will be in every group's interest to prevent any other group from acquiring more than an equal share. The mixed constitution as an institution for maintaining popular control depends on agents being motivated by a desire to maximize their political influence. It ensures that decisions on law and policy are based on interaction between different centers of political power, instead of being expressions of the concentration of power in any one of these centers.[3]

Pettit identifies other important institutions in his discussion of how to deal with three particularly worrisome threats to popular control. First, elected politicians might abuse their power to serve their own private interests.[4] Politicians are likely to be concerned with the next election and therefore focus on meeting citizens' immediate, short-term interests. To avoid bad long-term consequences, Pettit believes policy-making that can have such consequences should be given to unelected officials, who are appointed for fixed or open terms, and therefore need not serve so as to please those who appointed them. Other institutional remedies to these problems are, for example, supermajority requirements and majority support in two constituted houses of parliament.

A second threat is that of private lobbies using their influence to steer the government in directions without popular support.[5] A private lobby can deceive and manipulate decision makers, as well as threaten to harm the society, for example by threatening to move industry elsewhere at a great cost to the society. Private lobbies can also make politicians dependent on their financial support in electoral campaigns. A parliamentary legislature is, in Pettit's view, better equipped than other systems for dealing with this problem, since it can use independent regulators to impose restrictions on private campaign contributions. It also tends to require the members of the majority party to vote together, which means the lobbies typically have to buy over a whole party or a couple of parties to become influential. In other systems, it is easier to identify pivotal figures for lobbies to concentrate on.[6]

A third danger is that unelected authorities established to counter the first two threats—such as judges, ombudsmen, a central bank, and various commissions—might gain power that undermines popular control.[7] These are institutions meant to guard against threats to popular control. But who will guard the guardians? People need to put pressure on these unelected authorities to make it unprofitable for them to serve their private interests. This task is particularly a responsibility for a press independent of private interests conflicting with avowal-ready interests. For example, Ronald Dworkin, in his defense of judicial review, argues that making sure unelected judges reach decisions benefiting their society depends on media coverage stimulating popular interest in the nomination of judges as well as in their decision-making.[8] Society can thus force judges to make decisions compatible with common interests.

We thus see how informal institutions, which inform people's behavior without the use of legal coercion, are especially important to counter this third threat. But informal institutions are crucial for any threat to popular control. If people are not motivated to make formal institutions function as they are supposed to, they will not operate in this way.

This takes us to Pettit's third core idea: citizens must themselves make sure the state remains committed to securing their freedom.[9] They must individually and collectively commit to a virtuous pattern of contesting political decisions and initiatives that promote personal interests at the expense of common interests. This is an essential part of another key republican institution: contestatory democracy. People must have an arena for publicly expressing their complaints so as to hold political powerholders accountable for their actions. Political decision-making, remember, must track common, or avowal-ready, interests. Groups and individuals will look for ways of acquiring more than an equal share of government control and they might succeed unless others keep an eye on them. The extent to which citizens

90 THE REPUBLICAN DILEMMA

succeed in such vigilance is a function of popular control, and therefore also of republican freedom.[10]

No matter how virtuous government officials have been, Pettit says citizens should "always insist on the authorities going through the required hoops in order to prove themselves virtuous."[11] "People must be on the watch for proposals or measures that are not suitably supported," he writes, "and they must be ready to organize in opposition to such policies."[12] They must be ready to contest the decisions of government officials—elected or unelected—via channels such as the courts, the press, demonstrations in the streets, or by contacting their representative in parliament or an ombudsman.[13]

Pettit leaves it ambiguous whether this third core idea means citizens need to take an active role in political decision-making or merely that formal institutions must be in place to give citizens the opportunity for such participation. The former interpretation requires that citizens commit to a behavioral pattern of keeping an eye on the powerholders and being ready to speak out whenever they become aware of decisions or intentions undermining their common interests. On this view, republican freedom and popular control require the informal institution of norms of virtue—that is, norms making citizens commit to such virtuous behavior. The latter interpretation, on the other hand, requires no such norms or any other informal institution. On this view, making sure citizens have the opportunity to observe and actively participate is sufficient.

Pettit seems to favor this formal interpretation when he says people are free as long as "they are *able* to contest decisions at will and, if the contestation establishes a mismatch with their relevant interests or opinions, *able* to force an amendment."[14] That is, no one can prevent them from accessing relevant information or from expressing their concerns publicly. As we saw in Section 4.4, Pettit thinks citizens who have the opportunity to contest decisions undermining common interests but choose not to do so "only have themselves to blame."[15]

To blame for what, exactly? Presumably, for the loss of popular control. Pettit seems to think that if the citizens have chosen to sacrifice some popular control over their government to pursue other personal ends, they are themselves responsible for the loss and therefore remain as free as they were before. But on this account, republican freedom does not require popular control; it demands that it be up to the citizens themselves whether to have popular control or not. This understanding is implausible since enjoying republican freedom means being protected against uncontrolled interference. If people must themselves play a role in their protection but choose not to, then they have chosen not to be free, or to be less free than they otherwise would be.

We shall see that Pettit also recognizes the importance of norms of civic virtue and consequently appears to contradict his own view that formal opportunity to participate is sufficient.[16] On the comprehensive view of institutional protection, citizens' ability to contest is insufficient; protection against uncontrolled power requires that they must actually contest any attempt to undermine their common interests. Formal institutions are, in other words, insufficient for reaching and maintaining the power-sharing equilibrium.

The latter half of this chapter and the next chapter focus primarily on informal institutions that induce such acts of civic virtue without the threat of legal coercion. In the next chapter, we get a likely explanation for why Pettit is reluctant to fully accept the importance of a virtuous citizenry. In this chapter, I compare formal institutional protection of popular control to comprehensive institutional protection, which includes both formal and informal institutions. I show why the formal account is insufficient, and why both republicans and pure negative freedom theorists should take the comprehensive account.

5.3 The formal interpretation

If republican freedom is something one enjoys whenever certain formal institutions are in place, then it is a strictly legal status. To understand how republican freedom can be understood as a legal status, I apply List's distinction between three kinds of normative law: constitutional, ordinary legal, and moral.[17] Each of these kinds of law corresponds with a set of permissible worlds. The set of possible worlds permitted by constitutional law is greater than the set permitted by ordinary law, and the set permitted by moral law is likely to be the smallest.[18] The first two kinds of law determine the bounds of the formal interpretation of republican freedom, whereas the third kind determines the bounds of the comprehensive interpretation.

The sets of constitutional and ordinary legal permissible worlds, then, contain the worlds where people enjoy formal republican freedom. Here citizens are protected against uncontrolled interference by legal rights that guarantee a certain opportunity set across all permissible worlds. What matters

92 THE REPUBLICAN DILEMMA

is not that citizens never experience such interference, but that such inter-ference be appropriately penalized. As already discussed in Section 3.4.2, re-publican freedom requires protection against uncontrolled interference with impunity. A vigilant and effective police force, for example, can make it a modal fact that criminals are caught in most socially possible worlds, thus enhancing the modal robustness of the protection against interference con-flicting with the citizens' avowal-ready interests.

List takes the formal understanding and examines republican freedom as a legal status.[19] On his interpretation, republican freedom requires that society be organized so that no agent can disrespect another agent's legal status by interfering with him as it pleases her. List contrasts this status with pure neg-ative freedom since legal protection against interference is not a necessary condition for freedom on that account. While pure negative freedom focuses on an agent's contingent freedom in a particular world, republican freedom focuses on the agent's freedom made robust under law.[20]

This distinction is inaccurate. List, like many other sympathizers of re-publican freedom, understands pure negative freedom solely to be about an agent not *actually* being prevented from performing specific actions. However, we have seen, especially in Sections 3.5 and 3.6, that pure nega-tive freedom theorists also count subjunctive prevention as a source of un-freedom. For example, they do not consider B free to do x simply because A does not actually prevent him from doing x in the world in which he does not try to do x. They must also look at possible worlds where B does try to do x to determine whether he is free to do x. Furthermore, pure negative overall freedom is a measure of the probability of performing actions, especially conjunctively. If B is not prevented—either actually or subjunctively—from doing x, his overall freedom is, in part, a measure of the probability of A not preventing him from doing other actions in conjunction with x. B's institu-tional protection against such interference makes it occur in fewer possible worlds, which indicates a reduction in the probability of interference. Pure negative freedom theorists therefore cannot focus only on the actual world, as List claims. They must also look at other possible worlds.

However, List's view of republican freedom as a legally protected status nonetheless offers a way of distinguishing the two freedom concepts. While formal republican freedom explicitly requires the presence of formal institutions, pure negative freedom can rely on whatever kind of institu-tion that reduces the probability of agents interfering with one another. The law states what is permissible, and these statements are modal facts that are true in all permissible worlds, which form a subset of all possible worlds.[21] We measure formal republican freedom in terms of the robustness of these modal facts across accessible worlds.[22] The larger the set of accessible worlds in which the uncontrolled interferer will be punished under law, the more robust is the protection against uncontrolled interference. Only when the rule of law is sufficiently robust do people enjoy republican freedom. B must therefore be institutionally protected even against the most remote chance of A interfering with him. The republican robustness condition, as List interprets it, requires these modal facts to be true in all of the possible worlds A can access. What matters on the pure negative account, on the other hand, is whether A will interfere, and thus subjunctively prevent B from performing some action, or, with respect to overall freedom, the probability of A accessing an impermissible world. In neither case are pure negative freedom theorists concerned with whether A *can* prevent B or not; they are concerned with whether she will do so or with its probability.

As Pettit notes, non-domination cannot be understood in terms of probability of uncontrolled interference, since A can dominate B even if A has no interest in interfering with B, and the probability of such interference is no higher than that of B interfering with A.[23] Republican freedom requires "the sort of security which means, not just that people with a power of arbitrary [uncontrolled] interference will probably not exercise it, but that the agents in question will lose that power."[24] While Pettit accepts that a higher probability of interference makes the domination worse, B remains no less dominated as long as A can interfere as it pleases her.[25]

We thus see why Pettit repeatedly stresses that while people can have pure negative freedom under a benevolent dictator, they cannot have republican freedom, since a dictator, by definition, possesses the uncontrolled power to interfere with them as it pleases her. This legal understanding of republican freedom also makes sense of Pettit's use of the example of the slave as someone who is necessarily unfree. Government under popular control—especially its individualized control component (Section 4.4)—implies the rule of law and can never be compatible with the unconstrained, uncontrolled power of some group or individual. Republican freedom can therefore be understood as a status people enjoy under the law. On the pure negative account of freedom, on the other hand, any interference is a source of unfreedom, whether it is legal or not. A way of distinguishing the two freedom concepts is therefore to understand the rule of law as a necessary condition for republican freedom, as on List's understanding.

94　THE REPUBLICAN DILEMMA

More precisely, formal republican freedom requires the rule of *good* law, since law as such need not protect citizens' common interests. Joseph Raz provides a list of characteristics of the rule of law.[26] For the law to rule, it must be predictable, clear, publicly known, consistent, and stable; it must be made under the guidance of open, stable, clear, and general rules; it must be interpreted by an independent judiciary; courts must be unbiased and easily accessible; and the police must enforce the law effectively. The law defines the permissible use of state power and thus constrains it.[27] This is no doubt a good, but the law can be made and enforced for oppressive, malevolent purposes.[28] The law *should* be just, serve the common good, and protect moral rights, but it need not do so. Leslie Green calls this "the fallibility thesis."[29]

Pettit accepts the fallibility thesis. Protection against uncontrolled interference entails the rule of law, but the rule of law does not entail protection against uncontrolled interference. The law protecting against uncontrolled interference is forced to track citizens' avowal-ready interests.[30] But the law need not be subject to popular control, and legal coercion can therefore be an exercise of uncontrolled power. This is why Lovett calls Pettit's account of non-domination "substantive": the law must serve the common good. Alternatively, Lovett explains, the rule of any law, good or bad, protects people from "procedural" domination, as its constraints on government power makes legal coercion predictable, however unjust it might be.[31] On the substantive account of non-domination, the law must be appropriately made and applied to force the government, the citizens, and other actors in society not to interfere with others contrary to their common interests, thus providing the robust protection republican freedom requires.[32] And such legal protection against uncontrolled power is sufficient for republican freedom, on the formal interpretation, regardless of the extent to which it actually prevents interference.[33]

This formal interpretation of republican freedom consequently supports the common view among republicans that slavery is categorically an affront to republican freedom, but not to pure negative freedom. "Slave" is, after all, the legal status of a person who is owned by another person who is legally permitted do whatever she wants to her slave. Pettit and Skinner use the slave example to distinguish republican freedom from pure negative freedom, since the slave's master might be benevolent and choose not to interfere with her slave. The master consequently does not necessarily make the slave unfree in the pure negative sense.[34] If republican freedom is a legal status ensured by formal institutions, then this contrast makes sense, since the slave, by definition, lacks such institutional protection.

If republicans accept this formal understanding of republican freedom, they can make judgments about people's freedom that will conflict with those of pure negative freedom theorists. For example, in an anarchical utopia where people are reliably cooperative and non-interfering despite the absence of legal constraints, people have much pure negative freedom, but they have no formal republican freedom.

5.4 The gentle giant

To get a better understanding of this formal understanding of republican freedom, let us consider Kramer's example of a village where a giant is fully capable of making himself a tyrant who can interfere with the other villagers as it pleases him.[35] Fortunately, the giant prefers to live in a cave secluded from other people. He loathes the idea of social interaction, let alone the idea of interfering with others. The probability of him interfering with others is therefore "effectively zero," Kramer says.[36] People in this society know that it is possible for the giant to interfere with them, but they also know he is very unlikely to do so. They therefore go about living their lives with no fear of the giant. They leave the giant alone, and the giant leaves them alone.

The giant, Kramer notes, "is a dominator (according to Pettit's criteria for that status), but he is not significantly reducing the overall liberty of anyone else."[37] Since pure negative freedom is strictly empirical, as we saw in Section 2.3, it cannot build a need for formal institutions into its definition. It is only concerned with individuals' actions, and if formal institutions do nothing to increase the number of actions people can perform, then they do not contribute to pure negative freedom.

A formal understanding of republican freedom, on the other hand, has a built-in requirement of formal institution. On this account, the mere fact that the giant is not constrained under the rule of law makes the villagers unfree. After all, as Pettit says, the dominator need not want to interfere with the dominated. "I may wish not to dominate you," he says, imagining himself in a position of superior power, "but whether I like it or not you are dependent and I exercise domination."[38]

This view is consistent with Skinner's view of Kramer's gentle giant example. For Skinner, "the community is wholly enslaved . . . [i]f the giant

96　THE REPUBLICAN DILEMMA

could interfere at will and with impunity."[39] Like Pettit, Skinner argues that "it is the mere possibility of your being subjected with impunity to arbitrary [uncontrolled] coercion, not the fact of your being coerced, that takes away your liberty and reduces you to the condition of a slave."[40] Coercive, legal institutions are required for republican freedom, but since such institutions need not reduce the probability of interference, as in the gentle giant case, they are not strictly required for pure negative freedom. The giant's gentleness is sufficient.

We therefore see how the gentle giant example is a case where republican and pure negative freedom can make different judgments about the villagers' freedom. The probability of the giant interfering is so low that it has no impact on anyone's pure negative freedom, but the giant nonetheless makes the villagers unfree in the republican sense.[41] Kramer notes that domination usually comes with a reduction in the dominated person's overall freedom. And when it does have this effect, as opposed to in the gentle giant case, pure negative freedom theorists will obviously recognize it as a loss of freedom.[42] However, the gentle giant example shows, as Kramer observes, that someone can be a dominator "without significantly impairing the overall freedom of anyone else."[43]

If we compare this scenario, S_1, to an alternative scenario, S_2, where formal institutions protect the villagers against the giant's interference, we see that the villagers' pure negative freedom is no greater in S_2 than in S_1. In fact, pure negative freedom overall in society will be reduced by these institutions, as they necessarily impose constraints on the giant's opportunity set, as well as on the opportunity sets of villagers made to establish and maintain these institutions. On the formal republican account, on the other hand, it does not even make sense to talk about freedom in S_1, since freedom is constituted by the institutions only brought into existence in S_2.

5.5 Protection and common interests

While the gentle giant example shows how republicans can make freedom judgments that conflict with those of pure negative freedom theorists, doing so requires republicans to commit to an account of freedom we have seen they are reluctant to endorse. In Chapter 3, I identified the path for republicans to follow in order to falsify the equivalent-judgments thesis: define freedom so that it requires the protection against interference to be so

ETHOS 97

robust that it reduces the number of actions individuals can perform. This is the path Pettit and Skinner follow by insisting on the giant making his fellow villagers unfree.

However, Pettit takes a different path when he says freedom only requires protection to the extent that the eyeball test is met. If this is all that is required, then the villagers will be free in S_1, since the villagers seem able to look the giant in the eye without good reason for fear or deference. If they did have such a reason, the giant would reduce their pure negative freedom by making a set of actions exercisable only in conjunction with deferential behavior toward the giant. Lovett also understands the villagers to remain free as long as it is common knowledge among them that the giant is gentle and non-interfering.[44]

In light of the previous chapter, we see another reason why Pettit's account of republican freedom conflicts with a transition from S_1 to S_2. Since the institutions protecting the villagers against the gentle giant only reduce what the villagers can do, it would be reasonable for them to object to these institutions. Constructing and maintaining the institutional protection is, in other words, not in their common interest, and the interference it involves would therefore be uncontrolled. The formal understanding of republican freedom should require formal institutions to protect citizens against interference only insofar as it actually promotes citizens' common interests. But that means deviating from the path republicans must stick to in order to falsify the equivalent-judgments thesis.

We see why this is so by recognizing that also pure negative freedom theorists look favorably on institutional protection in cases more realistic than the gentle giant example. By assuming more ordinary circumstances, pure negative freedom theorists would also think institutional protection against interference can contribute to people's freedom. In particular, they will require that individuals possess legal rights that protect certain freedoms by threatening others with legal punishment if they interfere with any of these freedoms.

A right protecting B against A's uncontrolled interference is a claim that A cannot interfere without legal permission with a correlative duty on A not to interfere with B contrary to B's instructions. If this is what republican freedom is, then it relates to pure negative freedom in the same way as liberal rights. B's right will contribute to B's freedom insofar as it reduces the probability of A's interference, and consequently increase B's number of conjunctively exercisable actions. The legal enforcement of such rights takes away

98 THE REPUBLICAN DILEMMA

certain freedoms, but it can nonetheless enhance individuals' pure negative freedom overall.

This means that while we might say that republican freedom differs from pure negative freedom because it has an in-built rule of law requirement, this difference does not lead republicans and pure negative freedom theorists to make different judgments of how free people are as long as legal institutions enhance what people can do. In other words, the difference does nothing to challenge the equivalent-judgments thesis.

5.6 The insufficiency of legal protection

A more general problem with a strictly formal interpretations of any freedom concept is that it fails to explain cases we expect the concept to explain. With a formal understanding of republican freedom, we will fail to see obvious cases of domination for what they are. Pettit says a free person can "walk tall amongst others and look any in the eye without reason for fear or deference."[45] The legal protection formal institutions can offer is simply insufficient for securing this status.

This conceptual shortcoming becomes particularly apparent in Dowding's example of two societies with equal levels of formal republican freedom but different levels of overall pure negative freedom.[46] The two societies, Dowding explains, have "the same constitutions, regulatory institutions, and enforcement practices." These two societies have the same amount of formal republican freedom, he says, "even if in the first one class of people (say women) had continually to resort to the law if they wanted their liberties respected, whereas in the other they rarely had to do so."

The two societies differ in terms of pure negative freedom, however, since women in the first society must go to the courts in order to enjoy institutional protection, whereas in the other, they need not do so. Women consequently have more combinations of conjunctively exercisable actions in the second society than in the first. That is, they need not go through the court system to perform whatever actions discriminatory practices would otherwise prevent them from doing. But since the formal institutions are the same in both societies, women have the same level of formal republican freedom. Dowding therefore concludes that while pure negative freedom is compatible with the intuitive view that women are freer in the second society than in the first, formal republican freedom is not.

But it is also implausible to think the women in the two societies are equally able to "walk tall amongst others and look any in the eye without reason for fear or deference." Women clearly have a different social standing in the two societies, even though the laws and law enforcement are the same. Formal institutions therefore cannot alone secure the status of non-domination. This status must depend, in part, on informal institutions. Pettit also realizes that formal institutions cannot secure full protection against uncontrolled power. "Ultimately," he says "the republic has to rely on safeguards that are less tangible in nature, and perhaps less satisfying to the imagination." The republican ideal cannot be built only with "the heavy materials of institutional protection . . . we must also build with materials of civic virtue and trust."[47]

5.7 The comprehensive interpretation

The comprehensive interpretation of republican freedom is therefore more plausible. This account takes republicanism into List's third category of normative law: moral law. What is permissible behavior—that is, compatible with republican freedom—is specified by not only constitutional and ordinary law, but also unwritten codes for practice, especially expressed in social norms. A moral law demands people's obedience to moral standards prevailing in the society without the threat of formal punishment. By applying republicanism also to moral law, the scope of republican freedom shrinks, and the ideal becomes more demanding. How demanding is the focus of the next chapter.

As Pettit recognizes, republican freedom depends on "socially established norms"[48] and on "a certain sort of community."[49] The government's power will be under popular control as long as norms induce citizens to reliably resist decisions not tracking their avowal-ready interests.[50] Without norms motivating citizens to keep political power in check, legitimate government remains "an unattainable ideal," Pettit says.[51] Citizens' republican freedom, then, is protected "not just by a susceptibility to legal sanction, but also by a spontaneous, culturally reinforced civility."[52] The institutions required for realizing republican freedom, Pettit says, "are by no means restricted to the more or less legal instruments whereby the state operates; they also include various institutions of civil society."[53]

The social norms existing within a society constitute the social ethos, which specifies common attitudes toward questions of ethics and

100 THE REPUBLICAN DILEMMA

morality—that is, how one ought to live and how one ought to treat others. The ethos normalizes beliefs about how others will behave, and beliefs about others' beliefs about how others will behave, and so on. The ethos is therefore an important social coordinator and institution, as it enables people to expect a certain behavioral pattern from each other. In the second society of Dowding's example, people are expected not to discriminate against women, and to generally refrain from doing so to avoid contempt, and possibly also because they endorse values conflicting with such discrimination.

Social norms are rules for what individuals should and should not do, such as not to tell a lie, to keep one's promises, to wear black to funerals, and so on. Norms are regularities in behavior within a society that most citizens are aware of and conform to.[54] Requirements expressed by norms, Brennan et al. explain, are expressed either as deontic sentences ("A must do x in situation s" or "A must not do x in s") or as imperatives ("Do x in s" or "Do not do x in s").[55] Regularities are public rules in the sense that everyone knows what the rules demand of oneself and of others, and that everyone knows that everyone else knows this. These rules are activated, or enforced, when people's behavior deviates from them.[56] They form a system of rules that define roles in a society and are regularly acted on in accordance with a public understanding of that system. A person knows what the rules demand of her and of others, she knows that others know this, they know that she knows this, she knows that they know that she knows, and so on. The system also imposes penalties whenever rules are violated.

This publicity of norms and other public institutions thus establishes a shared basis for mutual expectations. This expectation is based on the common belief that others benefit from the norms and will therefore contribute to maintaining them. They expect one another to conform to existing norms, and to approve of others' conformity and to disapprove of deviations.[57] Individuals' desire to meet such expectations makes norms easy to abide by and difficult to violate. As Brennan et al. write, norms are "easy to operate within, hard to get out of."[58] This stickiness of norms enables people to form beliefs about how others will behave.

Although norms thus enable coordination, they need not be beneficent; they might be unjust, immoral, or costly.[59] They might, for example, enforce asymmetric power relations and thus entrench domination into the social fabric and consequently undermine republican freedom. Republican freedom therefore depends on a specific kind of norms, which underpins what Brennan and Pettit call an "economy of esteem," where individuals desire each other's esteem, which they gain by being vigilant and by contesting behavior perceived to conflict with avowal-ready interests. Conversely, they lose esteem by behaving contrary to such virtue.[60] Assuming that people crave each other's esteem, no one will have an incentive to depart from a virtuous pattern. Virtue thus becomes an equilibrium strategy.[61] This equilibrium is self-perpetuating, as the belief in conformity generates conformity.[62]

5.8 Norms of virtue

Republican freedom depends on norms constituting what we might call a "republican ethos." These are norms making possible the robust protection against uncontrolled interference necessary for realizing republican freedom, as understood on a comprehensive interpretation.

I distinguish between two kinds of social norm: legal and moral. Legal norms are norms of law abidance and are the distinguishing feature between Dowding's two societies. People engage in illegal discriminatory practices in one society, but not in the other. Pettit clearly sees the importance of legal norms. Society's basic institutional structure, he says, is likely to advance republican freedom only if individuals act in accordance with the rights and duties it provides.[63] The absence of uncontrolled power will not be robust without norms inducing law abidance.[64] Laws cannot work effectively, he says, unless they are "embedded in a network of norms that reign effectively, independently of state coercion, in the realm of civil society."[65]

Moral norms are also important for establishing robust protection against uncontrolled interference. These are norms people adhere to, and expect others to adhere to, independently of whether they are supported by law or not. However, as Pettit notes, a clean separation between legal and moral norms is problematic, since the law typically shape moral norms, and moral norms shape the law.[66] The law can enhance commitment to a moral principle, and so help establish moral norms, while the law can also have an impact on what is commonly considered morally acceptable. Laws supported merely by legal norms might over time shape citizens' moral beliefs so as to make law abidance compatible with moral standards. Pettit is not the first republican to make the connection between moral and legal norms. Machiavelli wrote that "just as good customs require laws in order to be maintained, so laws require good customs in order to be observed."[67] If

102 THE REPUBLICAN DILEMMA

existing norms, or customs, do not complement good laws, society will not be free, since the norms will corrupt the laws.

Pettit's third core idea of republicanism, which says that citizens must themselves make sure the state remains committed to securing their freedom, requires more than appropriate legal norms. This is evident in the observation I made earlier in this chapter, in Section 5.2, where we saw that popular control must involve citizens' commitment to making sure the government promotes their common interests. Their republican freedom must therefore depend on citizens committing to a behavioral pattern so that they force the government to function in this way.

Only moral norms can make this pattern robust by inducing citizens to remain vigilant of their government and to contest any decision they perceive to conflict with the promotion of the common good. The law, Pettit says, can protect people "only insofar as they manage to stay in the legal limelight, away from the darker corners where interference can go unresisted and unpunished."[68] "People must be on the watch for proposals or measures that are not suitably supported," Pettit writes, "and they must be ready to organize in opposition to such policies."[69] Ordinary citizens, he says, "need to be ready to blow the whistle."[70] Such publicity is made robust only by citizens continuously demanding that decisions be made openly. Popular resistance, Pettit says, requires a common awareness that if the government abuses its power, then some individual or group will protest and prevent this use of uncontrolled power.[71]

We have seen that Pettit emphasizes the importance of formal institutions, such as the mixed constitution and an arena for contestation, but he also stresses the necessity of specific informal institutions. Among these, he mentions "trade unions, consumer movements, prisoners' rights organizations, environmental movements, women's groups, civil liberties associations, and even competitive market forces."[72] And as already noted, citizens must be ready to contest political decisions via channels such as the courts, the press, demonstrations in the streets, or by contacting their member of parliament or an ombudsman. Pettit also mentions the importance of cultural practices making it easy for women and members of minority groups to access formal protection again uncontrolled interference.[73]

Republican freedom therefore depends on moral norms that give citizens incentives to commit to such vigilance and contestation. It depends on an economy of esteem where people win each other's approval by reliably acting on this commitment. Ideally, citizens will internalize this reward structure to the extent that they are unaware of it and will only become aware of it should they deviate from esteemed behavior and then experience disesteem. Attempts to use one's power to serve private ends at the expense of common interests will then be met with "shame and ignominy."[74] Such disapproval could be an effective form of punishment.[75] Brennan and Pettit call this social phenomenon of social control "the intangible hand."[76] Republican freedom, Pettit argues, requires us "to create a regulatory environment within which the intangible hand flourishes."[77]

Of course, the intangible hand need not induce virtuous behavior. For it to serve the desirable function Pettit has in mind, it must promote the specific behavior of vigilance and contestation. The norms, Pettit says, must have "a republican character."[78] Political philosophy, in Pettit's view, should design institutions that encourage civic virtue, especially by encouraging an economy of esteem, in which citizens' pro-social behavior satisfies their desire for others' esteem, and for avoiding disesteem.[79]

Citizens' desire for approval and for avoiding disapproval can thus motivate them to remain vigilant and ready to contest decisions they understand to conflict with common interests.[80] Society depends on effectively enforced good norms that provide citizens with the knowledge that others will act in accordance with the ideal. Otherwise, behavior in accordance with the ideal will not be incentive-compatible, and therefore unstable.[81] Only with the common knowledge that all, or at least most, people will cooperate on fair terms can virtue be an equilibrium strategy.

5.9 Two kinds of constraint

We might think of the constraining effect of social norms on people's behavior as strictly "external" in the sense that they establish expectations people want to live up to regardless of whether they are "internally" committed to the moral values the norms promote. To return to Dowding's example, people are externally constrained if they refrain from discriminating against women only because they think they will be taken to court for it, and that they will lose the court case (legal norms), or because they think they will be disesteemed by their fellow citizens (moral norms). Alternatively, they are internally constrained if they refrain from discrimination because it conflicts with the moral values they hold.

104 THE REPUBLICAN DILEMMA

Pettit takes a strictly external view when he, with Lovett, writes that "virtuous self-restraint would not remove domination."[82] Internal constraints do not *force* people to act for the common good. As Pettit says elsewhere, "mere morality" can protect no one against the uncontrolled will of another.[83] Citizens must therefore continuously give government officials reasons to use their power for the common good, so that a pattern of popular control remains robust whether officials have internalized a moral commitment to serving the common good or not.[84] Powerholders must be compelled to use their power in accordance with avowal-ready interests for the specific reason that they will get in trouble if they use it for other purposes. If A is constrained only by her own moral conviction, she might interfere with B if her moral views should change. So, for B to be free from A's domination, a third-party must prevent A from interfering. A's moral convictions is therefore neither a necessary nor a sufficient reason for B's protection. B's freedom consequently depends on A being forced to do something A is not required to do voluntarily.

Acts on such personal commitments are acts of mere goodwill, which Pettit repeatedly emphasizes adds nothing to the robust protection against uncontrolled interference. I might be morally committed not to interfere with you, he says, but "it remains the case that I may prefer to practise interference, whether out of weakness of will, out of malice, or out of a will for evil; the option continues to lie within my capacity."[85] A constraint is only relevant, on this view, if it takes the external form of convincing me that I will be penalized if I violate it. Internal constraints are too unreliable to enhance the robust protection against uncontrolled power. We might imagine government officials who serve the common good due to their republican commitments. But that, Pettit argues, does not mean the people are in control of their government.[86] Without denying that government officials can be genuinely virtuous, Pettit takes the relevant constraint to be the motivation to constrain others.

This emphasis on external constraints reveals a mistrust in powerholders that is characteristic of republican thought. Pettit asks, "Which of us would remain virtuous if we had access to the ring of Gyges—the ring that makes a wearer invisible—and could commit a variety of offences with complete impunity?"[87] He believes few would remain virtuous under such circumstances.[88] Apathetic citizens are therefore a problem. Even those deeply committed to non-domination might occasionally fall for the temptation of using their power in ways conflicting with common interests.[89]

Now, while external constraints no doubt seem useful for establishing and maintaining popular control, such constraints are unlikely to materialize unless they are accompanied by internal constraints. A cooperation scheme based strictly on external constraints is possible. People may collectively promote the common good strictly because of the widely held expectation that anyone who defects will receive moral disapproval or be legally punished. In principle, then, no one need be morally committed to promoting the common good. Civic virtue can be in equilibrium strictly due to social expectations. This would be a case of pluralistic ignorance: no one believes in a proposition—in this case, "We ought to promote the common good"—but everyone believes that everyone else believes in it. And everyone's virtuous behavior on the belief that everyone else believes in the proposition is taken as confirmation of this belief.

This scenario might seem unlikely to come about and likely to be unstable if it does. As M. Victoria Costa notes, "while this is a theoretical possibility, there is little reason to think that it is achievable . . . without presupposing a sufficient number of virtuous citizens."[90] In practice, she says, "a sufficient degree of personal virtue" will be necessary for making sure individuals comply with the norms of promoting the common good.[91] However, there are examples of remarkably stable practices based on pluralistic ignorance. In his famous study, Gerry Mackie shows how practices of foot binding and female genital mutilation have persisted despite no one actually preferring them. Because of the widely held belief that others valued the practices, no one dared to challenge them.[92] But while pluralistic ignorance can be stabilizing, genuine conviction of the rightness of a practice is an additional stabilizing factor.

And such internal constrains do have an impact on the two factors Pettit identifies to indicate the level of popular control and, consequently, on the extent to which people enjoy republican freedom.[93] First, how disposed people are to resisting perceived abuses of governmental power is in part determined by moral convictions. The same goes for the second factor: how disposed government officials are to be inhibited by actual or potential resistance. If citizens are motivated by republican values, they will be more disposed to such resistance than if they were motivated by external pressure alone. And government officials with internalized republican values will be more respectful toward the citizens and therefore more sensitive to their avowal-ready interests and to the prospect of their resistance.

106 THE REPUBLICAN DILEMMA

Ignoring personal commitment would also be unwise because inculcating individuals not to want to dominate is a more efficient strategy than enforcing the moral code through law or the economy of esteem. After all, people will find ways to cheat no matter how strictly these external mechanisms are implemented. A society of knaves is therefore highly unlikely to function in the way republicans want it to. Making people personally disposed to behave in accordance with republican values will always contribute to the probability of institutions functioning in the way republicans want them to. Such dispositions enforcing internal constraints should therefore be part of the republican ethos alongside dispositions to enforce external constraints.

I should note that if cooperation occurs strictly due to pluralistic ignorance, then people might come to internalize republican values. That is, they might come to sincerely believe what they at first wrongly believed all others to believe. Individuals believing that most others disagree with them have been found to be more doubtful of their views and more disposed to changing their beliefs. And conversely, believing that most others agree with them makes them more confident.[94] This might stabilize the cooperation, but it does so only due to the emergence of internal constraints.

5.10 Are good norms sufficient?

For pure negative freedom theorists, good norms can make formal institutions superfluous insofar as the latter do nothing to enhance the number of people's available combinations of conjunctively exercisable actions. This is evident in the anarchical utopia I have referred to earlier. It is now clear that good norms can also function as external constraints that enhance the robustness of popular control. But Pettit denies that norms can ever be so effective that formal institutions become unnecessary for republican freedom. He gives two reasons for this view.[95] First, relying strictly on norms does not guarantee that people will agree on which liberties are to count as basic liberties and on how to provide the resources people need to exercise these liberties. And second, without formal institutions, citizens will have to depend on each other's goodwill.

This view is compatible with the comprehensive understanding of republican freedom, of course, since that account sees both formal and informal institutions as necessary for popular control. However, in Section 5.5, we saw that the importance of formal institutions in Pettit's republicanism is contingent on certain facts about the particular society in focus. Pettit's first reason for considering informal institutions insufficient is obviously relevant only in societies where people cannot agree on the liberties they are to collectively promote and protect. The fact of pluralism is likely to make this reason relevant. This first reason is therefore a contingent rather than categorical reason for the necessity of formal institutions.

To give strength to his second reason, Pettit refers to Immanuel Kant's Kingdom of Ends, where everyone is morally committed to respecting each other as ends, and a state is therefore unnecessary for maintaining law and order. But a state under collective control is still necessary, Pettit argues, since only a state can ensure the modally robust protection against uncontrolled interference that republican freedom requires.[96] Without a state, the individuals populating the Kingdom of Ends will depend on each other's goodwill. Especially weaker parties will be "in the position of dependants, not equals, in relation to [stronger] parties."[97] Crucially, coercive law means weaker parties can enjoy protection against stronger parties not as acts of benevolence they should be grateful for, but as an institutionally guaranteed claim. So, while good norms are necessary for republican freedom, they are only sufficient in conjunction with a state forced to track common interests.

The Kingdom of Ends is similar to Joel Feinberg's "Nowheresville."[98] In Nowheresville, people are "as attractive and virtuous as possible."[99] But importantly, they have no legal rights. They therefore lack the institutional structure that

> enables us to "stand up like men," to look others in the eye, and to feel in some fundamental way the equal of anyone. To think of oneself as the holder of rights is not to be unduly but properly proud, to have that minimal self-respect that is necessary to be worthy of the love and esteem of others. Indeed, respect for persons (this is an intriguing idea) may simply be respect for their rights, so that there cannot be the one without the other; and what is called "human dignity" may simply be the recognizable capacity to assert claims.[100]

Feinberg's emphasis on the importance of legal rights thus seems to capture exactly what Pettit has in mind when he says law is necessary for protecting people against domination—for making sure they pass the eyeball test— even in a society where people are generally virtuous despite there being no legal constraints.

108 THE REPUBLICAN DILEMMA

Even if everyone commits to a pattern of virtuous behavior, moral norms might still be insufficient for assuring everyone that everyone else will act virtuous. Social cooperation, as also Rawls points out, is therefore likely to depend on coercive state power also in a well-ordered society.[101] A modern pluralistic society is characterized by "burdens of judgment"—that is, disagreement about the good among reasonable persons—and coercive political power is needed to enforce the principles they agree on in overlapping consensus.[102] Reasonable persons' shared moral commitments do not entail full confidence in one another's consistent virtue. And citizens' suspicion that others will not do their part could make citizens tempted not to do theirs. What Rawls calls an "effective penal machinery" might therefore serve an important role "as men's security to one another" even in a society where people are generally virtuous.[103]

We have seen, however, that Rawls never abstracts away from the fact of pluralism. Pettit also seems to take this fact for granted.[104] Everyone respecting each other as ends in themselves need not, of course, mean that they will continue to do so come what may. However, if citizens conform on a view of the basic liberties and how to ensure that everyone enjoys them, and if social norms make it common knowledge that it is highly improbable that anyone will ever interfere with another in an uncontrolled manner, and that formal institutions can do nothing to further reduce this probability, then it would be incompatible with Pettit's republicanism. Formal institutions will then be reasonably objectionable, as they impose constraints on people without offering them any meaningful protection.

To be sure, Pettit's insistence on the importance of formal institutions to accompany, and even give support to, informal institutions is no doubt plausible. But its plausibility is contingent on certain facts about the particular society in focus. A strictly informal view of republican freedom therefore cannot be ruled out categorically; its implausibility must be demonstrated empirically. The alleged categorical distinction from pure negative freedom on the matter of institutional protection therefore collapses.

5.11 Ethos and pure negative freedom

We saw in Section 5.5 that the formal institutions required for Pettit's republicanism will also contribute to people's pure negative freedom. The same is the case with respect to informal institutions. Informal, as well as formal, institutions will also be beneficial for pure negative freedom. Any institution that will reduce the probability of interference with people's combinations of conjunctively exercisable actions will make people freer in the pure negative sense. We have no good reason for thinking that informal institutions—such as norms against interference—will not contribute to this end.

In the anarchical utopia where people voluntarily refrain from preventing others from pursuing any course of action, people are inclined to cooperate and thus enable each other to perform actions they can only perform jointly.[105] While people will not be formally, or legally, penalized for acting otherwise, they prefer to act this way, and therefore have a maximally high number of combinations of conjunctively exercisable actions. This freedom utopia is realized by a firm commitment to norms increasing the probability of cooperation and non-interference to an extent that it is commonly expected as a matter of course. Any introduction of formal institutions would come at the cost of people's freedom.

This is just what we saw in the discussion of Kramer's gentle giant example earlier in the chapter. We cannot just look at the formal constraints on the giant. We must also look at his preferences. As Kramer tells us, the giant has no desire to interfere with anyone; he just wants to be left alone. In this case, the giant's non-interference is not due to social norms, as his desire to live by himself is not based on the belief that he will be shunned by others if he were to interfere with someone. Perhaps some republicans will therefore say that since there are no external constraints, either formal or informal, on the giant, he makes the villagers unfree. However, we have seen that norms plausibly depend on, or are at least made more robust by, people endorsing the values they promote. And since the giant wants to be left alone, he is committed to non-interference. We could try to make the giant care more about what other people think about him, but we would probably all be better off just leaving him alone. Under more realistic circumstances, however, both internal and external constraints will likely contribute to pure negative freedom. Formal institutions will be necessary to make people cooperate and not interfere. We therefore see again, as we first observed in Section 3.5, that republicans and pure negative freedom theorists both see formal institutions as only contingently important for the promotion of freedom.

What matters for republicans, as for pure negative freedom theorists, is therefore the probability of being prevented from performing certain actions or combinations of actions. So, how free we judge someone to be in the presence of a more powerful agent does not differ whether we hold the

110 THE REPUBLICAN DILEMMA

republican or the pure negative definition of freedom. This observation obviously strengthens the equivalent-judgments thesis.

5.12 Conclusion

In this chapter, I have distinguished between two interpretations of the robustness condition of republican freedom. On the formal interpretation, republican freedom requires that people be protected strictly by formal institutions. This interpretation fits well with the understanding of republican freedom as the absence of uncontrolled interference *with impunity*. On a strong interpretation of this view, formal institutions are strictly necessary for republican freedom. By taking this view, republicans' judgments of how free people are will differ from those of pure negative freedom theorists. Pettit, however, cannot take this strong interpretation, since he defines the scope of freedom in terms of common interests, which do not necessarily justify such institutions. He takes a moderate view on which formal institutions are necessary for freedom only contingently on relevant social facts. On this view, the equivalent-judgments thesis holds, as the required formal institutions enforce individuals' liberal rights in a way that corresponds with the promotion of their pure negative freedom.

But in any case, as also Pettit says, a strictly formal protection is insufficient for popular control. Popular control also depends on informal institutions, especially in the form of social norms. These required norms must serve a dual role: give citizens and public officials incentives to abide by the law, as well as incentives to be vigilant and ready to contest attempts to act in ways that undermine common interests. But we have seen that also these informal institutions will contribute to pure negative freedom. So, while a republican ethos promotes republican freedom, it also promotes pure negative freedom.

We therefore see that we must reject the commonly held view that only a republican freedom concept can ground an argument for the importance of civic virtue. Costa rightly notes that "[l]iberals who champion freedom as noninterference" think "the exercise of virtue is indispensable in sustaining a liberal regime." She makes a mistake, however, when she goes on to say that this is because liberals "do not ground their claims solely on the value of freedom as noninterference, but also on other values such as personal autonomy."[106] We can now see that freedom as non-interference, at least in its

pure negative form, does provide plausible grounds for defending the importance of civic virtue.

But while Pettit's moderate republicanism does not falsify the equivalent-
judgments thesis, a stronger interpretation of republican freedom can do so
by reducing the scope of freedom so as to make its robustness require greater
protection against interference than is compatible with promoting pure negative overall freedom. In the next chapter, I compare the different practical
implications of Pettit's moderate account of republican freedom to those of
this strong account.

6

Pluralism

6.1 Introduction

Taking the comprehensive interpretation of republican freedom gives us more flexibility in specifying its robustness. With a strictly formal interpretation, we can only say that legal institutions should promote whatever avowal-ready interests exist in society. This account is compatible with citizens pursuing a wide range of conceptions of the good. The ideal of republican freedom therefore becomes, in a sense, robust because undemanding, since it is realizable in a wide range of possible worlds, each of which defined by distinct preference ordering across the individuals populating it. This is not, however, the robustness I have focused on, which concerns the protection against uncontrolled power. We see this by noticing that within the wide range of possible worlds in which formal republican freedom is achieved, there will be worlds where citizens frequently experience the kind of domination that is regarded a source of unfreedom only on the comprehensive interpretation.

By taking the comprehensive view, we see republican freedom as compatible with a narrower range of possible worlds, as we are more specific about how people must behave. As we saw in the previous section, this is the set of possible worlds defined by a particular moral law, which is smaller than those specified by constitutional and ordinary legal law. By narrowing the set of possible worlds in which the ideal is realized, we make the protection against interference more robust, but only at the expense of narrowing the scope of freedom by making it compatible with more kinds of interference. In this chapter, I explore what it means in practice to reduce the scope of freedom for the sake of greater robustness.

We shall see that such reduction in scope implies a reduction in the range of conceptions of the good with which the ideal is compatible. Since promoting pure negative freedom also requires institutional protection into the set of morally permissible worlds, such scope reduction need not conflict with the promotion of freedom thus understood. However, as I have already

The Republican Dilemma. Lars J. K. Moen, Oxford University Press. © Oxford University Press 2024.
DOI: 10.1093/oso/9780197757024.003.0006

argued, restricting the scope of republican freedom beyond a certain point will enable republicans to make judgments about people's freedom that conflict with those of pure negative freedom theorists. Scope reduction, with a corresponding increase in robustness, is therefore the way for republicans to falsify the equivalent-judgments thesis and separate their freedom ideal from the promotion of pure negative freedom. This chapter explores the practical implications of this move.

6.2 Strong and moderate interpretations

To consider the implications of this scope reduction, Ingham and Lovett's distinction between strong and moderate interpretations of republicanism will be useful.[1] Recall from Chapter 3, where I first introduced this distinction, that on the strong interpretation, republican freedom requires institutions making sure that uncontrolled interference with impunity occurs in fewer socially possible worlds than it does on the moderate interpretation.[2] But for republican freedom to remain a possible ideal, we cannot take it to require that uncontrolled interference occurs in no socially possible world, since that implies maximal robustness, which we have seen makes freedom impossible. But a strong interpretation can demand greater robustness than moderate republican freedom while remaining possible.

Moderate republican freedom requires that it be common knowledge that uncontrolled interference will generally be punished. It is achieved when the probability of institutional protection failing is so low that it will have "no significant practical consequences."[3] People can then behave toward each other "as if" they knew that interference will result in a penalty no one will be willing to take. We might assume with Ingham and Lovett that this is roughly what it takes to meet Pettit's eyeball test and that Pettit therefore holds this moderate view of republicanism.[4] On Pettit's account, inaccessibility of uncontrolled interference requires something significantly less demanding than perfect law enforcement. Passing the eyeball test requires only that institutional "safeguards should enable people, by local standards, to look one another in the eye without reason for fear or deference."[5] The test, Pettit explains, requires "a degree of protection against others that makes the interference option ineligible, if not actually impossible, and that does this more and more effectively with progressively more serious forms of interference." It "identifies the criterion for determining what is enough by way

114 THE REPUBLICAN DILEMMA

of safeguarding."[6] Safeguards should ensure that everyone passes the eyeball test and can robustly exercise the basic liberties in accordance with avowal-ready interests.

List, on the other hand, takes a very strong interpretation by understanding republican freedom to require that punishment for acting in conflict with common, avowal-ready interests be so regular it occurs in all socially possible worlds.[7] If punishment in response to such behavior occurs in all socially possible worlds, it is a positive social law. Positive social laws, List explains, are regularities in human behavior, such as the law of supply and demand.[8] The set of all socially possible worlds is a subset of all biological possible worlds, which form a subset of all physically possible worlds, which are a subset of all logically possible worlds. Each of these sets is defined by positive—as opposed to normative—laws. While uncontrolled interference will always remain biologically, physically, and logically possible, List takes republican freedom to require that it be socially impossible. While making uncontrolled interference strictly impossible is itself impossible, the measures required for maximizing robustness include a very effective police force, extensive surveillance, and, as we shall see, a highly vigilant citizenry.

As we saw in Section 3.4, Pettit rejects this strong interpretation by requiring only that punishment be effective enough for citizens to pass the eyeball test. It is therefore puzzling that he nonetheless thinks List "offers a wonderfully clear (and to me, congenial) view of how the liberal and republican approaches compare in their treatment of possibility."[9] Ingham and Lovett also endorse a moderate view. The strong interpretation, they say, "is too strong."[10] The moderate understanding is the only reasonable one, they argue. It is subject to a "pragmatic constraint" that makes it a useful ideal that has "critical force without being hopelessly demanding."[11]

The strong and moderate interpretations are different trade-offs between the scope and robustness dimensions of freedom. We have seen that the scope of freedom on Pettit's moderate view is tied to the people's common interests as defined in the procedure of political constructivism. This procedure ensures a respect for pluralism well-suited for modern conditions. But it thereby produces a freedom ideal that cannot demand enough robustness to conflict with the promotion of pure negative freedom. By taking the strong interpretation, however, we strengthen the robustness requirement and, correspondingly, weaken the scope requirement. This scope reduction means that more acts of interference will be understood to promote common interests and therefore considered compatible with republican freedom. It will become clear in this chapter that strong republican freedom conflicts with the promotion of pure negative freedom, but only because it compromises the pluralism of modern society.

6.3 Rawls and republican protection

Pettit's concern with preserving the pluralism that characterizes modern society leads his republicanism into the framework of Rawls's political liberalism. But while Pettit recognizes certain similarities between his own and Rawls's theories, he thinks Rawls's protection against uncontrolled power fails to meet republican standards. Rawls, as Pettit understands him, only requires that punishment for interfering with others' basic liberties reduce the probability of such interference. For Rawls, Pettit says, people should be made sufficiently sure that the powerful will not interfere with them, and that could be achieved while leaving the powerful "able to interfere at a relatively low cost."[12] Republicans, on the other hand, demand that such interference with impunity be made inaccessible, not merely improbable. Passing the eyeball test, Pettit says, involves a level of protection "certainly higher than anything envisaged by Rawls."[13]

But Pettit should not be so certain about that. First of all, it is unclear why Pettit thinks Rawls's political liberalism does not require that this test be met. Securing protection against interference up to this level seems to be what liberal rights are for. As Feinberg notes, rights should enable "us to 'stand up like men,' to look others in the eye, and to feel in some fundamental way the equal of anyone."[14] Another reason for thinking Rawls requires that the eyeball test be met is his repeated emphasis on the importance of ensuring the social bases of self-respect. Rawls says, for example that, self-respect "includes a person's sense of his own value,"[15] and that it "normally depends upon the respect of others."[16] If you cannot look other people in the eye without fear, that is a good indication that they do not respect you, that you do not have a sense of your own value, and that your self-respect is diminished as a result.

Pettit gives two reasons for why his republican theory cannot "be cast as an attempt to espouse Rawls's first principle [of justice] and to dispense with his second."[17] The first is that "Rawls's first principle does not require full resourcing for the basic liberties."[18] We saw in Chapter 4, however, that this concern with the basic liberties is exactly what Rawls takes any political conception of justice to require. The second reason, however, concerns the

116   THE REPUBLICAN DILEMMA

topic of this chapter. Pettit says that Rawls's first principle "does not require [the basic liberties'] protection against domination, only their protection in a weaker sense."[19] In other words, Pettit thinks his republicanism requires more robust and demanding protection against uncontrolled interference than political liberalism does.

But since Pettit defines the scope of republican freedom in terms of avowal-ready, common interests, as we saw in Chapter 4, he cannot require citizens to commit to maintaining institutional protection beyond what is compat-ible with these interests. And since Rawls's political liberalism requires that these same interests be promoted and institutionally protected, it can require the same level of institutional protection as Pettit's republicanism.[20] The view that republicanism requires a greater level of institutional protection than political liberalism does must therefore depend on a stronger version of re-publican robustness than Pettit's moderate eyeball-test version.

Rawls sees no tension between his political liberalism and republicanism. The latter, he says, presupposes no particular comprehensive doctrine, as it defends the protection of basic rights and liberties without making polit-ical participation part of the ideal.[21] They are both therefore contrasted with what Rawls calls "civic humanism," in which political engagement is a neces-sary component of a good life.[22] Given his commitment to neutrality, Pettit must also reject this doctrine, which he also does.[23]

But like Pettit, Rawls stresses the importance of political participation by informed citizens for protecting society against misrule. Without widespread political engagement, he says, "even the best-designed political institutions will eventually fall into the hands of those who hunger for power and mil-itary glory." Citizens wanting to remain "free and equal . . . cannot afford a general retreat into private life."[24] They must do what is needed to establish and maintain just institutions.[25] A well-ordered society, as Rawls sees it, "encourages a political character that . . . sustains the political virtues of social cooperation."[26] Political engagement is thus considered merely instrumen-tally valuable for its contribution to protection against political misrule. It is not promoted as a part of the ideal itself, as in civic humanism. Rawls there-fore finds "no fundamental opposition" between his own liberalism and the republican tradition he associates with Machiavelli and Skinner.[27] But strong republicanism is too demanding for political liberalism, as we shall see later in this chapter.

Achieving distance from the promotion of pure negative freedom also requires strong republicanism. If you cannot look another in the eye without reasonable fear or deference, then that other person restricts the number of actions you can perform conjunctively with looking her in the eye, and with other non-deferential actions. That is, B's failure to pass the eyeball test will be due to A credibly threatening to interfere with B unless B chooses a course of action that A approves of. And that is a case of A reducing the number of B's available combinations of conjunctively exercisable actions, and therefore his pure negative freedom. To maintain that republican freedom demands more robust protection that does the promotion of pure negative freedom, Pettit must go beyond the eyeball test and require that the protection of a set of particular opportunities be so demanding it reduces the number of available courses of action people can pursue.

That means endorsing the strong interpretation of republican freedom. No such restriction would be compatible with the moderate interpretation, since it would not be acceptable to all reasonable persons. On the strong account, citizens must conform to a particular behavioral pattern in response to institutions designed to reduce their number of opportunities. By coercive or non-coercive means, these institutions shape people's preferences so as to make them reliably do what they can to make sure no one gets away with behavior conflicting with the common good. On the strong interpretation, the set of actions understood to conflict with common interests grows as the scope of freedom shrinks, since it must allow for restrictions on behavior conflicting with the specified level of robust protection. On this interpretation, then, republicanism gives individuals smaller opportunity sets than does a theory promoting pure negative freedom. But the smaller opportunity sets will be more robustly protected.

6.4 Specifying republican preferences

Reducing scope to achieve strong republican robustness implies a restriction on the domain of preferences individuals can satisfy. A scope reflecting only a Rawlsian reasonableness condition is smaller than the maximum scope of pure negative freedom, but to make a trade-off with robustness that conflicts with the promotion of overall pure negative freedom, republicans must reduce the scope further. I shall now consider which preferences are compatible with this strong interpretation of republican freedom and which are not.

To see how much republicans must restrict the scope of their definition of freedom in order to falsify the equivalent-judgments thesis, we must

118 THE REPUBLICAN DILEMMA

consider what robust protection against uncontrolled power requires of people. The key issue, in other words, is what preferences a distinct, because highly robust, understanding of republican freedom can allow people to act on, and what preferences are at odds with such an ideal.

Recall that government interference does not make citizens unfree, in the republican sense, as long as the government is under popular control. On the strong interpretation of republicanism, popular control requires that citizens be committed to making sure that public officials, who carry out the state's actions, act strictly in accordance with the people's common interests. Each citizen must also make sure that all other citizens remain devoted to this task. Citizens must keep an eye out for behavior incompatible with promoting their common interests, and they must be ready to contest such behavior and make sure it ceases. With respect to the government–citizen relationship, the government's power is under popular control, and the citizens remain free, as long as the citizens will invariably succeed in resisting decisions not tracking their common interests.

We saw in the previous chapter that the institutional protection against uncontrolled power must include citizens' behavior and disposition, and not just formal institutions. No matter how virtuous government officials have been, Pettit says citizens should "always insist on the authorities going through the required hoops in order to prove themselves virtuous."[28] "People must be on the watch for proposals or measures that are not suitably supported . . . and they must be ready to organize in opposition to such policies."[29] They must be ready to contest decisions of government officials—elected or unelected— via channels such as the courts, the press, demonstrations in the streets, or by contacting an ombudsman or their representative in parliament.[30] But on Pettit's moderate interpretation of republicanism, popular control is "virtual control," which means citizens need not actively look for abuse of political power, they just have to be ready to blow the whistle should they become aware of power abuse.[31] They can therefore go about their lives as they wish, as long as they remain in standby mode by being ready to speak out if "the red lights go on," as Pettit says.[32]

On the strong interpretation, on the other hand, the republican robustness requirement goes beyond virtual control. People cannot just be ready to contest any abuse of political power they become aware of; they must be actively on the lookout for it. They cannot wait for the red lights to go on, they must be ready to switch them on by carefully watching political processes and how decisions are made and carried out. Citizens must also watch each other and put pressure on those perceived not to do their bit in keeping powerholders virtuous. Greater commitment to such behavior will always have a positive effect on the two factors indicating the level of republican freedom people enjoy.[33] That is, people's disposition for vigilance and contestation will increase the firmer their commitment is, and government officials will have better reason to feel inhibited. Anything less than such "active control" means the external constraints on political power will be weaker than they can be.

Active control necessarily strengthens the check on the powerholders to a greater extent than does virtual control. Virtual control is better than no control, of course, but it falls short of meeting a distinctly republican robustness condition. In reality, even active control might not fully realize the robust protection required on the strong interpretation of republican freedom. But the more vigilant and ready to contest the citizens are, the greater is their protection against uncontrolled rule. On strong republicanism, then, the republican motto "the price of liberty is eternal vigilance" is taken quite literally.

Active control must itself be maximally robust—that is, citizens must be vigilant and ready to contest in all socially possible worlds. And such robustness is achieved by the informal institutions discussed in the previous chapter. Without norms motivating citizens to keep political power in check, legitimate government will remain "an unattainable ideal," as Pettit notes.[34] Recall from the previous chapter that social norms are constituted by people's expectations of one another to conform to certain behavior, their desire to meet these expectations, as well as their approval of such conformity and disapproval of deviations. Under the norms required for strong republican freedom, citizens will expect one another to act so as to maintain active control—that is, to be as vigilant and ready to contest as they can be. Any deviation from this behavioral pattern will be met with social disapproval.

We now see that strong republicanism requires that citizens adopt a set of preferences compatible with active control—that is, preferences compatible with maximal vigilance and readiness to contest their government, as well as monitoring their fellow citizens to make sure they are equally committed to active control. This is the set of distinctly republican preferences. Considering what citizens must sacrifice to act strictly on these preferences, List is right when he suggests that "republicans may have to reduce the scope of freedom to such an extent that very little individual freedom can be preserved if maximal robustness is to be achieved."[35] Or, more precisely, he is almost right, since any conception with maximal robustness is untenable. But to try to achieve strong republicanism to the greatest extent possible involves

120　THE REPUBLICAN DILEMMA

shaping their preferences so as to make them willingly promote a highly robust protection against uncontrolled power. In return for such preference-shaping, strong republican freedom promises people greater certainty that their preferences will be satisfied than if we instead aim to promote their pure negative freedom.

Liberals will complain that this level of security involves restricting individuals' opportunity sets to such an extent that there will be little freedom left to secure.[36] They will want to give individuals legal rights protecting them against being made to contribute to institutional protection, and to enable citizens to pursue a variety of conceptions of the good. Many conceptions of the good—including many reasonable ones, as understood in political liberalism—will conflict with strong republicanism. Political liberals will therefore give individuals a wider and less protected range of permissible actions than is compatible with strong republicanism.

Strong republicanism cannot allow for the extensive individual rights of liberalism. List notes, on the basis of his strong interpretation of republican freedom, that if republicans grant every member of the society a set of rights she or he can exercise in all socially possible worlds, "the resulting rights set may turn out to be vanishingly small."[37] Citizens cannot have rights giving them corresponding duties to sometimes undermine institutional protection, as that would weaken the robustness of this protection.

6.5　Republicanism and neutrality

Strong republicanism reduces the scope of freedom to strengthen the robustness condition, and some conceptions of the good consequently becomes incompatible with this restricted scope. Promoting strong republicanism therefore involves undermining the development and pursuit of some possible conceptions of the good and promoting conceptions compatible with a firm commitment to vigilance and contestation. It therefore conflicts with liberal neutrality, which requires the state to give no special advantages or disadvantages to particular conceptions of the good.[38] It also conflicts with the perfectionist branch of liberalism focused on individual autonomy, as its concern is with ensuring citizens collective, and not their individual, self-rule.[39] This strong interpretation of republicanism seems consistent with Cass Sunstein's view of classical republicanism, according to which the polity is supposed to inculcate civic virtue to an extent modern observers would regard as an impermissible "imposition of a 'comprehensive doctrine' on the population."[40] Machiavelli, for example, saw great importance in citizens devoting their lives to protecting their city from corruptive private interests as well as from foreign intrusion. For Machiavelli, one's liberty and the greatness of one's city both depend on total devotion to civic virtue.[41]

Pettit, however, follows Rawls in defining his political ideal in a process of political constructivism, and therefore supports individual rights against such inculcation that would have seemed foreign to classical republicans. For Pettit, the government should promote citizens' common interests, which are those interests no one can reasonably reject. We have seen that Pettit understands these interests to be "avowal-ready," not "avowal-worthy." The latter suggests a moral standard people should conform to whatever their moral convictions, whereas the former is more permissive, as it refers to the interests people actually have and are ready to publicly avow, rather than to the interest they ought to have.[42] Pettit's account is therefore more compatible with the plurality of conceptions of the good existing in a modern society. As he says, his understanding the ideal of republican freedom is "compatible with modern pluralistic forms of society."[43]

Reasonable persons respect this pluralism, and they realize that imposing a particular conception of the good on the whole population would be possible only by oppressive and illegitimate use of political power.[44] Just as Rawls requires that a political conception be acceptable to all reasonable members of society, Pettit considers freedom as non-domination "a pluralistic ideal" we can expect "to command allegiance across a wide spectrum of contemporary interest and opinion."[45] We can therefore, on his view, appeal to freedom as non-domination to support "multicultural concerns."[46] The ideal of republican freedom, Pettit says, "is capable of commanding the allegiance of the citizens of developed, multicultural societies, regardless of their more particular conceptions of the good."[47]

Pettit understands this as a modern approach to republicanism that looks at "political institutions with quite a different attitude from that of premodern republicans."[48] On this approach, non-domination is considered a primary good, which is a good everyone would want no matter what her or his conception of the good might be.[49] Anyone in a pluralistic society wants freedom as non-domination, Pettit argues, and he therefore considers it "a neutral political ideal."[50] Whatever you might like to do with your life, Pettit thinks freedom from domination will be important. This view of republican

122   THE REPUBLICAN DILEMMA

freedom confirms its compatibility with pure negative freedom, which we have seen is served by letting people pursue a wide variety of personal plans.

Pettit further notes that everyone possesses "a deep and universal human desire for standing and dignity," even those who simply want to follow "the mainstreams of a contemporary, pluralistic society."[51] It is "reasonable to hold," he writes, "that people are everywhere concerned with avoiding domination, as it is reasonable to hold that they are everywhere concerned with avoiding deprivation. . . . There is no society where involuntary subjection to the power of others can be welcome, as there is none where involuntary deprivation of material resources can be appealing." Freedom as non-domination is therefore "a universal and supreme value."[52]

By taking this view, Pettit can say that republicanism is neutral in the liberal sense, as it seeks "a relatively neutral brief for the state—a brief that is not tied to any particular conception of the good."[53] And this view seems plausible in the sense that having a right to exercise one's basic liberties is in everyone's interests. And like Rawls's political liberalism, Pettit's moderate republicanism takes today's pluralistic society for what it is. This is why Ingham and Lovett consider it a "pragmatic" ideal: it is not too demanding for society as it is.[54]

But that observation does nothing to distinguish republicanism from the promotion of pure negative freedom. It instead confirms that a modern kind of republican freedom sensitive to pluralism must promote pure negative freedom. Strong republicanism, on the other hand, requires more homogeneity. In a small, isolated society where everyone holds the same conception of the good, the set of people's shared, or avowal-ready, interests might be significantly smaller and provide support for institutions making sure they commit to strong republicanism. In a modern, pluralistic society, by contrast, many citizens will be content with a sufficiently low probability of someone constraining their exercise of the basic liberties. Sufficiently low to pass the eyeball test, we might conjecture. But the extensive vigilance necessary for the robust protection against uncontrolled power that strong republicanism requires will to most people involve a too costly sacrifice of personal pursuits. People want to pursue ends that conflict with devoting their lives to making sure no one gets away with abusing political power. So, while the basic liberties might constitute a primary good, non-domination does not.[55] It looks more like a public good, as individuals want their basic liberties to be protected in all socially possible worlds, but few might want to make the necessary contribution to the extensive vigilance such protection requires. Even the public-good view is questionable, however, since the required vigilance involves extensive surveillance of citizens, not just of government officials, to make sure everyone contributes to active control.

Non-domination looks different from the perspective of Pettit's moderate republicanism, of course, since he takes it to require no more than virtual control, and not the far more demanding active control. And virtual control might very well be sufficient protection to the extent the eyeball test requires. Citizens need not constantly be on the watch for abuse of political power to feel confident enough to relate to others as their equals. And since virtual control allows people to lead their lives in accordance with a wide range of conceptions of the good, Pettit can understand his theory to be compatible with liberal neutrality. Virtual control lets people pursue their conceptions of the good, since they must only remain in standby mode, "ready to intervene on a need-to-act basis."[56] They need only commit to blowing the whistle whenever they become aware of power abuse; they need not actively search for it. On this account, the virtue republican freedom requires from citizens does not imply a comprehensive doctrine. Citizens can pursue a wide range of conceptions of the good while, as we have seen, being ready to act when "the red lights go on."

This moderate virtual-control view of republican freedom therefore meets Pettit's criterion that "any plausible political ideal must be an ideal for all."[57] That is, at least for all who are reasonable. The republican ideal, in Pettit's view, is "capable of commanding the allegiance of the citizens of developed, multicultural societies, regardless of their more particular conceptions of the good."[58] This view clearly conflicts with strong republicanism, the pursuit of which involves making the citizens conform to a republican comprehensive doctrine that most citizens will probably oppose.

To achieve strong republican robustness, people must be more vigilant than Pettit requires them to be, as there will be cases when the red lights should go on but do not. Any relaxation in the monitoring of how decisions are made and carried out means opportunities for uncontrolled power. Once people start prioritizing other interests at the expense of vigilance and contestation, they give others opportunities to increase their share of political power. Strong popular control therefore goes beyond virtual control; it is an active form of control that seeks to rid as many socially possible worlds as possible of uncontrolled interference. Government officials are carefully monitored so that no decision conflicting with the common good is unopposed.

124 THE REPUBLICAN DILEMMA

Since respect for pluralism would make republicans' judgments of people's freedom the same as those of pure negative freedom theorists, falsifying the equivalent-judgments thesis requires a strong interpretation of republican freedom. Republican freedom, on this account, cannot be the basis for what Rawls calls a liberal theory, which "allow[s] for a plurality of different and opposing, and even incommensurable, conceptions of the good." It is instead a non-liberal theory holding that "there is but one conception of the good, or . . . there is but one conception of the good which is to be recognized by all persons, so far as they are rational."[59] By taking the liberal side of this distinction, Pettit's moderate view confirms the equivalent-judgments thesis.

6.6 Liberal constraints on virtue

Neither Pettit nor Rawls treats people's preferences as fixed. They both believe social institutions should induce voluntary virtuous behavior. Even political liberals must require a certain level of political participation from citizens to make sure that institutions remain neutral between different conceptions of the good. People's preferences are not "fixed or given," as Rawls says.[60] Just institutions should not seek to satisfy existing desires, but instead try to alter these desires so as to better meet the principles of justice. Just institutions reproduce certain desirable norms over time. "[T]he institutions of the basic structure," Rawls says, "have deep and long-term social effects and in fundamental ways shape citizens' character and aims, the kinds of persons they are and aspire to be."[61] Just institutions tend to "eliminate or at least to control men's inclinations to injustice."[62] Just institutions, for Rawls, should induce "political virtues," including political participation, to ensure that people remain committed to maintaining these institutions over time, thus ensuring the protection of their own liberties.[63] Pettit also supports such a role for just institutions. He, for example, sees the need for a programme of civics education.[64]

But there are restrictions in political liberalism and moderate republicanism on how virtuous just institutions can require citizens to be. These constraints are identified in political constructivism, as the principles it generates are acceptable to all reasonable persons as they are, here and now, regardless of their comprehensive doctrines. As Rawls says, political constructivism "proceeds from what is, or can be, held in common."[65] People can reasonably reject principles for being too demanding. They can reasonably reject the superiority of a principle requiring the robustness of strong republican freedom, because that entails too great a restriction on their opportunity sets. The principles must express fair terms of cooperation that reasonable persons can expect one another to abide by.[66] The political ideal must therefore be defined so that people benefit from just institutions and are therefore motivated to comply with them and to maintain them.[67] A fundamental principle is thus rooted in society's public political culture and might therefore differ from one society to another.

This appears to be Pettit's view as well, which is no surprise, of course, given the commitment to political constructivism he shares with Rawls (Chapter 4). An ideal, he argues, must be feasible and sustainable, and must consequently be defined with sensitivity to what people can actually be expected to live up to.[68] The ideal of non-domination cannot require norms that contradict people's personal interests, since they will then try to avoid acting on them, thus undermining them.[69] This is exactly the concern Rawls expresses when he says a conception of justice must be sensitive to reasonable pluralism, as it will otherwise be unstable.[70]

Pettit distinguishes between two questions of feasibility. He first asks, "which institutions are likely to attract full or at least adequate compliance?"[71] For the ideal to be feasible, compliance must be "sufficient, at the very least, to keep the institutions in place and to enable them to promote the benefits for which they are designed."[72] A feasible ideal is, or can be made, incentive-compatible—that is, we can expect individuals to be motivated to act as the ideal demands.

Pettit's second question of feasibility is, "which are the institutions that, once in place, we can be confident will remain in place?"[73] The ideal is stable to the extent that it is incentive-compatible over time. Ordinary people must be able to sustain the ideal arrangements when they are in place.[74] For Rawls, similarly, principles of justice are stable to the extent that reasonable persons are motivated to comply with them.[75] Rawls requires that everyone can rationally expect others to comply with the ideal over time, or otherwise the scheme of cooperation will break down. Pettit admits he is unable to specify exactly what is feasible and not.[76] He just says the feasibility set cannot contain everything that is logically possible, but it must contain more than just what people are likely to go along with. In any case, what the ideal of republican freedom requires is "certainly within people's reach," he says.[77]

Pettit thinks political ideals must be politically feasible—that is, they must be achievable by democratic means in an actual society.[78] We cannot define

126 THE REPUBLICAN DILEMMA

an ideal without accounting for real problems of implementing it in a society of citizens with different, conflicting interests. Laws are effective only if they work in synergy with norms that actually can be established in real societies.[79] This is to take people as they are instead of as they should be to fit a political ideal. Along the same lines, Rawls says "[c]onceptions of justice must be justified by the conditions of our life as we know it or not at all."[80] The ideal must, in other words, be sensitive to facts about the objects it is supposed to regulate.

For Rawls, we have a natural duty to comply with just institutions, as well as to assist in establishing such institutions "when this can be done with little cost to ourselves."[81] He does not specify what he means by "little cost," but since he thinks of justice as reciprocity, which is apparent in the reasonable acceptance test, it cannot be greater than what we can reasonably expect from reasonable and rational persons given facts about their personal ends, which are defined by their desire to establish just institutions. Just institutions are stable institutions, for Rawls, and they therefore cannot demand more than people can reasonably expect from each other. The natural duties are supposed to "insure the stability of just arrangements" and can therefore only be so demanding that reasonable persons have a persistent desire to fulfill them.[82]

Pettit also denies that we can determine how much protection non-domination requires prior to "empirical investigation."[83] The virtuous behavior required must be rational for all individuals given their actual motivations. And the political ideal must be stable, in the sense that it is satisfied in a broad range of possible worlds.[84] The less specific the ideal, the more stable it will be, since it will then be realized in more possible worlds. Compared to an ideal based on reasonable expectations, an ideal specifying people's preferences beyond such reasonableness will be less stable. Achieving the ideal he prescribes requires people's coordination, and people can only coordinate on behavior they can expect from one another. As rational beings, they will only sacrifice their personal interests if they expect others to make similar sacrifices. People's coordination will only stabilize on what they expect from others, others expect from them, they expect others to expect from them, and so on. It therefore makes sense for Pettit to require virtual control, not active control.

We can now see that strong republicanism is less stable and less achievable under the conditions of a modern pluralistic society. The difference between moderate republicanism and strong republicanism is a difference in the trade-off between requirements for political participation and the scope of people's opportunities for pursuing personal ends. Strong republicanism gives more weight to political participation as a way of protecting society against misrule, while moderate republicanism is more permissive with respect to political engagement. Strong republicanism thus becomes dependent on a more specific set of people's preferences, which makes it less stable and less realizable given the wide range of conceptions of the good with which it is incompatible.

6.7 Pettit's rejection of active control

This problem of realizing active control might appear fatal for strong republicanism. For Pettit, demanding active control will actually undermine the robust protection against abuse of political power. He implicitly denies the distinction between strong and moderate forms of republicanism. I have found three reasons in Pettit's work underpinning this view. I show how they either fail or lead to a support for the promotion of pure negative freedom.

First, Pettit argues that not being constantly monitored gives government officials a feeling of being trusted, which motivates them to make decisions in accordance with common interests.[85] The trustee wants the good opinion of the trustor, or of others witnessing the act of trust, and will therefore be motivated not to let the trustor down.[86] The idea is that if B trusts A, then A will be more motivated to act on B's instructions than if B had not shown A that he trusts her. Active control is incompatible with such showing of trustworthiness, and therefore prevents this beneficial effect.

Whether or not trust actually has this beneficial effect is, of course, an empirical question.[87] But I need not go into that here because I can respond conceptually by pointing out that trust can add nothing to the modal robustness of government officials acting for the good of society. Trust might reduce the probability of uncontrolled interference, but it does not impose an external constraint on the government officials so as to make their power abuse absent from more socially possible worlds. Trust might lower the probability of government officials exercising uncontrolled power, but it does not make the use of such power less accessible.

Pettit's second and third reasons for objecting to active control reflect the constructivist constraints on virtue requirements I have just discussed. His second reason is that promoting active control would conflict with citizens'

128 THE REPUBLICAN DILEMMA

common, or avowal-ready, interests, and consequently involve domination. It would be pointless to try to make citizens this virtuous since that would cause more domination than it prevents.[88] Interference to improve citizens will be uncontrolled, as it will cause a greater loss in overall non-domination than it gains in robust protection against uncontrolled power. Pettit can therefore appeal to non-domination in granting individuals rights protecting them against being forced to contribute to ends they do not endorse. So, if A faces a choice between doing x or y, and only x-ing is compatible with active control, republicans might still grant A the right to choose for herself whether to do so or not.

In response, I refer to earlier chapters showing that Pettit's respect for people's avowal-ready interests is the basis for his political constructivism, which we have seen leads to moderate republicanism and to freedom judgments equivalent to those of pure negative freedom theorists. Pettit's second reason for rejecting strong republicanism therefore effectively implies support for the promotion of pure negative freedom. To distance themselves from pure negative freedom, republicans must therefore reject Pettit's second response and endorse the strong interpretation of republican freedom.

Pettit's third and final reason for rejecting active control is closely related to his second reason. He points out that forcing people to contribute to ends they do not endorse will make them less motivated to contribute than if they had the opportunity to do so voluntarily.[89] After all, there is no point in trying to widen the range of possible worlds without uncontrolled interference if doing so involves interference conflicting with people's common interests in the actual world. Republicanism requires that the state be forced to track the citizens' interests, and these interests, as Pettit understands them, conflict with full commitment to protecting their society against uncontrolled power.

But this response just says that the commitment to vigilance and contestation must be voluntary. It does not say that republicanism must be preference-neutral. Republicans can grant citizens legal rights that protect them against uncontrolled interference while still trying to motivate them to use the freedoms these rights grant them in a specific way. Republicans need not be indifferent to how individuals make uncoerced choices.[90] So, if a right makes A free to choose x or y, and y will best promote non-domination, then republicans can look for non-coercive ways of making A voluntarily choose y rather than x. But institutions designed to motivate such behavior, even if only non-coercively, will not be supported by political constructivism, and are therefore not justified in Pettit's moderate republicanism. This is

PLURALISM   129

particularly due to the transparency of intentions required by the procedure's publicity condition, which I discuss in the next chapter.

6.8 Motivating active control

Republicans taking the strong interpretation should support subtle ways of altering citizens' preferences to make them willingly commit to the behavioral pattern of active control. Such strategies might be considered compatible with Viroli's vision of the *res publica* as "a community of individuals in which no one is forced to serve, and no one is allowed to dominate."[91] Well-designed interventions might include nudges, which arrange individuals' options so as to make them more likely to choose beneficial options without undermining their sense of autonomous decision-making.[92] But perhaps more obviously, such measures will include a compulsory civic education. Political liberalism and liberal republicanism will also give an important role to education. In particular, they can emphasize the importance of the basic liberties and of respecting various ways people exercise them.[93] But liberal neutrality constrains them from going as far as strong republicanism in specifying how people are to exercise their liberties and in creating citizens who devote much of their lives to political activity. On the strong account, a compulsory civic education might gradually take the form suggested by American revolutionary Benjamin Rush: "It is possible . . . to convert men into republican machines." A republican pupil, Rush said, should "be taught that he does not belong to himself, but that he is public property."[94]

Pettit, however, is concerned that an education designed to stimulate civic virtue can "easily deteriorate into the sort of propaganda that bores or alienates."[95] This view is compatible with moderate republicanism, which, like political liberalism, is focused on not alienating anyone from the governing structure of their society. And, of course, if the education bores rather than inspires children to become active citizens, it must be reconsidered and altered. But if such education is introduced gradually in correspondence with gradual preference-shaping, it need not have this effect.

Some republicans criticize Pettit's view of education. Lovett challenges Pettit's commitment to neutrality by arguing that civic education restricted by the constraints of neutrality will not ensure institutional protection against domination across various social and political environments.[96] Republican education, in Lovett's view, might involve encouraging a patriotic

130 THE REPUBLICAN DILEMMA

attachment to local political order and tradition to preserve institutions of non-domination. Lovett defends toleration of certain conceptions of the good that conflict with such education by providing opt-outs and imposing no legal or economic disabilities. But he holds that the public funding needed for adequate civic education violates neutrality by advantaging certain conceptions of the good.

Costa argues that "Pettit virtually ignores the potential of education to provide citizens with the knowledge and skills required for effective political action." Schools, she says, "are in a unique position to encourage democratic virtues among their students."[97] While such virtues can also be taught in other institutions, such as in the family home or churches, it is difficult to control that these institutions promote the right kind of values. Costa considers concerns about schools in democratic societies brainwashing children to be exaggerated. She grants that "certain policies of moral and political education might turn into a kind of propaganda, or might have negligible effects," but adds that "this is a reason to reject only those sentimental approaches that make no room for the development of critical thinking. It is not a reason to reject all forms of moral and political education."[98] Costa does not seem to have the promotion of strong republicanism in mind, however, as she focuses on education as a means to counter a narrower range of vices, including sexism and racism. But her view of education as a way of making citizens adopt the right kind of values is something strong republicans cannot ignore.

Now, strong republicanism might actually require a kind of education that discourages the critical thinking Costa wants to stimulate. This kind of civic education is designed to create citizens fully devoted to protecting their society against uncontrolled power. And that might indeed undermine individuals' capacity to think critically and, as we have seen, to develop and pursue their own conception of the good.

Moderate republicans will likely object to this view by stressing that because of the plurality of modern society, such education would itself be an exercise of uncontrolled power. Any attempt to impose the conformity of strong republicanism on a diverse population would amount to uncontrolled interference, and therefore be unjustifiable. But this objection would once again confirm moderate republicanism's strong ties to political liberalism. It might indeed be right to say that since society is what it currently is, realizing strong republicanism is impermissible, and perhaps impossible. But taking that view means conceding to the pure negative freedom theorists that political decision-making should promote their conception of freedom.

6.9 Freedom and efficiency

Stimulating the active control strong republicanism requires will likely come at a high cost in terms of not only pluralism but also efficiency. As Brennan and Lomasky note in their critique of republicanism, requiring citizens to devote their lives to political participation necessarily reduces their capacity to produce goods people value. Brennan and Lomasky ask, "Do we really want pilots to spend less time on take-off techniques and surgeons to stint on practicing suture tying so that they can devote the odd hour or two to the consideration of foreign policy?"[99] To promote a kind of republicanism that conflicts with the promotion of pure negative freedom, we must give an affirmative answer to this question.

As we saw in Section 3.8, List also expresses this concern. His strong republicanism blocks an optimal trade-off between scope and robustness with respect to efficiency.[100] Strong republicanism suggests we should move toward a society where people enjoy fewer opportunities than they do in a society where people can pursue a wide range of conceptions of the good. People prefer to live in the latter society, but strong republicans would argue they are wrong to do so. Promoting a conception of republican freedom that conflicts with Carter's equivalent-judgments thesis therefore means opting for a kind of society most people do not want to live in.

The kind of "civic friendship" republicanism requires, Brennan and Lomasky argue, makes little sense in large modern states with diverse populations. It might have worked in small republics of the pre-industrial era, where citizens had plenty of time for politics because most of the labor was performed by women and slaves. However, such political duties are incompatible with the larger and more egalitarian modern society. Thinking that this republican ideal can be applied to such a society, Brennan and Lomasky argue, "is to allow nostalgia to turn into fantasy."[101] Modern society needs a liberal freedom ideal. "Liberty as non-interference is," in their view, "more responsive to individual diversity than is liberty as non-domination, and it thereby is more responsive to people's self-perceived interests."[102]

As I noted in the introductory chapter, Pettit responds to Brennan and Lomasky by arguing that their critique of his theory is misdirected, as it focuses on a "Continental form of republicanism," or what Rawls calls "civic humanism."[103] This kind of republicanism sees freedom as self-government and political participation: citizens need to take an active role in the political decision-making by which they are bound. It is associated with positive

132   THE REPUBLICAN DILEMMA

liberty and self-mastery. Pettit's "Italian-Atlantic" form of republicanism, on the other hand, sees political participation only as instrumentally important, and not as a part of the ideal itself.[104] Pettit's model is therefore not vulnerable to Brennan and Lomasky's critique, as it allows citizens to largely absent themselves from political involvement if they so prefer, at least insofar as political decision-making goes "reasonably well."[105] On this moderate account, citizens appreciate that some level of political participation is required in order to sustain important institutions, but they will not compromise their personal projects to devote themselves to political engagement. We have seen that these liberal views are compatible with virtual control. And such control, Pettit argues, is compatible with citizens distributing political participation to their representatives.[106]

The problem with Pettit's response is that it avoids Brennan and Lomasky's criticism only because it turns republicanism into a liberal theory promoting pure negative freedom. Pettit's response to the inefficiency concerns therefore amounts to giving citizens pure negative freedom to undermine a republican freedom ideal that actually does conflict with the promotion of pure negative freedom. That is, citizens are given a generous scope within which to choose to what extent they commit to popular control, thus being granted more combinations of conjunctively exercisable actions than under strong republicanism.

6.10 Conclusion

This chapter concludes the analysis of the scope and robustness dimensions of republican freedom. A freedom concept with an in-built protection requirement against interference necessarily has a restricted scope. The greater the robustness of this protection, the greater is the restriction on individuals' opportunity sets. The scope restricted only by a reasonableness condition, as on Pettit's moderate interpretation of republican freedom, can only be coupled with the robustness requirement of an institutional protection constituted by institutions promoting the citizens' virtual control of their government. Like political liberalism, this moderate republicanism is neutral between conceptions of the good, but only because it promotes pure negative freedom.

A strong commitment to robustness, and corresponding reduction in scope, does all the work in forming an account of freedom as non-domination

PLURALISM   133

on which republicans can make judgments of people's freedom that conflict with those of pure negative freedom theorists. So, to avoid the equivalent-judgments thesis, republicans must define freedom in a way that restricts scope for the sake of robustness to the extent that it has a negative impact on individuals' number of combinations of conjunctively exercisable actions. And that, I have now demonstrated, means making citizens conform to a conception of the good compatible with active control.

So, republicans can endorse liberal neutrality by supporting the promotion of pure negative freedom, or they can reject pure negative freedom by violating neutrality and undermining the pluralism that characterizes modern society. The former alternative leads to moderate republicanism, and the latter to strong republicanism. We have seen that Pettit favors moderate republicanism with virtual control and therefore ends up promoting institutions also pure negative freedom theorists would see as freedom-enhancing. And if Pettit is right that there is a point at which political liberalism goes one way and republicanism another, then he follows the former, not the latter.

In response, Pettit might say that given the pluralistic nature of modern society, avowal-ready interests will not allow for strong republicanism. As we have seen, avowal-ready interests are the interests people actually share, not those they ought to share, as seen from some controversial moral viewpoint. Since republican freedom requires the protection of avowal-ready interests, then, it is compatible only with a moderate understanding. Republican freedom requires the tracking of people's actual interests, and therefore does not legitimize extensive preference-shaping. If this is right, then republicanism is bound to be a form of political liberalism, and bound to promote pure negative freedom. To avoid this result, Pettit must abandon his respect for reasonable pluralism and instead support institutions that shape people's preferences so as to make them more devoted to protecting their society against uncontrolled political power. Here we see the real choice between promoting pure negative freedom or republican freedom.

In her support of Pettit, Costa writes that his republicanism is often mistakenly understood as a theory requiring a citizenry committed to a level of political participation that is too high for modern society. Although accepting that this is one version of republicanism, Costa argues that Pettit's theory "offers a very promising reconstruction of republican insights which can be extended to include a feasible politics of virtue."[107] I have said nothing to challenge this view. My argument is rather that these insights are

134 THE REPUBLICAN DILEMMA

compatible both with political liberalism and with the promotion of pure negative freedom. Moderate republicans may continue to see "freedom as non-domination" as their ultimate ideal, but they cannot say that this ideal conflicts with, or adds anything of importance to, the liberal ideal of pure negative freedom.

We can therefore understand why Costa thinks Rawlsian liberalism promotes republican freedom.[108] Pettit's moderate understanding of non-domination makes a trade-off between scope and robustness that is compatible with the liberal neutrality Rawls defends. However, Costa also argues that because Rawls promotes freedom as non-domination, he does *not* promote freedom as non-interference. It should now be clear why this is incorrect.

7

Ideal

7.1 Introduction

What do we need strong republicanism for? As an ideal, it seems unsuited for the modern, pluralistic society we live in. Realizing it would have an intolerably high moral cost, and if we could find a way of making citizens commit to the active control it requires, we would have a sure recipe for an inefficient society. Since this is the ideal republicans must endorse to show how pure negative freedom is an inadequate freedom ideal for our society, they seem forced to concede that freedom as non-domination can add nothing of importance to contemporary political discourse. So, while I have shown how republicans can reject the liberal freedom concept they like to criticize, it seems unlikely that many of them will endorse this strong account of freedom as non-domination.

In this chapter, however, I identify a way in which we can usefully employ this distinctly republican freedom ideal in contemporary political theory. I do so by considering how we ought to use political ideals, or what purpose we want ideals to serve, in political theorizing. The political constructivism I have discussed in earlier chapters generates principles to guide the progress of the societies to which they apply. We saw in Chapter 4 that Pettit follows Rawls in employing this method, and how it leads him to promote an ideal that will seem attractive in a modern society. We have also seen how this method is the basis for a liberal theory promoting pure negative freedom. A republican rejection of pure negative freedom therefore calls for a different methodological approach to political ideals.

Now, strong republicanism can be the outcome of political constructivism, but only in societies very different from our own, where people share a conception of the good and are already highly committed to vigilance and contestation. It is because people are as they are in society as we know it that political constructivism is the basis for the liberalism of Pettit and Rawls. Rawls indeed assumes liberal values and a liberal culture, and he is therefore guaranteed to construct a liberal conception of justice. But under different

The Republican Dilemma. Lars J. K. Moen, Oxford University Press. © Oxford University Press 2024.
DOI: 10.1093/oso/9780197757024.003.0007

136 THE REPUBLICAN DILEMMA

conditions, political constructivism can generate a non-liberal conception. By assuming republican preferences, as defined in the previous chapter, political constructivism could deliver strong republicanism. Moderate and strong republicanism would then be inseparable. For this reason, it might be more accurate to use the term "liberal republicanism" rather than "moderate republicanism" to refer to Pettit's theory. Of course, the reason why we cannot make such unrealistic assumptions in political constructivism is that we would get an outcome the implementation of which would be both infeasible and undesirable. Political constructivism would then consequently fail to offer the guidance it promises.

But by rejecting this guidance requirement for political ideals, we can abstract away from people's actual preferences. We can then define an ideal without concern for how feasible its realization would be. We can say the ideal is what it is, independently of facts about actual societies, while recognizing that trying to realize it in a particular society might be an uncertain and even undesirable endeavor. On this approach, republicans can think of strong republicanism as the ultimate ideal, while accepting that it might be unwise to try to implement it under current conditions.

The reason why it ought not, and perhaps cannot, be implemented is that doing so would come at an unacceptable cost in terms of other values. On this alternative approach, values conflict and give contrary directives, and in the abstract, we have no way of prioritizing one or another of these values. Only by taking relevant facts about specific societies into account can we pursue the most attractive trade-offs between values to produce all-things-considered guidance. It is when these facts are taken into consideration that strong republican freedom begins to look unattractive. But we shall see that the converse is also true: strong republican freedom can make the facts look unattractive. While it cannot provide all-things-considered directives, strong republican freedom can give republicans grounds for evaluating society and for criticizing citizens for their failure to live up to this ultimate republican ideal.

7.2 The two approaches

Cohen identifies three kinds of question in political philosophy: "(i) What is justice?; (ii) What should the state do?; and (iii) Which social states of affairs ought to be brought about?"[1] These questions, he adds, "are not distinguished as often as they should be."[2] Political philosophers should be aware that these questions demand distinct answers, and they should be conscious of which question they try to answer.

But Cohen's view is controversial. In fact, keeping these questions separate leads to a rejection of constructivism.[3] Constructivists, and Rawls in particular, think of the promotion of justice as constitutive of the legitimate state, or the basic structure. As Rawls famously says, "[j]ustice is the first virtue of social institutions."[4] Pettit, likewise, sees the promotion of republican freedom, his grand ideal, as the essence of the legitimate state. We have seen that promoting a political conception of justice is what Rawls requires the state to do to meet the liberal principle of legitimacy, and that Pettit's account of freedom is a kind of political conception. Ingham and Lovett indeed call it a "political conception of freedom."[5]

But on Cohen's "radical pluralism," we define justice, or any other value, without considering how it should inform our thinking about how social institutions should operate under actual conditions.[6] Values are fundamentally insensitive to facts about our actual society, as we can consider the extent to which we ought to realize the values after we have defined them.[7] We do not ask what freedom or justice requires given what society and the people within it are actually like. Such facts are not accounted for when we define the value itself. Defined independently of facts, justice or freedom becomes just one value in a plurality of values. And without relevant facts, we do not know how to prioritize one value at the expense of another in actual decision-making.

On this approach, we treat Cohen's three questions separately. Justice, or freedom, is what it is, regardless of what the state ought to do or what states of affairs actually ought to be brought about. The advantage of this fundamental, or radical, value pluralism is that it clarifies what we promote and what we forgo when we make the trade-offs and the all-things-considered decisions we inevitably have to make to run our society.

Critics might argue that this approach is impractical. Political constructivism is more useful since it develops an attractive and feasible ideal for society as it is. It is defined for the purpose of guiding real political practice. Pettit endorses this pragmatism when he says a political ideal should be an aim for the state to pursue by the use of legitimate means. A state promoting republican freedom, he says, will be legitimate and just.[8] The ideal, in his view, must be achievable by democratic means in an actual society.[9] This is also the view Rawls takes when he says the ideal must be within the bounds

138 THE REPUBLICAN DILEMMA

of "practicable political possibility."[10] It must be achievable by legitimate, democratic means in society as it is.

And what is practicable in one society might not be practicable in other societies. We therefore cannot expect political constructivism to deliver the same principles in different societies. What is reasonably objectionable in one society might be not be reasonably objectionable in another. It follows that different societies might construct different political conceptions of justice or of republican freedom. As Pettit says, "political philosophers should give particular attention to reform proposals that are psychologically and institutionally within reach of the community to which they are addressed."[11] Political ideals must be sensitive to sociological and psychological facts that determine what agents will go along with over time.[12] On Pettit's view, we therefore cannot determine what republican freedom requires prior to "empirical investigation."[13]

The ideal must particularly be sensitive to facts about how we can expect people to behave without the use of oppressive power. And given the diversity characterizing modern society, we are unlikely to transparently and democratically adopt policies intended to alter citizens' preferences in the way we have seen strong republican robustness requires. This approach to defining ideals, then, takes people and their preferences as they are rather than what they ought to be.

By understanding values as basic and prior to empirical investigations, on the other hand, we regard them as independent of "practicable political possibility." Values are insensitive to facts about people's preferences or other features of society that determine such possibility. When we consider what can be achieved under actual conditions, and what all things considered ought to be done, we will therefore often find that facts restrict the extent to which we can realize a value, or an optimal trade-off between values.

No such conflict with facts occurs in constructivism, which defines a conception of the most prominent value—justice for Rawls, freedom for Pettit—so as to make it practice-guiding under actual circumstances. But for Cohen, this is no way of understanding what the value is; it is rather the less basic and more practical exercise of working out "rules of regulation."[14] Such rules are no doubt important, but Cohen denies that they can be fundamental in the sense constructivism takes them to be, since "they cannot tell us how to evaluate the effects by reference to which they themselves are to be evaluated."[15] We ought to be able to evaluate the extent to which the regulation we consider optimal under current circumstances is compatible with justice, or freedom, or equality, but we forgo any such opportunity by defining our values in terms of this regulation. While we need facts about society to create rules of regulation, such facts are irrelevant for understanding, or discovering, our basic values. Facts about practicable political possibility do not affect the content of these values; they only play a role when we determine the extent to which we ought to satisfy them.[16] While Rawls thinks a principle of justice is "seriously defective" if people are not motivated to act on it, Cohen takes such lack of motivation to mean only that the principles are defective as rules of regulation, not as principles of justice.[17] Facts about human motivation do not affect the meaning of justice, only the extent to which it is, can be, or ought to be achieved.

Values are thus considered logically prior to rules of regulations. We do not start by asking what principles ought to regulate our society, as on the constructivist approach. Instead, we first formulate the value, and then ask whether, or to what extent, it would be desirable to try to satisfy it under current conditions. Figuring out how institutions ought to operate given existing conditions involves trading values off against each other in response to these conditions. "Justice," Cohen says, "is an input into, not an output of, these trade-off decisions."[18] We should design rules of regulation to promote justice, but only to a reasonable extent.[19] Facts therefore become relevant only at the stage at which we determine the rules of regulation, which is posterior to the stage at which we formulate the values.

We might understand this difference between constructivism and Cohen's radical pluralism by noting how they produce two different kinds of claims. Constructivism gives us *prescriptive* claims that are falsified when people cannot fulfill them.[20] A constructivist principle, in other words, does not apply in contexts where people are not motivated to satisfy it. In radical pluralism, on the other hand, we make *evaluative* claims about states of affairs that only give us *pro tanto* reasons for actions. From this perspective, a principle is not falsified merely because we cannot make institutions conform to it.[21] We can therefore say that while satisfying a principle would be good, actually trying to satisfy it under current circumstances would be undesirable and perhaps impossible because it would require people to make unreasonably large sacrifices.

We consequently see why Cohen rejects Rawls's justice–truth analogy. "Justice," Rawls says, "is the first virtue of social institutions, as truth is of systems of thought. A theory however elegant and economical must be rejected or revised if it is untrue; likewise laws and institutions no matter

140 THE REPUBLICAN DILEMMA

how efficient and well-arranged must be reformed or abolished if they are unjust."[22] But for Cohen, a statement's being true is neither a necessary nor a sufficient condition for it being a justifiable utterance.[23] Whether or not we should tell the truth depends on the circumstances we are in. And the same goes for whether we should promote justice or some other value in the way we set up our social institutions. We should tell the truth whenever the costs of doing so are not too high, just as we should make our institutions just only to the extent that doing so does not involve sacrifices too great in terms of other values.

7.3 Constraints

In this section, I consider two kinds of constraint and show how they feature in a constructivist understanding of values, but not in a radical-pluralist one. These constraints are often understood as deontic constraints essential in non-consequentialist theories, as they constrain the collective pursuit of an agent-neutral good.

My use of the term "constraint" might be challenged by those favoring these constraints on value formation insofar as it suggests that we cannot permissibly require that people do what they can to realize the ideal. On the constructivist approach, "constraints" are built into the ideal itself, which means they are not constraints on the extent to which we can require people to fulfil the requirements of the ideal. What I call constraints are therefore constraining in this sense only on from a radical-pluralist perspective. On this view, the ideal is free from constraints, although we might very plausibly find good reasons for constraining the pursuit of the ideal. This is what we discover when we work out the appropriate rules of regulation, which is an exercise posterior to the formulation of values. As Cohen says, "[t]he desired theory tells us how much justice we should strive to realize.... Constructivism promotes the extraneous (to justice) considerations that properly figure in the justification of rules of regulation to the status of constraints on what justice *is*."[24] From Cohen's point of view, then, the constructivist ideal is not the pure ideal but a diluted ideal with constraints built into it.

These reasons for not wholeheartedly pursuing the ideal are moral reasons pointing out that such promotion involves undesirable means. Rawls's ideal of justice, for example, must be realizable in "morally permissible" ways.[25]

I shall now discuss a personal prerogative and a publicity condition as two constraints taken to ensure such moral permissibility in political constructivism. If we abstract away from facts about people's preferences, however, as we do on a radical-pluralist approach, these constraints are not built into a practice-guiding ideal; they are instead value considerations that can constrain the extent to which we can permissibly promote a value like freedom or justice.

7.3.1 Personal prerogative

Several commentators of Rawls's theory have pointed out that it includes a personal, or agent-centered, prerogative.[26] A personal prerogative gives individuals a certain scope for choosing how much to contribute to the overall good.[27] It allows individuals to decide for themselves what an ideal demands of them. This condition is more generally expressed in what Rawls calls the "strains of commitment," according to which compliance with the principles of justice cannot require citizens to abandon their fundamental interests.[28] The principles are therefore not "all controlling," Rawls says.[29] Laws and institutions implementing principles that are too demanding will make citizens feel alienated from their own society, and fail to motivate compliance while treating the citizens as free and equal persons.[30] We have seen that Pettit understands such alienation as domination. So, for neither Rawls nor Pettit can principles be so demanding that the laws and institutions implementing them will leave citizens feeling alienated from their own society. Such laws and institutions, Pettit says, would cause more domination than they prevent.[31]

The personal prerogative is what Ingham and Lovett have in mind when they say political ideals ought to be subject to a "pragmatic constraint." By defining freedom in response to this constraint, we get a "political conception of freedom" that we have seen they perceive to be "useful, meaning roughly that it should have critical force without being hopelessly demanding."[32] The ideal of freedom should not be so demanding that we cannot reasonably expect people to live up to it. Subject to this constraint, the ideal can guide political practice.

The prerogative allows individuals to give special consideration to their own personal projects. It therefore plays an important role in an ideal compatible with the diversity of modern society by ensuring that different courses of action be left open for citizens. In political constructivism, we can expect a principle that is too restrictive in this sense to be reasonably rejected. We have seen, particularly in Chapter 4, that both Rawls and Pettit are concerned with stability, and we cannot expect a principle that does not allow reasonable individuals to pursue their own personal ends to meet the stability requirement, as individuals will comply with it only reluctantly and look for ways of undermining it.[33] The constructivist procedure, however, filters out principles that are too demanding, thus ensuring a personal prerogative that gives individuals scope for deciding for themselves how to lead their own lives.

It is important to note that the personal prerogative does not make constructivism an "anything goes" approach to political or moral ideals. As Samuel Scheffler writes, the prerogative gives you permission to give M times more weight to your own interests than to anyone else's. You may therefore do y provided the total net loss to others resulting from your doing y instead of x is less than M times your net loss resulting from doing x instead of your preferred y.[34] In some cases, however, the concerns of others are weighty enough to require you to compromise your personal projects. In constructivism, such requirements must be reasonable. Both Rawls and Pettit define the boundaries of reasonableness in terms of the basic liberties: promoting the ideal cannot involve reducing individuals' capacity to exercise their basic liberties.[35]

But if we take Cohen's radical-pluralist view, we understand fundamental values independently of what any particular society is like, and without sensitivity to a reasonable rejection test. But here the issue is not whether or not a normative theory specifying how social institutions ought to operate, all things considered, should grant individuals a personal prerogative. It is rather whether to build the prerogative into values themselves. We can take this view of basic values, but then introduce the personal prerogative at the level of theorizing at which we consider how values are to be traded off against each other for the purpose of making rules of regulation. Cohen, for example, supports the personal prerogative because, as he says, "we are not nothing but slaves to social justice."[36] Requirements of social justice, in other words, are not constrained by the prerogative, but the extent to which rules of regulation should require people to act justly is.[37] So, while the prerogative is not built into the radical-pluralist definition of justice, it might come into play as a permission for people not to always do what justice requires of them.

Moderate republicanism builds the personal prerogative into the freedom ideal by taking the ideal to require popular control only up to the extent of virtual control to allow people to pursue a wide range of conceptions of the good. The ideal of republican freedom is therefore satisfied to no greater extent when individual citizens exercise virtue beyond this minimum threshold. Pettit bases the personal prerogative on a concern for the dignity and respect of actual people of real societies. For A to treat B with dignity, Pettit believes B must preserve "a certain dominion over how he fares at [A]'s hands."[38] A must treat B with concern for B's avowed interests; B should have a say in how he is treated. We can therefore understand moderate republicanism as strong republican freedom constrained by concerns with individual dignity and respect. Moderate republicanism ensures such dignity and respect by giving individuals legal rights that protect them against being used for ends they do not endorse. If B cannot exercise the veto a right gives him against A's interference, then "he is merely a pawn in the enterprise of [A]," as Pettit sees it.[39] By understanding republican freedom as independent of this constraint, however, we see rights as rights not to contribute to republican freedom; they give individuals freedom to choose not to contribute to this ideal.

Strong republican freedom includes no personal prerogative, as it simply requires people to monitor both their government and their fellow citizens to establish and maintain an active popular control of political powerholders. This requirement is not softened by considerations of how motivated citizens might be for such behavior. On this view, then, the moderate-republican respect for people as they are must enter the stage after we have formulated the freedom ideal itself. It will then make sense to say that people are not slaves to republican freedom and should therefore be granted some scope for deciding for themselves to what extent they satisfy its active-control requirement. So, instead of treating moderate republican freedom as the ideal itself, we see it as a trade-off between republican freedom and other values based on facts relevant for producing desirable all-things-considered action guidance.

This is how pure negative freedom enters a theory suited for current circumstances. Facts about modern society tell us that it is constituted by individuals with a desire to pursue different ends, and in response to this plurality of conceptions of the good, a constructivist ideal must ensure that they be provided with opportunities to pursue a wide range of different courses of action. The fact of pluralism therefore draws constructivists towards liberal principles for promoting individuals' pure negative freedom.

144 THE REPUBLICAN DILEMMA

We now see how the personal prerogative is crucial for distinguishing strong and moderate republicanism. We might nonetheless say, of course, that strong republicanism is too demanding given facts about what people are actually like, and that it is therefore not a suitable ideal to pursue, or that it is attractive only as a component of a theory in which it is weakened by trade-offs with other values. The personal prerogative thus plays a different role in a theory with the moderate republican freedom ideal than in one with the strong republican freedom ideal. And recognizing this difference enables us to see why promoting pure negative freedom conflicts with the latter but not with the former.

7.3.2 Publicity

The other kind of constraint I consider, publicity, requires that the public have access to information about how institutions operate. This condition is met when it is common knowledge how the principles of justice apply, what they require, and to what extent individuals conform to the principles.[40] By applying this constraint to the definition of justice, we can say that "justice must be seen in order to be done."[41] If we cannot specify what justice requires of each of us, and if we cannot observe whether or not everyone does what she or he is required to do, then we must alter our definition of justice.

This is an important condition in constructivism. Publicity, Rawls says, "arises naturally from a contractarian [or constructivist] standpoint."[42] People can reasonably reject a principle if it is unclear what it requires of them, and they "cannot agree to a principle if there is a real possibility that it has any outcome that one will not be able to accept."[43] The same goes for a principle one cannot tell whether others comply with, since one might then unknowingly end up as the sucker who complies when others do not. Assurance of others' compliance is, as Rawls notes, essential for motivating compliance.[44]

People must therefore be able to see that society's institutions satisfy the principles of justice. Only then is every reasonable person assured that these institutions work to her or his benefit, which is essential for motivating general compliance. A political conception of justice citizens lack motivation to comply with is unstable.[45] And an unstable conception of justice, for Rawls, is no conception of justice at all. Promoting justice in ways requiring secrecy is therefore self-defeating. General awareness of universal acceptance, Rawls

IDEAL   145

says, "should have desirable effects and support the stability of social cooperation."[46] In a just society, "nothing need be hidden."[47]

The publicity condition is central also in Pettit's republican theory. It is expressed in its requirement that people know the intentions behind government interference. If what government officials do is not publicly known and understood, the people lack a basis for keeping an eye on the powerholders and for contesting actions they understand to violate avowal-ready interests.[48] Government would then not be on the people's terms. Political decisions will not always please everyone, but it must be clear to everyone how decisions track common, avowal-ready interests.[49]

Both Rawls and Pettit see dignity and respect as reasons for the importance of publicity. People are not adequately respected unless they can see that their government promotes their interests. Only when it is clear that every decision is compatible with avowal-ready interests, Pettit argues, will those unhappy with the decision recognize it as a case of tough luck, and not as systematic disrespect and violation of their dignity.[50] And Rawls notes that "the public recognition of the two principles [of justice] gives greater support to men's self-respect."[51] In his view, "a desirable feature of a conception of justice is that it should publicly express men's respect for one another."[52]

The publicity condition makes moderate republicanism resistant to active control since its intentional promotion cannot in a modern society be openly publicly presented as what it is. People can reasonably oppose the measures for stimulating active control I discussed in Section 6.8, which include a comprehensive civic education designed to indoctrinate republican preferences. Strong republicanism, on the other hand, can require that citizens commit to the high level of vigilance and contestation of active control, as it is unconstrained by facts about actual preferences. Publicity refers to transparency concerning what an ideal requires of people. But since strong republican freedom is insensitive to what people can actually accept and be expected to comply with, it is unconstrained by any concern for publicity. Of course, with active control, citizens will be so skilled at monitoring their government and at making sure it functions in their interest, that the publicity condition will be met. This does not, however, make publicity a constraint on strong republicanism. It is rather a consequence of citizens actively forcing their government to publicly explain its practices.

The publicity condition has significant limitations due to practical problems both with specifying what rules, or principles, require, and with observing whether people comply with them. Cohen, for example, discusses

146 THE REPUBLICAN DILEMMA

racism, which is obviously unjust, but racist practices can be hard to recognize for what they are because we cannot know other people's attitudes. As he says, "[w]e could not legally institute a principle that says: 'cleanse your soul of racist bias,' because we could not tell, sufficiently well, whether people (including we ourselves) were being true to it. But that doesn't mean that racism isn't unjust, or that 'do not practice racism, even *in foro interno*' is not an injunction of justice."[53] Rawls seems to recognize this limitation of publicity when he says "it is possible that all should understand and follow a principle and yet this fact not be widely known or explicitly recognized."[54] However, for present purposes, we can safely assume that there will be certain cases of promoting strong republicanism that can be seen as what they are and will therefore be considered impermissible in moderate republicanism.

7.4 Consequentialism

The personal prerogative and publicity constraints are commonly regarded as constraints on the pursuit of an impersonal, or agent-neutral, account of the good. They are therefore understood to conflict with consequentialism. This issue is not essential to the main purpose of this chapter. I bring it up here as a brief digression because Pettit is a staunch defender of consequentialism in moral and political philosophy.[55] He is also clear about his republicanism being a consequentialist theory.[56] But if the theory incorporates characteristically non-consequentialist constraints, then Pettit seems unable to maintain that his republicanism is consequentialist. We shall see, however, that Pettit sees the constraints as compatible with consequentialism. For Rawls, however, they are part of his rejection of consequentialism. Rawls and Pettit would therefore disagree about whether Pettit's republicanism is consequentialist or not. But we shall see that this dispute does not take the theory out of the framework of Rawlsian liberalism.

In moral philosophy, "the good" concerns reasons for what we want the world to be like—that is, the state of affairs we would like to bring about. It refers to an agent-neutral value, such as happiness or welfare. A value is agent-neutral, as opposed to agent-relative, when it can be recognized from an impersonal standpoint, and not necessarily from any particular agent's standpoint. "The right," on the other hand, refers to actions we are permitted or obligated to do. Non-consequentialist theories keep the right and the good distinct by permitting or requiring agents not to act for the good.

Consequentialism, on the other hand, unifies the two by taking the right action to invariably be that which best promotes the good. An agent is always obligated to choose the available option that most effectively serves the good.

Scheffler distinguishes between two kinds of constraints on the pursuit of the good that characterize non-consequentialism and conflict with consequentialism. He calls them "agent-centered prerogatives" and "agent-centered restrictions."[57] We have seen that the agent-centered, or personal, prerogative gives you a certain scope for choosing to what degree you promote the good. An agent-centered restriction, on the other hand, forbids certain actions even when they promote the good.[58] It specifies actions it is wrong for an agent to perform regardless of their likely consequences. Lying is a classic example.[59] Publicity is also often understood as such a restriction, since it says that it is wrong to hide what a principle requires even if doing so would produce the best consequences.

Note that a non-consequentialist theory need not treat these constraints as absolute. Rawls, who opposes consequentialism, says not being concerned with consequences "would simply be irrational, crazy."[60] What distinguishes consequentialism from non-consequentialism is that the former focuses only on consequences, whereas the latter can also draw on other considerations. Rawls rejects consequentialism for failing to give individuals sufficient respect as persons with their own conceptions of the good.[61] With a sole focus on agent-neutral value, consequentialism gives agents no scope for regarding their own personal projects as more important than anyone else's. A non-consequentialist theory, on the other hand, can give individuals permission to systematically devote more attention to their own projects even when doing so will not produce the best overall outcome.[62]

An important point is that while consequentialism requires individuals to act so as to best promote an agent-neutral good, the best way of doing so depends, in part, on the sacrifice it involves for these individuals. Without concern for A's preferences, we might say that A would best promote the good by doing x rather than y. But consequentialists must also take A's preferences into account and treat them equally with anyone else's preferences. It therefore does not follow that the good is necessarily best promoted by forcing A to do x, or by making it very costly for A to do y rather than x. A's preference for y-ing rather than x-ing might be so strong that making her do x would involve means that would cause an overall loss of the good we are trying to promote. This is essentially the insight of "sophisticated consequentialism," according to which the best way of maximizing the overall good

148   THE REPUBLICAN DILEMMA

may be to allow individuals to not always choose the action that will best promote the good, since denying such choice could be self-defeating.[63] We thus see how the personal prerogative might be introduced into a consequentialist theory.[64]

Pettit bases his republican theory on sophisticated consequentialism. His theory is consequentialist, he explains, as it treats non-domination as a target rather than as a constraint.[65] That is, the aim is to minimize domination, which means an act of uncontrolled interference is justified insofar as it "represents the most effective means of increasing non-domination overall."[66] But the core emphasis in his theory on protecting everyone's ability to effectively exercise the basic liberties may seem to conflict with this view. Rawls thinks the priority of his first principle of justice, which ensures everyone's capacity to exercise the basic liberties, grants them a prerogative to choose whether or not to act so as to maximize the good. Just institutions will therefore not be set up to maximize the good.[67] If this is so, then Pettit's concern with the basic liberties would make also his theory non-consequentialist. But in Pettit's view, giving individuals rights to exercise the basic liberties in ways that will not optimally serve the good does contribute to the overall good, since these rights promote individuals' dignity, which has a beneficial effect on the overall good.[68] Violating these rights in an attempt to promote the good would upset their dignity, and therefore be counterproductive.

Pettit therefore thinks we are mistaken if we understand maximizing the overall good to involve sacrificing our personal projects.[69] The good is best served, in his view, if people commit to a pattern without thinking much about whether their actions contribute to the good or not. They serve the good indirectly by making choices with the intention of promoting an agent-neutral good.[70] This pattern, Pettit says, should be broken only when "the red lights go on."[71] When acting in accordance with the pattern will jeopardize the agent-neutral good, we ought to change our behavior. What distinguishes consequentialism from non-consequentialism is after all the former's requirement of maximizing the overall good, and behavioral patterns should therefore only be sustained insofar as they contribute to this end. This view seems roughly compatible with Rawls's respect for individual's personal conceptions of the good, while still keeping an eye on consequences.

Pettit also defends publicity on the grounds that it ensures individuals' dignity in a way that promotes the good. For Rawls, publicity is related to civility, and Pettit thinks civility has "extremely beneficial consequences."[72] People are civil toward one another when they publicly justify their actions. They treat each other with respect as reason-givers and reason-takers, as Pettit says. Promoting the good is therefore very unlikely to involve violations of publicity.

Rawls, however, is not impressed by the kind of consequentialism Pettit defends. Seeing consequentialism to require people to act in accordance with non-consequentialist principles, and so promote the good only indirectly, is to concede the inadequacy of consequentialism, in his opinion. You are no consequentialist, Rawls argues, unless you think social institutions ought to be organized in accordance with a conception of justice that can be publicly defended in terms of a consequentialist principle.[73] And such a principle would not be publicly defendable in a pluralistic society. So, while tracking people's avowal-ready interests may produce the best consequences in a pluralistic society, as Pettit argues, his republican theory does not conform with Rawls's definition of consequentialism. John Christman also argues that Pettit's theory is not consequentialist, since non-arbitrariness "is defined in terms of the proper respect for citizen's interests."[74]

So, if Rawls and Christman are right, then a theory based on political constructivism cannot be consequentialist. But against their view, one might question why the action of publicly defending a principle should not also be evaluated in terms of consequences.[75] And if Pettit is right in his assessment of civility, then consequentialists can require the publicity that ensures it. Only in rare cases will consequentialism justify violation of publicity, and in such cases, Rawls might also accept the concern for good consequences.[76] I shall not pursue this matter further, however, as the purpose of this section is merely to show how Pettit, at least, thinks he can build the constructivist concerns for publicity and a personal prerogative into a consequentialist theory. The differences between Pettit's and Rawls's views of consequentialism therefore do nothing to separate their theories' substantive requirements.

7.5 In defense of evaluative claims

Returning now to the discussion of constructivism and radical pluralism, a key difference between these approaches to understanding values concerns their views of what a value is meant to do. The constructivist approach is meant to give us a grand ideal, like justice or freedom, that can guide the development of social institutions, all things considered. On the

150　THE REPUBLICAN DILEMMA

radical-pluralist approach, on the other hand, we understand a value without concern for how significant it will turn out to be when we consider how institutions actually ought to function; when we work out the "rules of regulation," as Cohen would say. On this view, a value gives us only a pro tanto reason for pursuing one course of action rather than another.

Constructivism therefore aspires to producing prescriptive claims, while radical pluralism can only provide evaluative ones. Recall that a prescriptive claim is false if it states an obligation we do not know how to fulfill, while an evaluative claim cannot be falsified by such practical considerations.[77] Strong republicanism, due to facts about modern society, is rejected in a constructivist procedure, as it seems ill-suited for delivering prescriptive claims. But it can nonetheless express a fundamental normative conviction on which we can base evaluative claims. Citizens' active control over their government can be considered valuable independently of the political possibility of motivating such virtue. The usefulness of strong republicanism therefore depends on a justification of evaluative claims. This is what I turn to in the remaining sections of this chapter.

The critics of strictly evaluative claims are numerous. For Rawls, a conception of justice that does not specify whether, or to what extent, we ought to satisfy it is "but half a conception [of justice]."[78] William Galston suggests that a principle not suited for guiding real practice is either false or useless.[79] Brennan and Pettit, similarly, question why we should care about an ideal "that is nowhere to be found and that might be counter-productive to try to establish."[80] Gerald Gaus joins these critics by arguing that political philosophy should only be concerned with how social institutions actually ought to operate, and not with evaluating institutions without this essential purpose in mind.[81]

David Miller thinks Cohen's fact-insensitive approach develops a perverted account of justice, since it might have no role to play in institutional design.[82] "All we are left with," Miller writes, "is regret that we are powerless to achieve true justice."[83] Like Galston, Miller asks why we should care about justice if it has no impact on principles governing our institutions. "If justice is unobtainable," Miller concludes, "that is simply something that we must regret."[84] If we can only say that our society is unjust without suggesting a way of making it just, we are left with nothing but pointless regret. Miller dismissively refers to this approach as "political philosophy as lamentation."[85]

Cohen does little to silence these critics with statements such as "[t]he question of political philosophy is not what we should do but what we should think, even if what we should think makes no practical difference."[86] But he actually makes his approach appear less practical than it is. It is more precise to say with Holly Lawford-Smith that "what we should think will have implications ... for what we should do."[87] I shall argue that we ought to think about values without concern with their all-things-considered attractiveness, since that will generally improve our all-things-considered decision-making. By defining a value without concern for facts about our society might make it unsuitable as a guiding ideal, but it can nonetheless help us appreciate what is at stake and what we inevitably must forgo when we make hard decisions. We see one way the state of affairs can be improved, which is worth taking into consideration even if there are other, weightier reasons for pursuing a different course of action.

This approach makes us more aware of what we are forced to forgo in political decision-making, and Miller is therefore right to say the fact-insensitive approach he criticizes gives us reasons for regret. It is unclear, however, why such regret is pointless, since it instead appears to be a consequence of appreciating the costs involved in making difficult decisions.[88] Awareness of both what we can and cannot achieve is important even if we do not get clear directives regarding how we actually ought to make these decisions.[89] Values should enable us to reflect on how all-things-considered judgments arise from the trade-offs we must inevitably make when values conflict.

We are ill-equipped for appreciating the costs involved in prioritizing one value over another if we follow the constructivist way of defining ideal principles in accordance with what we can achieve by the legitimate use of political power given relevant facts about society. The constructivist approach provides a way of working with people's preferences as they are, and it is therefore no surprise that Pettit says promoting republican freedom is to simultaneously promote other political values, such as justice and legitimacy.[90] But this happy unity of values blurs from view the costs involved in pursuing one course of action rather than another. Making a hard decision involves undermining certain values we otherwise could have realized to a greater extent. This is what makes the decision hard. And so we see an important reason for insisting on the separation between ideals and rules of regulation that constructivists deny. It is actually unclear what the benefits of rejecting this distinction are. No one can deny that a political decision in favor of one course of action rather than another involves costs as well as benefits. A fact-insensitive approach makes us well-equipped for evaluating these costs and benefits.[91]

152 THE REPUBLICAN DILEMMA

A useful way of employing basic values and fact-insensitive principles is to fit them together into what Alan Hamlin and Zofia Stemplowska call a "theory of ideals."[92] Such theorizing, they explain, begins by identifying ideals without concern for feasibility and whether the ideals and principles can be perfectly realized. It then moves on to considering whether values and principles are commensurable and how they can be traded off against one another. For example, Hamlin and Stemplowska consider how a greater focus on welfare might come at the expense of equality, and vice versa. We can then evaluate different feasible states of affairs on the basis of the different trade-offs of welfare and equality they represent.

Such theorizing is valuable because it shows how principles are co-satisfiable and how they are not. It does so without resulting in all-things-considered action guidance. While it is always preferable to realize any value to a greater rather than to a lesser extent, we are very often forced to make trade-offs. This process enhances our understanding of the issue at hand by illuminating costs of co-satisfying the principles, as well as inevitable costs in trade-offs between principles that are not co-satisfiable. The theory can help us see whether, or to what extent, the principles' co-satisfaction is morally permissible and politically possible, which we have seen political constructivism requires principles to be. This kind of theory of ideals does not claim to provide solutions to real-world problems, but it can nonetheless help us consider to what extent they should inform real political decision-making by specifying what the promotion of one value might cost in terms of another.

Cohen develops such a theory by showing why the values of equality, Pareto efficiency, and freedom of choice of occupation need not conflict.[93] What is required to co-satisfy them, Cohen argues, is that people internalize egalitarian values, and consequently choose occupations so as to achieve Pareto efficiency without demanding inequality-producing incentives.[94] This theory illuminates the benefits of an "egalitarian ethos" that informs citizens' behavior. As Cohen says, "[l]iberty, Pareto, and equality join a happy quartet when we add inspiration by principle and/or fellow feeling to the trio."[95]

Why should we not try to make this happy result a reality? One reason is that people in the real world are not all devoted egalitarians, and we might therefore want to satisfy a greater level of preference-neutrality than is logically compatible with Cohen's possibility theorem. By introducing preference-neutrality, we turn Cohen's result into an impossibility theorem. This is essentially what Samuel Bowles does in his "liberal trilemma": any two of the values of voluntariness, efficiency, and preference-neutrality can be co-satisfied, but not all three.[96] I should note here that preference-neutrality, for Bowles, refers to the permissibility of any possible preference being socially decisive. It is, in other words, synonymous with universal domain, and therefore not what political philosophers typically refer to as "neutrality," which, following Rawls, is a domain restricted by a reasonableness condition. But also this set of reasonable preferences, under modern circumstances, contain preferences incompatible with Cohen's theory of ideals. Bowles's and Cohen's theories therefore help us see the cost of neutrality.

When we bring facts into consideration, as we obviously must do in responsible political decision-making, we become aware of how values and principles might conflict due to factual contingencies. While equality, efficiency, and freedom of choice of occupation are logically compatible, as Cohen shows, they will likely be incompatible when people's actual preferences are taken into consideration. Turning people into devoted egalitarians, for example, will likely involve restricting their freedom. But while we therefore cannot realize all three of these values, we are at least aware of what we lose out on when we decide not to try, and we can therefore make a well-informed decision.

7.6 Critical republicanism

Facts about people's actual preferences will likely make it reasonable to reject a course of action intended to lead toward strong republicanism. People in a pluralistic society have a common interest in pure negative freedom, and that is therefore what they get from moderate republicanism. Republicans desiring to reject pure negative freedom and give freedom as non-domination distinctive importance in political theorizing should therefore reject political constructivism and adopt a fact-insensitive understanding of their freedom ideal.

On this approach, the meaning of republicanism is universal. It does not, as on the constructivist approach, take on different meanings depending on the circumstances to which it applies. A conformist society, where most people share a republican conception of the good, will enjoy stronger protection against uncontrolled power than a pluralistic society will. By taking this approach, then, we can say that people in the conformist society have more republican freedom than people in the pluralistic one.

154   THE REPUBLICAN DILEMMA

Republicans can then criticize people in the pluralistic society for their lack of republican preferences. In the same way, we can criticize others in our society for not acting justly enough, while recognizing that other considerations, such as most people's motivations, prevent a collective pursuit of the improvements called for. We can thus use the value of justice to condemn the rich for their greed and undeserved wealth, but not necessarily as a guide in dealing with the problems of greed and inequality. Similarly, republicans can use their freedom ideal to criticize people for not being active participants in their political community.

However, we need not see a practicable, or desirable, route from our current world to another possible world in which the value is satisfied in order to consider the value a value. Strong republicans need not think the state, or any other actor, ought, all things considered, to intervene to make citizens' preferences more republican. Their approach is therefore compatible with Pettit's view that it would be "a big mistake" to aim for an ideal we do not know how to achieve.[97] Radical pluralists do not see values as targets, since targets can plausibly only be defined in response to relevant facts, and these facts enter the theorizing only after the values have been defined. But strong republicanism conflicts with Pettit's view that an ideal that cannot offer guidance for institutional designers has "a very serious problem."[98] For strong republicans, this is not the problem. The problem is rather the facts making the ideal unsuited for the realization of strong republican freedom.

Pettit overlooks how we can appeal to an ideal without expecting people to go along with it. We can lament, as Miller would say, the absence of republican preferences in the population, and use that to explain the comparatively weak protection against abuse of political power. We can also appeal to strong republican freedom to argue for an educational system better designed for turning children into good citizens, while accepting the legitimacy of the political procedures failing to introduce such a system. We can thus appeal to republicanism to criticize a liberal system that promotes citizens' freedom to develop and pursue a wide range of conceptions of the good at the expense of republican freedom. Republicans can thus criticize liberalism for being too individualistic.[99]

By making republican freedom fact-insensitive, we can say that it is a more attractive ideal in the conformist society, A, than in the pluralistic society, B. If the reason is that people in A are more political engaged than the citizens of B, we have an explanation for why people in B are more vulnerable to abuse of political power than are people in A. We can also criticize citizens of B for not caring enough about this vulnerability.

We have just seen that Bowles uses a theory of ideals to criticize preference neutrality by showing how it comes at the expense of either efficiency or voluntariness. He thus illuminates the importance of caring about individuals' preferences, which leads him to argue that the cost of neutrality is too high. He goes on to argue that policymakers ought to think about how they design incentives, and points to evidence in behavioral economics showing how certain kinds of incentives "crowd out" motivations for virtuous behavior and instead, counterproductively, induce selfishness. Republicans, similarly, ought to think carefully about incentives' effects on people's preferences. We have seen, in Chapter 5, that even Pettit's moderate republicanism depends on a republican ethos. Bowles proposes no measures in obvious conflict with a liberal plurality of conceptions of the good; he merely stresses that we must be aware of how incentives might have unexpected effects. Republicans can take the same approach to the design of incentive structures whether they accept Pettit's moderate republicanism or the strong version.

If we fit strong republican freedom into a theory of ideals with liberal neutrality, we are, of course, bound to get an impossibility result, since the conflict between them, as we saw in the previous chapter, is conceptual rather than contingent. That is, strong republican freedom depends on preferences that are more specific than the preferences within the domain defined by reasonableness in political liberalism. The conflict is not merely due to the contingent fact that people in an actual society happen to have preferences conflicting with the strong republican ideal of freedom. That simply follows from the need for distinctly republican preferences. The theory thus identifies what we must forgo to realize strong republicanism, but without saying strong republicanism is something we should actually aim for, all things considered. Strong republicanism thus becomes a critique of people's preferences, while moderate republicanism is more respectful of people's preferences as they are.

But the strong republican criticism might not demand a change in how social institutions actually function. Strong republicans can, and indeed ought to, accept a trade-off between values when they argue for or against actual political decisions. They might accept that republican freedom has less influence than it would have had in a more ideal society where citizens have more republican preferences. We see, then, that they can remain connected to the real world without weakening their ideal.

156 THE REPUBLICAN DILEMMA

They can therefore continue to criticize people's unwillingness to live up to it. As Cohen also notes, we need not consider it wise to pursue an ideal in order to regret not realizing it.[100] An ideal does not vanish simply because we do not prefer to realize it in full, or because we do not know how to realize it. That only counts against attempting to realize it. We might criticize people for lacking civic virtue without thinking we ought to, all things considered, try to make them more virtuous. On any account, republicanism remains "a normative theory for assessing political regimes," as Pettit says it is.[101] But it need not give us all-things-considered prescriptions.

Republicans can consider non-republican preferences a disease for a society that no known treatment will cure.[102] Just because there is no known cure, republicans need not take the moderate line of concluding that the disease is not actually a disease after all. Republicans need not understand the ultimate ideal to be the minimal level of domination that happens to be achievable given people's actual preferences. They can instead see it as the level of domination they would enjoy if citizens had ideally republican preferences. Only then is society entirely healthy.

Strong republicanism will, of course, be prescriptive insofar as we take it to specify a target that society, all things considered, ought to pursue. But this need not be—it is, indeed, unlikely to be—an attractive theory for large modern societies. The strong republican freedom ideal is more plausibly understood as one value in a plurality of values, and it might be used to express a concern about low levels of virtue and popular control, as just described. This is a common-sensical consequence of value pluralism: values conflict, and when we prefer one to another, we still have reason to regret forgoing the all-things-considered inferior value. So, if we endorse Rawls and Pettit's liberal neutrality, we should not lose sight of what we cannot have, such as better protection against uncontrolled power in virtue of a more conformist society in which citizens' preferences are informed by a republican ethos.

This focus on preferences makes republicanism, to a far greater extent than political liberalism, a theory of the ideal citizen. It therefore seems compatible with Cécile Laborde's view that "[r]epublicanism . . . is primarily a theory of citizenship."[103] Laborde's "critical republicanism" insists on people's social attitudes being "as important as just institutions and laws in creating and sustaining the ideal society."[104] Achieving non-domination depends on people's preferences, and not only on a just institutional structure within which individuals are permitted to act on their non-republican preferences. Critical republicanism is thus importantly different from liberalism.

7.7 Conclusion

The republican dilemma has important implications for how republicans can use freedom as an ideal. By taking the moderate view, they understand it as an attractive ideal to pursue in society as it is, since it protects citizens' opportunities to develop and pursue their own conceptions of the good. On the strong view, on the other hand, republican freedom is an ideal requiring a specific kind of society that we might not want to try to bring about under current circumstances. Given facts about our actual society, strong republican freedom might be an ideal it would be neither feasible nor desirable to pursue.

But while strong republican freedom ought not be targeted in society as it is, seeing this ideal within a plurality of conflicting values can still be useful. By fitting it into a theory—a theory of ideals—with other values, we see whether or not it is logically compatible with these other values. And when we also bring in facts about a particular society, we become aware of desirability and feasibility concerns involved in actually trying to realize it. Conflicts with facts and with other values might thus tell us that we ought not pursue strong republicanism. The strong republican freedom we forgo as a consequence of the decisions we make based on all-things-considered judgments can nonetheless be a loss for republicans to regret. And they can criticize their fellow citizens for making strong republican freedom an infeasible and undesirable aim.

8

Conclusion

8.1 Republican trade-offs

Republicans want a freedom ideal that makes a distinct contribution to political theorizing, and now they have one. It is not Pettit's moderate account of freedom as non-domination, which we have seen does not conflict with the promotion of pure negative freedom. It is rather a stronger, more demanding account that requires citizens' commitment to a high level of vigilance to make sure powerholders act for the common good. This ideal is unlikely, however, to replace pure negative freedom as the cornerstone of a theory suitable for modern conditions. Strong republican freedom seems unsuited for a modern society, and it looks unattractive from a liberal perspective.

This is the republican dilemma. Republicans can make republican freedom an all-things-considered ideal well-suited for modern society, but they must then accept that their assessments of people's freedom will align with those of pure negative freedom theorists. Their freedom concept will then not provide a distinct consideration in the making of political prescriptions and evaluations. It will not have "serious payoffs in normative thought," as Pettit takes it to have.[1] But by defining republican freedom so that it becomes such a distinct basis for normative considerations, it will be unsuited for guiding the political practice of a modern society.

In the process of repositioning republican freedom along the scope and robustness dimensions in search of a trade-off point at which it does conflict with the promotion of pure negative freedom, I have developed Ingham and Lovett's distinction between moderate and strong republicanism. We can think of the difference between strong and moderate republican, and between their distinct trade-offs between scope and robustness, as different interpretations of how institutions make interference "inaccessible." On the moderate account, as Ingham and Lovett say, it means it is common knowledge that people will not be interfered with in a way they have not instructed, because the probability of being punished is sufficiently high. They can therefore go about living their lives without feeling vulnerable to uncontrolled

The Republican Dilemma. Lars J. K. Moen, Oxford University Press. © Oxford University Press 2024.
DOI: 10.1093/oso/9780197757024.003.0008

CONCLUSION 159

interference. On the strong account, on the other hand, inaccessible means occurring in no socially possible world. Institutions must be so effective that any use of uncontrolled power will be noticed and appropriately penalized. And we have seen how this level of protection requires people to commit to a higher level of vigilance and political engagement than we can expect in a modern, pluralistic society.

Strong republicanism requires greater protection against uncontrolled power even when that does nothing to relieve people of the fear of being interfered with. They might feel sufficiently safe and able to pursue their plans in life, and therefore lack any desire for protective measures that will restrict their opportunity sets. This is why strong republicanism seems unattractive. And we should understand people's unwillingness to conform to this ideal as an expression of their desire for pure negative freedom. Further protection will reduce their number of combinations of actions they can exercise conjunctively and therefore reduce their pure negative overall freedom. This is exactly why strong republicans can make judgments that conflict with those of pure negative freedom theorists, but it is also why their freedom ideal will not appear attractive under modern conditions.

Perhaps because of the nature of modern society, we might think of strong republican freedom as an absurd way of conceptualizing freedom. It might seem counterintuitive to many people to say that we are free when we contribute to institutional protection against interference to an extent that entails a significant restriction on what courses of action we can pursue. But that just tells us our intuitions are more in line with the pure negative way of thinking about freedom. A distinctly republican way of thinking of freedom would probably have been more intuitive to people of small, conformist city-states of earlier centuries.

8.2 Political liberal republicanism

Strong republicanism is not a liberal ideal, as it calls for people to conform to a distinct republican way of life and to forgo opportunities to pursue other conceptions of the good. Moderate republicanism, on the other hand, is a liberal theory that is compatible with a pluralistic society where people have a wide range of different personal ends. This range is restricted only by a collective pursuit of the common good understood to incorporate this plurality

160 THE REPUBLICAN DILEMMA

of conceptions of the good. We have seen that this understanding of the common good is indistinguishable from that of Rawls's political liberalism.

Brennan and Lomasky write that republican freedom, as Pettit defines it, "is compatible with extensive paternalistic control." Republicans can define citizens' interests as they see them, and thus give "no limit to the state's authority to override individuals' preferences." "To the extent that this is resisted," they go on, "it is because a lingering, unacknowledged tinge of liberalism distorting the natural implications of the theory."[2] But Pettit does acknowledge this "tinge of liberalism," at least in his later work. And this is what keeps him away from the paternalism that we have seen strong republicanism is compatible with. If the citizens' avowal-ready interests define the common good that republican freedom requires the government to promote, then the result is a liberal neutrality inseparable from that of Rawls's political liberalism.

That means Pettit does not go "beyond Rawls," as he claims to do.[3] He claims to do so for two reasons. First, he says Rawls does not require "full resourcing for the basic liberties"—that is, while he sees these liberties as important, he does not ensure that every citizen can exercise them.[4] But this is exactly what Rawls says any political conception of justice must do. And it follows that any legitimate government, on his account, will make sure the citizens can make effective use of their basic liberties. Pettit's second reason for rejecting Rawls's theory is that "it does not require [citizens'] protection against domination, only their protection in a weaker sense."[5] A central point of this book, especially in Chapter 6, has been to show why this cannot be right. Since Rawls and Pettit share a liberal understanding of the common good, which they require institutions to promote, one is not able to demand greater institutional protection than the other.

I should note, however, that while Rawls is mostly occupied with abstract theorizing, Pettit explores to a greater extent what institutions can actually make his theory work in practice. We saw particularly in Chapter 5 that Pettit is quite specific about what institutions can realize his republican ideal, including the mixed constitution, a contestatory democracy, and an economy of esteem. But while such practical considerations are no doubt important insofar as we want political philosophy to guide real-world political practice, it does not take Pettit's theory out of the abstract framework of political liberalism. We can therefore say that Pettit's moderate republicanism is political liberalism in the Rawlsian sense, or that Rawls's political liberalism is republicanism in the moderate, or Pettitian, sense.

CONCLUSION   161

8.3 Rhetoric

In Brennan and Lomasky's view, "[e]ither republicanism is non-threatening [to liberalism] because it is little more than a somewhat archaic rhetorical skin for a body of modern liberalism or, if substantively distancing itself from liberal precepts, is overtly oppressive to a troubling degree."[6] Moderate republicanism is liberal and in harmony with pure negative freedom. It therefore fits the former interpretation. Strong republicanism, however, applies comprehensively to citizens' lives; it is specific about how citizens are to behave than is compatible with any liberal theory. It therefore seems to fit the latter interpretation that worries Brennan and Lomasky.

Some republicans might endorse moderate republicanism but nonetheless insist on important ways in which it conflicts with liberalism and pure negative freedom. For these republicans, the "archaic rhetorical skin" of republicanism is well worth reviving. Viroli, for example, complains about political theory having turned into analytic philosophy when it really should be an exercise of rhetoric.[7] In his view, "classical republican wisdom" tells us that "political theory is not a department of philosophy, or law, or science but of rhetoric."[8] Machiavelli and other classical republicans, he says, "composed their works with the purpose of persuading their readers to accept or reject particular political ideals by winning their rational assent but also by moving their passions."[9] The classical republicans' arguments were "fundamentally aimed at moving their listeners' passions."[10] This "old way" of doing political theory, Viroli says, "was better than the new one." He sees the move away from rhetoric and towards analytic philosophy as "a decay not a progress."[11]

The observation that the republican ideal of freedom as non-domination is actually reducible to the promotion of a strictly empirical concept of freedom as non-prevention is of interest to analytical philosophers, but arguments for this reducibility might have little persuasive force in real political deliberation. Viroli might be right when he says appealing to "feelings and emotions" will give us "a better chance of persuading our leaders and our fellow citizens to accept and to put into practice the political principles congenial to the life of a democratic republic."[12] I have tried to pick two concepts apart to explore whether, and ultimately to show how, they can lead us to make the same judgments about the world. However, while pure negative freedom and moderate republicanism are bases for equivalent freedom judgments, one might still *appear* to be a more attractive political ideal than the other.

162   THE REPUBLICAN DILEMMA

Even one philosopher associated with the analytic tradition, Ronald Dworkin, has little time for an empirical freedom concept, which he dismissively describes as "flat."[13] Dworkin endorses a moralized view on which "liberty" refers to the freedoms we think people ought to have. He denies that preventing or punishing people for wrongful acts, such as murder and theft, are restrictions on liberty, since liberty is only compatible with respectful and dignified treatment of individuals. On close scrutiny, we might find that Dworkin's "liberty" is actually reducible to the promotion of "flat" freedom. But by understanding liberty as an attractive ideal conflicting with morally impermissible behavior, we might give it greater rhetorical appeal.

Pettit implicitly follows Dworkin by preferring his moralized conception of freedom as non-domination because of its harmony with a theory of justice. Constraints compromise an agent's freedom only if they are not justified by a legitimate procedure, while constraints that are justified in this way do not. Republican freedom is therefore an attractive ideal people can willingly devote themselves to promote. Pettit rejects pure negative freedom for having, for him, the unappealing implication that constraints make people unfree no matter how justifiable they might be. Applying this understanding of freedom or unfreedom might require more careful analysis than is sensible, or even possible, in a political speech intended to attract people to one's cause.

Insofar as moderate republicans want to implement their program into real political practice, they might therefore be well advised to present it as based on the ideal of freedom from domination rather than on pure negative freedom. Analytically, they will be mistaken to insist on significant differences between republican freedom and pure negative freedom. But rhetorically, the differences they identify might be more significant.

8.4 Analyzing moralized concepts

But as we saw in Chapter 2, we have good reasons for rejecting a moralized definition of freedom. A non-moralized freedom concept might seem rhetorically less appealing, but it can do an important job in clarifying political disputes. Only with an empirical, "flat" definition of freedom can we appeal to freedom to justify a moral claim on grounds our opponents can accept.

We saw in Chapter 2 an example of how moralizing freedom might lead to stalemate. While Pettit holds that to be free is to be protected against

CONCLUSION   163

interference citizens have not collectively instructed, Nozick thinks being free is to live in a society where private property rights are well enforced. Despite this difference, they can agree on a strictly empirical measurement of freedom that counts the number of actions people can perform without being prevented by others. And given their liberal inclinations, they will both see value in this kind of freedom. Empirical observation can then, at least roughly, determine which of Pettit and Nozick's freedom ideals gives people the most unhindered opportunities. Pettit and Nozick can continue to argue about whether republicanism or libertarianism is more just, but one of them will have the advantage of promoting less overall interference, whereas the other must face the challenge of justifying why more interference is a good thing.

More important for this book, pure negative freedom also enables us to see why liberals will see moderate republicanism as more compelling than strong republicanism. People value the opportunity to pursue a wide range of different courses of action, and an ideal narrowing down this range will therefore be unattractive.

We see here an important strength of the analytic argumentation Viroli shakes his head to. Analytic philosophy has in its toolkit what we need to reveal the substance underlying rhetorically powerful terms and to consider how they compare with what underlies other terms. By using this analytic tool, we have seen that the ideal of moderate republican freedom calls for the promotion of pure negative freedom. This tool, then, helps us clarify our thinking, which is the main purpose of philosophy. We should aim for clarity about the meaning of the terms we use independently of how they might affect people's emotions. By deviating from this aspiration, we risk causing confusion and engaging in pointless verbal disputes.

Viroli says political theorists ought to "think of disputes over political liberty as conflicts between partisan interests and conceptions, not as philosophical debates whose goal is to ascertain or demonstrate the truth."[14] Now we see what that can lead to: a debate on how to promote freedom between parties who agree on how to promote freedom.

Notes

Chapter 1

1. See especially Philip Pettit, *Republicanism: A Theory of Freedom and Government* (Oxford: Oxford University Press, 1997); Quentin Skinner, *Liberty before Liberalism* (Cambridge: Cambridge University Press, 1998).

2. Pettit, *Republicanism*, 4–5, 57–58.

3. To avoid potential awkwardness and ambiguity of using "she or he" or "they," I shall consistently refer to the dominated agent, or the agent interfered with, as "he" and to the dominating or interfering agent as "she."

4. Pettit makes this argument in most of his many works defending republican freedom. See, for example, his *On the People's Terms: A Republican Theory and Model of Democracy* (Cambridge: Cambridge University Press, 2012), 8–11; *Republicanism*, 41–50; "The Instability of Freedom as Noninterference: The Case of Isaiah Berlin," *Ethics* 121, no. 4 (2011): 693–716. See also Skinner, *Liberty before Liberalism*, 77–99; Maurizio Viroli, *Republicanism*, trans. Antony Shugaar (New York: Hill & Wang, 2002), 8–12, 40–41.

5. Viroli, *Republicanism*, 43, 61.

6. Pettit, "The Instability of Freedom as Noninterference," 704.

7. Throughout the book, I use "freedom" and "liberty" interchangeably.

8. Ian Carter, "How Are Power and Unfreedom Related?," in *Republicanism and Political Theory*, ed. Cécile Laborde and John Maynor (Oxford: Blackwell, 2008), 58–82; Matthew H. Kramer, "Liberty and Domination," in *Republicanism and Political Theory*, ed. Cécile Laborde and John Maynor (Oxford: Blackwell, 2008), 31–57.

9. For republican freedom, see especially Philip Pettit, *Just Freedom: A Moral Compass for a Complex World* (London: W. W. Norton, 2014); Pettit, *On the People's Terms*; Pettit, *Republicanism*. For pure negative freedom, see Ian Carter, *A Measure of Freedom* (Oxford: Oxford University Press, 1999); Matthew H. Kramer, *The Quality of Freedom* (Oxford: Oxford University Press, 2003); Hillel Steiner, *An Essay on Rights* (Oxford: Blackwell, 1994). I acknowledge that Carter, Kramer, and Steiner do not hold identical accounts of freedom and how to measure it. One important difference is that while Carter and Steiner defend a strictly quantitative measurement of freedom, Kramer includes both quantitative and evaluative, or qualitative, considerations in his measurement. However, this difference is insignificant in the debate about republican freedom, in which Carter and Kramer completely agree.

10. Philip Pettit, "Freedom and Probability," *Philosophy and Public Affairs* 36, no. 2 (2008): 211–212.

11. Pettit, "Freedom and Probability," 216.

166   NOTES

12. Pettit gives two reasons for this change in terminology. First, he wants to avoid the association with "arbitrary" as it is often used to describe actions not conforming to established rules. Interference conforming to established rules may still be uncontrolled, Pettit argues, since rules need not serve the interests of those subject to them. Second, he wants to avoid the connotation of arbitrary with morally wrong or objectionable. See Pettit, *On the People's Terms*, 58.

13. Steiner, *An Essay on Rights*, 38–41.

14. Carter, *A Measure of Freedom*, 173; Hillel Steiner, "How Free: Computing Personal Liberty," *Royal Institute of Philosophy Supplement* 15 (1983): 74–75.

15. For an account that does include natural obstacles as sources of unfreedom, see, for example, Amartya Sen, *Development as Freedom* (Oxford: Oxford University Press, 1999).

16. Besides Carter, Kramer, and Steiner, other accounts of negative freedom as a social relation include, for example, Isaiah Berlin, *Liberty*, ed. Henry Hardy (Oxford: Oxford University Press, 2002), 169; Kristjan Kristjánsson, *Social Freedom: The Responsibility View* (Cambridge: Cambridge University Press, 1996); Felix E. Oppenheim, "Social Freedom and Its Parameters," *Journal of Theoretical Politics* 7, no. 4 (1995): 5–37.

17. Matthew H. Kramer, "Why Freedoms Do Not Exist by Degrees," *Political Studies* 50, no. 2 (2002): 230–243; Steiner, "How Free," 78–79. By saying you are either free or unfree to perform an action, I follow Carter and Steiner in regarding freedom as a bivalent relation. Kramer, on the other hand, argues for trivalence by holding that you can not only be free or unfree, but also neither free nor unfree (not free) when your inability to perform the action is not due to another's prevention. I shall not go into this debate, as nothing turns on this disagreement with respect to the question of whether promoting republican freedom differs from the promotion of pure negative freedom. For the most recent exchange on this matter, see Ian Carter and Hillel Steiner, "Freedom without Trimmings: The Perils of Trivalence," in *Without Trimmings: The Legal, Moral, and Political Philosophy of Matthew Kramer*, ed. Mack McBride and Visa A. J. Kurki (Oxford: Oxford University Press, 2022), 239–267; Matthew H. Kramer, "Looking Back and Looking Ahead: Replies to the Contributors," in *Without Trimmings: The Legal, Moral, and Political Philosophy of Matthew Kramer*, ed. Mack McBride and Visa A. J. Kurki (Oxford: Oxford University Press, 2022), 453–483.

18. Pettit, *Republicanism*, 65–66.

19. Pettit, *Republicanism*, 63–64.

20. Carter, "How Are Power and Unfreedom Related?"; Kramer, "Liberty and Domination."

21. Carter, "How Are Power and Unfreedom Related?," 58.

22. Carter, "How Are Power and Unfreedom Related?," 59.

23. The republican freedom ideal can still be more rhetorically powerful, but as I argue in the concluding chapter (Section 8.3), that gives political philosophers no good reason for preferring it to pure negative freedom.

24. Christian List, "Republican Freedom and the Rule of Law," *Politics, Philosophy & Economics* 5, no. 2 (2006): 217–218; Christian List, "The Impossibility of a Paretian Republican? Some Comments on Pettit and Sen," *Economics and Philosophy* 20, no. 1

NOTES 167

(2004): 65–87; Philip Pettit, "Capability and Freedom: A Defence of Sen," *Economics and Philosophy* 17, no. 1 (2001): 1–20.

25. Gerald C. MacCallum, "Negative and Positive Freedom," *Philosophical Review* 76, no. 3 (1967): 314.

26. As I show in Sections 2.3 and 3.5.1, the prevention relevant here can be either actual or subjunctive.

27. Lars J. K. Moen, "Freedom and Its Unavoidable Trade-Off," *Analytic Philosophy*, published online, DOI: 10.1111/phib.12301.

28. Geoffrey Brennan and Loren Lomasky, "Against Reviving Republicanism," *Politics, Philosophy & Economics* 5, no. 2 (2006): 222.

29. Pettit, *On the People's Terms*, 11, fn. 8.

30. Pettit, *Republicanism*, vii.

31. Pettit, *On the People's Terms*, 8–11. Pettit may therefore have satisfied some early critics who pointed out that his republican theory is liberal. Roger Boesche, for example, writes in his review of *Republicanism* that "I can only conclude that [Pettit's] whole ideal of freedom as nondomination is simply one variant of liberalism, a conclusion that certainly deflates and diminishes the central argument of the book." See Boesche, "Thinking about Freedom," *Political Theory* 26, no. 6 (1998): 863. Charles Larmore, similarly, writes that "Pettit belongs to the very liberal tradition that he imagines he has transcended." See Larmore, "A Critique of Philip Pettit's Republicanism," *Philosophical Issues* 11, no. 1 (2001): 235.

32. In a recent paper, I reach this conclusion by restating Rawls's and Pettit's positions without the use of vague and ambiguous terminology. See Lars J. K. Moen, "Eliminating Terms of Confusion: Resolving the Liberal–Republican Debate," *Journal of Ethics* 26, no. 2 (2022): 247–271. Other commentators have also found common ground between Pettit and Rawls. See, for example, Andrés de Francisco, "A Republican Interpretation of the Late Rawls," *Journal of Political Philosophy* 14, no. 3 (2006): 270–288; Anthony Simon Laden, "Republican Moments in Political Liberalism," *Revue Internationale de Philosophie* 3, no. 237 (2006): 341–367; Charles Larmore, "Liberal and Republican Conceptions of Freedom," *Critical Review of International Social and Political Philosophy* 6, no. 1 (2003): 117; Larmore, "A Critique of Philip Pettit's Republicanism"; Alan Thomas, *Republic of Equals: Predistribution and Property-Owning Democracy* (Oxford: Oxford University Press, 2017).

33. Pettit, *On the People's Terms*, 10–11.

34. Philip Pettit, "Neo-Liberalism and Neo-Republicanism," *Korea Observer* 50, no. 2 (2019): 197.

35. Pettit, "Neo-Liberalism and Neo-Republicanism," 204.

36. G. A. Cohen, "Capitalism, Freedom and the Proletariat," in *The Idea of Freedom: Essays in Honour of Isaiah Berlin*, ed. Alan Ryan (Oxford: Oxford University Press, 1979), 9–25.

37. Cohen, "Capitalism, Freedom and the Proletariat," 12. Others have also made this or a closely related point. Jeremy Bentham points out that "[a]ll rights are made at the expense of liberty. . . . How is property given? By restraining liberty; that is, by taking it away so far as necessary for the purpose. How is your house made

168 NOTES

yours? By debarring every one else from the liberty of entering it without your leave." See Bentham, "Anarchical Fallacies: An Examination of the Declaration of Rights Issued during the French Revolution," in *The Works of Jeremy Bentham*, ed. John Bowring (Edinburgh: William Tait, 1843), 2:503. See also his *The Theory of Legislation*, ed. C. K. Ogden, trans. Richard Hildreth (London: Kegan Paul, Trench, Trubner & Co., 1931), 93–95. H. L. A. Hart also argues that private property rights restrict freedom in his "Rawls on Liberty and Its Priority," in *Reading Rawls: Critical Studies on Rawls' "A Theory of Justice,"* ed. Norman Daniels (New York: Basic Books, 1975), 234.

38. Philip Pettit, "Two Republican Traditions," in *Republican Democracy: Liberty, Law and Politics*, ed. Andreas Niederberger and Philipp Schink (Edinburgh: Edinburgh University Press, 2013), 169–204; Quentin Skinner, "The Republican Ideal of Political Liberty," in *Machiavelli and Republicanism*, ed. Quentin Skinner, Gisela Bock, and Maurizio Viroli (Cambridge: Cambridge University Press, 1990), 293–309; Viroli, *Republicanism*.

39. John Rawls, *Justice as Fairness: A Restatement* (Cambridge, MA: Belknap Press of Harvard University Press, 2001), 144; John Rawls, *Political Liberalism*, expanded ed. (New York: Columbia University Press, 2005), 205–206.

40. Rawls, *Justice as Fairness*, 142–143; Rawls, *Political Liberalism*, 205–206.

41. Philip Pettit, "Reworking Sandel's Republicanism," *Journal of Philosophy* 95, no. 2 (1998): 73–96.

42. Pettit, "Two Republican Traditions."

43. Pettit, *On the People's Terms*, 11–16.

44. Pettit, "Reworking Sandel's Republicanism."

45. Pettit, *On the People's Terms*, 12–18.

46. Pettit, *Republicanism*, ch. 1; Quentin Skinner, "The Idea of Negative Liberty," in *Philosophy in History*, ed. Richard Rorty, J. B. Schneewind, and Quentin Skinner (Cambridge: Cambridge University Press, 1984), 193–221. Others have traced the origin of this tradition not to Ancient Rome but to Ancient Greece further back in time. See Annelien de Dijn, *Freedom: An Unruly History* (Cambridge: Cambridge University Press, 2020).

47. Pettit, *On the People's Terms*, 17. See also Quentin Skinner, "On the Slogans of Republican Political Theory," *European Journal of Political Theory* 9, no. 1 (2010): 98–100.

48. Rawls clearly has this "neo-Roman" or "Italian-Atlantic" tradition in mind, as he associates "classical republicanism" with Skinner and Machiavelli and distinguishes it from "civic humanism," which he associates with Arendt, Rousseau, and Taylor. See Rawls, *Justice as Fairness*, 142–144; Rawls, *Political Liberalism*, 205–206.

49. Pettit, *On the People's Terms*, 12, 200; Philip Pettit, "Republican Freedom: Three Axioms, Four Theorems," in *Republicanism and Political Theory*, ed. Cécile Laborde and John Maynor (Oxford: Blackwell, 2008), 127–128, n. 19.

50. Pettit, *On the People's Terms*, 20.

51. Pettit, "Neo-Liberalism and Neo-Republicanism," 197–199; Pettit, *On the People's Terms*, 8–11; Pettit, *Republicanism*, 41–50.

NOTES   169

Chapter 2

1. Since scope concerns the number of types of interference that makes you unfree, it might make just as much sense to speak of the scope of *un*freedom as the scope of freedom. I prefer the latter, however, simply because it will be more convenient to refer to both scope and robustness as dimensions of freedom than to say scope is a dimension of unfreedom and robustness a dimension of freedom.

2. I therefore use "scope" differently than does List, who takes it to refer to the size of an agent's capability set. I use the term to refer to the extent to which an agent is not interfered with by another agent. This difference is due to my focus on freedom as a social relation—that is, as a triadic relation between two actors and a possible action or set of actions. See List, "Republican Freedom and the Rule of Law"; List, "The Impossibility of a Paretian Republican?"

3. Pettit, *On the People's Terms*, 64–67; Pettit, "The Instability of Freedom as Noninterference."

4. Pettit, "The Instability of Freedom as Noninterference," 695–697.

5. John Bramhall, "Selections from Bramhall, *A Defence of True Liberty*," in *Hobbes and Bramhall on Liberty and Necessity*, ed. Vere Chappell (Cambridge: Cambridge University Press, 1999), 59; Thomas Hobbes, "Selections from Hobbes, *The Questions concerning Liberty, Necessity, and Chance*," in *Hobbes and Bramhall on Liberty and Necessity*, ed. Vere Chappell (Cambridge: Cambridge University Press, 1999), 81. See also Thomas Hobbes, *Leviathan*, ed. J. C. A. Gaskin (Oxford: Oxford University Press, 2008), ch. 16.

6. Berlin, *Liberty*, 31–32.

7. J. P. Day, "On Liberty and the Real Will," *Philosophy* 45, no. 173 (1970): 191.

8. Berlin, *Liberty*, 32.

9. Berlin, *Liberty*, 169.

10. Berlin, *Liberty*, 32.

11. Pettit, *On the People's Terms*, 54–56.

12. Joseph Raz, *The Authority of Law: Essays on Law and Morality* (Oxford: Oxford University Press, 1979), 221.

13. Philip Pettit, "Freedom as Antipower," *Ethics* 106, no. 3 (1996): 578; Pettit, *Republicanism*, 25–26.

14. Carter, *A Measure of Freedom*, 206; Kramer, *The Quality of Freedom*, 257–260. An agent's own psychological constraints on overcoming physical obstacles—such as phobias, compulsion, or ignorance—may be included in the measurement of the agent's overall freedom. See Kramer, *The Quality of Freedom*, 264–271.

15. Pettit, *On the People's Terms*, 64–65.

16. Pettit, *On the People's Terms*, 64.

17. Pettit, *On the People's Terms*, 64.

18. Pettit, "Freedom and Probability," 216–217.

19. Pettit, *Just Freedom*, 43–46; Pettit, *On the People's Terms*, 64–67; Pettit, "The Instability of Freedom as Noninterference."

20. Pettit, *On the People's Terms*, 65.

170 NOTES

21. Pettit, *Just Freedom*, xxvi–xxvii; Pettit, *Republicanism*, 22.

22. Pettit, "The Instability of Freedom as Noninterference," 705.

23. The mistakes of Pettit's "liberation by ingratiation" argument against freedom as non-interference will become especially clear in Section 3.6.

24. Pettit, *On the People's Terms*, 11.

25. Pettit, *On the People's Terms*, 62.

26. Pettit, *On the People's Terms*, 170–171.

27. However, Pettit adds that uncontrolled interference makes the agent interfered with "non-free." If A is appropriately forced to interfere only in accordance with B's instructions, A's interference makes B "non-free but not unfree." See Pettit, *Republicanism*, 26, fn. 1. Pettit says A's domination "compromises" B's freedom, whereas A's interference without domination merely "conditions" B's freedom. See Pettit, *Republicanism*, 76–77.

28. Pettit, *On the People's Terms*, 11.

29. Pettit describes the distinction between interference that makes you unfree and interference that does not make you unfree in many of his works. For example, *On the People's Terms*, 58.

30. Pettit uses this example repeatedly in his recent works, such as *On the People's Terms*, 57, 152–153, 155, 159–160, 165, 171, 176.

31. Pettit, *On the People's Terms*, 160–179.

32. Pettit, *On the People's Terms*, 176–179.

33. Carter, *A Measure of Freedom*; Kramer, *The Quality of Freedom*; Steiner, *An Essay on Rights*.

34. Carter, "How Are Power and Unfreedom Related?," 64.

35. Steiner, *An Essay on Rights*, 9–12, 17–21.

36. Kramer's measurement of freedom, however, is sensitive to the quality of liberties, not just their quantity.

37. Steiner, *An Essay on Rights*, ch. 2.

38. Kramer, "Why Freedoms Do Not Exist by Degrees," 233.

39. Kramer, "Liberty and Domination," 41; Kramer, *The Quality of Freedom*, 134–135.

40. Steiner, *An Essay on Rights*, 33–41.

41. Steiner, *An Essay on Rights*, 38.

42. Carter, *A Measure of Freedom*.

43. Felix E. Oppenheim defends the separation between the meaning and the value of a political concept in his *Political Concepts: A Reconstruction* (Chicago: University of Chicago Press, 1981).

44. I am far from the first to argue that republican freedom is moralized. Other critics who have made this argument include Ian Carter, "A Critique of Freedom as Non-Domination," *The Good Society* 9, no. 3 (2000): 45; John Christman, "Review of *Republicanism: A Theory of Freedom and Government* by Philip Pettit," *Ethics* 109, no. 1 (1998): 202–206; Keith Dowding, "Republican Freedom, Rights, and the Coalition Problem," *Politics, Philosophy & Economics* 10, no. 3 (2011): 303; David Estlund, "Review of *On the People's Terms: A Republican Theory and Model of Democracy*, by Philip Pettit," *Australasian Journal of Philosophy* 92, no. 4 (2014): 799–802; Kramer,

NOTES 171

"Liberty and Domination," 41; Christian List and Laura Valentini, "Freedom as Independence," *Ethics* 126, no. 4 (2016): 1058–1066; Christopher McMahon, "The Indeterminacy of Republican Policy," *Philosophy & Public Affairs* 33, no. 1 (2005): 69–70; Jeremy Waldron, "Pettit's Molecule," in *Common Minds: Themes from the Philosophy of Philip Pettit*, ed. Robert Goodin, Geoffrey Brennan, Frank Jackson, and Michael Smith (Oxford: Clarendon Press, 2007), 151–154.

45. Cohen, "Capitalism, Freedom and the Proletariat," 12; G. A. Cohen, *History, Labour, and Freedom: Themes from Marx* (Oxford: Oxford University Press, 1988), 294–296.

46. G. A. Cohen first referred to Nozick's account of freedom as a "moralised definition," but he later more specifically called it a "rights definition." See, respectively, Cohen, "Capitalism, Freedom and the Proletariat," and Cohen, *History, Labour, and Freedom*. For a recent discussion of rights-based definitions of freedom, see Ralf M. Bader, "Moralizing Liberty," in *Oxford Studies in Political Philosophy*, ed. Peter Vallentyne, David Sobel, and Steven Wall (Oxford: Oxford University Press), 4:141–166.

47. Robert Nozick, *Anarchy, State and Utopia* (New York: Basic Books, 1974), 160–164.

48. Pettit, "Neo-Liberalism and Neo-Republicanism," 200; Pettit, *On the People's Terms*, 8–11.

49. Cohen, "Capitalism, Freedom and the Proletariat," 12.

50. For example, Pettit, *On the People's Terms*, 58; Pettit, "Republican Freedom," 117; Philip Pettit, "The Determinacy of Republican Policy: A Reply to McMahon," *Philosophy & Public Affairs* 34, no. 3 (2006): 278–280.

51. I demonstrate how republican freedom is moralized at the individual and collective levels also in Moën, "Republicanism and Moralised Freedom," *Politics, Philosophy & Economics* 22, no. 4 (2023): 423–440.

52. Pettit, *On the People's Terms*, 170, fn. 34.

53. Pettit, "The Determinacy of Republican Policy," 276.

54. Carter, "How Are Power and Unfreedom Related?," 64–65; Christman, "Review of Pettit, *Republicanism*," 205; Estlund, "Review of Pettit, *On the People's Terms*," 799–802; List and Valentini, "Freedom as Independence," 1061–1063.

55. Carter, "How Are Power and Freedom Related?," 65.

56. Pettit, *Republicanism*, 66.

57. Pettit, *Republicanism*, 93.

58. Pettit, *On the People's Terms*, 167.

59. Pettit, *On the People's Terms*, 163–164.

60. Pettit, *Republicanism*, 56, fn. 3.

61. Pettit, "The Common Good," in *Justice and Democracy: Essays for Brian Barry*, ed. Robert E. Goodin, Keith Dowding, and Carole Pateman (Cambridge: Cambridge University Press), 152.

62. Pettit, *On the People's Terms*, 167.

63. Pettit, *Republicanism*, 93.

64. Here we can understand why Carter prefers the term "justice-based" definition of freedom rather than "moralized."

65. Pettit, *On the People's Terms*, 58–59.

66. Pettit, "Republican Freedom," 127–128, n. 19

172 NOTES

67. Pettit, *Republicanism*, 56; Pettit, "The Determinacy of Republican Policy," 279–280.
68. Pettit, "Republican Freedom," 117.
69. Pettit, *Republicanism*, 56–57; Pettit, "The Determinacy of Republican Policy," 278–280.
70. I say "we *might* agree" since Pettit is deliberately vague about the required degree of assurance that the other agent will not act contrary to your instructions. It must be determined, he says, "on an intuitive, context-sensitive basis." See Pettit, *On the People's Terms*, 32, fn. 8.
71. Pettit, *On the People's Terms*, 21.
72. Pettit, "The Common Good," 152.
73. Pettit, *On the People's Terms*, 157.
74. Assaf Sharon argues that Pettit's "equal control" requirement is very weak indeed, since equal control is consistent with no one having control. See Sharon, "Domination and the Rule of Law," in *Oxford Studies in Political Philosophy*, ed. Peter Vallentyne, David Sobel, and Steven Wall (Oxford: Oxford University Press, 2016), 140.
75. Pettit, *On the People's Terms*, 158. Skinner, however, thinks consent, not contestability, is what makes power non-arbitrary. See Quentin Skinner, "Freedom as the Absence of Arbitrary Power," in *Republicanism and Political Theory*, ed. Cécile Laborde and John Maynor (Oxford: Blackwell, 2008), 86–87. In Skinner's view, the law that governs free citizens should express the citizens' will, which they express in consenting to the law. Only then can a citizen "be said to remain a free-man in obeying it." See Skinner, "Freedom as the Absence of Arbitrary Power," 87.
76. Pettit, "Freedom as Antipower," 585.
77. Pettit, *Republicanism*, 62.
78. John Ferejohn, "Pettit's Republic," *The Monist* 84, no. 1 (2001): 77–97. See also McMahon, "The Indeterminacy of Republican Policy," 81.
79. Pettit, *On the People's Terms*, 216–217.
80. Pettit, *On the People's Terms*, 257.
81. Pettit, *On the People's Terms*, 189.
82. Pettit, *On the People's Terms*, 175.
83. Carter, "How Are Power and Unfreedom Related?," 65. See also Sharon, "Domination and the Rule of Law," 137–138.
84. Pettit, *On the People's Terms*, 57, fn. 33.
85. Dowding, "Republican Freedom, Rights, and the Coalition Problem," 308.
86. Lovett also rejects a welfarist understanding of republicanism, and says no republican holds such a view. See Frank Lovett, *The Well-Ordered Republic* (Oxford: Oxford University Press, 2022), 78–80.
87. Pettit, "Republican Freedom," 117.
88. Pettit, "Republican Freedom," 117.
89. Pettit, *On the People's Terms*, 160.
90. Pettit, *On the People's Terms*, 147.
91. Pettit, *On the People's Terms*, 20.
92. Carter, "How Are Power and Unfreedom Related?," 81.
93. Carter, *A Measure of Freedom*, 72. Emphasis in the original.

NOTES 173

94. Cohen, *History, Labour, and Freedom*, 296. This point also applies to other political values. Joseph Raz, for example, shows how "rule of law" becomes useless in our theorizing if we define it as "rule of good law." See Raz, *The Authority of Law*, 211.
95. Berlin, *Liberty*, 177.
96. Cohen, "Capitalism, Freedom, and the Proletariat"; G. A. Cohen, "Freedom, Justice, and Capitalism," *New Left Review* 126 (1981): 8–11.
97. Steiner, *An Essay on Rights*, 15.
98. Pettit, "Republican Freedom," 127, n. 19.

Chapter 3

1. Pettit, *Republicanism*, 63–64.
2. List, "Republican Freedom and the Rule of Law," 212.
3. List, "The Impossibility of a Paretian Republican?"
4. Amartya Sen, "The Impossibility of a Paretian Liberal," *Journal of Political Economy* 78, no. 1 (1970): 152–157.
5. Sen, "The Impossibility of a Paretian Liberal," 155.
6. This is at least the case if we want to define freedom so that it is possible for two individuals in the same society to both be free to perform any action. Robinson Crusoe on a desert island no one can access enjoys maximally robust absence of any kind of interference. But freedom will be of little value in political theorizing if it is only achievable for isolated individuals like Robinson Crusoe.
7. In their definition of "freedom as independence," List and Laura Valentini try to avoid this trade-off altogether. See List and Valentini, "Freedom as Independence." The result is that it is impossible for two or more people to be free to do anything. For this impossibility critique, see Ian Carter and Ronen Shnayderman, "The Impossibility of 'Freedom as Independence,'" *Political Studies Review* 17, no. 2 (2019): 136–146; Moen, "Freedom and Its Unavoidable Trade-Off."
8. Geoffrey Brennan and Alan Hamlin also make this rather obvious observation: "More resilient liberty will necessarily be at the expense of less liberty." See Brennan and Hamlin, "Republican Liberty and Resilience," *The Monist* 84, no. 1 (2001): 54.
9. Sen, *Collective Choice and Social Welfare*, 446.
10. Steiner, *An Essay on Rights*, 33.
11. Steiner, *An Essay on Rights*, 38–41.
12. Kramer, *The Quality of Freedom*, 131.
13. Carter, *A Measure of Freedom*, 180–181; Kramer, *The Quality of Freedom*, 137.
14. Kramer, "Why Freedoms Do Not Exist by Degrees," 233.
15. List, "Republican Freedom and the Rule of Law," 218.
16. Pettit, *On the People's Terms*, 50; Pettit, *Republicanism*, 88.
17. Pettit, *On the People's Terms*, 60.
18. Pettit, "The Instability of Freedom as Noninterference," 704.
19. Pettit, *Republicanism*, 57–58, 75–77, 103–106.
20. Pettit, *Republicanism*, 52.

174 NOTES

21. Pettit, *Republicanism*, 107.
22. Philip Pettit, "Keeping Republicanism Simple: On a Difference with Quentin Skinner," *Political Theory* 30, no. 3 (2002): 350.
23. Pettit, "Freedom as Antipower."
24. Pettit, "Freedom as Antipower," 583.
25. E.g., Lovett, *The Well-Ordered Republic*, 36–38; Pettit, *Republicanism*, 22; Pettit, *Just Freedom*, xxvi–xxvii.
26. Pettit, *Republicanism*, 24.
27. Kramer, "Liberty and Domination," 45.
28. Carter, "How Are Power and Unfreedom Related?," 71; Carter and Shnayderman, "The Impossibility of 'Freedom as Independence'," 139–140; Dowding, "Republican Freedom, Rights, and the Coalition Problem"; Gerald F. Gaus, "Backwards into the Future: Neorepublicanism as a Postsocialist Critique of Market Society," *Social Philosophy and Policy* 20, no. 1 (2003): 69–74; Robert E. Goodin and Frank Jackson, "Freedom from Fear," *Philosophy & Public Affairs* 35, no. 3 (2007): 249–265; Matthew H. Kramer, "Freedom and the Rule of Law," *Alabama Law Review* 61, no. 4 (2010): 844; Kramer, "Liberty and Domination," 45; Kramer, *The Quality of Freedom*, 138–139; Thomas W. Simpson, "The Impossibility of Republican Freedom," *Philosophy & Public Affairs* 45, no. 1 (2017): 27–53.
29. Pettit, "Freedom and Probability," 207.
30. Pettit, *Republicanism*, 214.
31. Pettit, "Freedom as Antipower," 578–580; Pettit, *Republicanism*, 22; Skinner, *Liberty before Liberalism*, 72.
32. Pettit, *On the People's Terms*, 71.
33. Pettit, "The Instability of Freedom as Noninterference," 708.
34. Pettit, "Freedom and Probability," 219.
35. Pettit, *On the People's Terms*, 72, fn. 41.
36. Pettit, *Republicanism*, 55.
37. Pettit, "Freedom as Antipower," 590.
38. Kramer, "Freedom and the Rule of Law," 838–845; List, "Republican Freedom and the Rule of Law"; Sharon, "Domination and the Rule of Law."
39. Pettit, *On the People's Terms*, 109–110; Pettit, "The Determinacy of Republican Policy," 281.
40. Dowding, "Republican Freedom, Rights, and the Coalition Problem," 311.
41. Sean Ingham and Frank Lovett, "Republican Freedom, Popular Control, and Collective Action," *American Journal of Political Science* 63, no. 4 (2019): 778.
42. List, "Republican Freedom and the Rule of Law."
43. Ingham and Lovett, "Republican Freedom, Popular Control, and Collective Action," 779.
44. Ingham and Lovett, "Republican Freedom, Popular Control, and Collective Action," 779.
45. Philip Pettit, "Free Persons and Free Choices," *History of Political Thought* 28, no. 4 (2007): 715.
46. Pettit, *On the People's Terms*, 32, fn. 8.

NOTES 175

47. Pettit, *On the People's Terms*, 68, fn. 38.
48. Pettit, *On the People's Terms*, 33–35.
49. Pettit, *On the People's Terms*, 68, fn. 38.
50. Pettit, *On the People's Terms*, 47, 72, 84.
51. Pettit, *On the People's Terms*, 71. Montesquieu, similarly, says, "[p]olitical liberty in a citizen is that tranquillity of spirit which comes from the opinion each one has of his security, and in order for him to have this liberty the government must be such that one citizen cannot fear another citizen." See Montesquieu, *The Spirit of the Laws*, ed. and trans. Anne M. Cohler, Basia C. Miller, and Harold S. Stone (Cambridge: Cambridge University Press, 1989), 157 (XI.6).
52. Pettit, *On the People's Terms*, 84.
53. Pettit, *On the People's Terms*, 3.
54. Pettit, *On the People's Terms*, 59–61.
55. Pettit, *On the People's Terms*, 84.
56. Pettit, *On the People's Terms*, 17.
57. Pettit, *Republicanism*, 85.
58. Philip Pettit, *A Theory of Freedom: From the Psychology to the Politics of Agency* (Oxford: Oxford University Press, 2001); Pettit, "Freedom and Probability"; Pettit, *Republicanism*, 85.
59. Philip Pettit, "The Domination Complaint," in *Nomos 46: Political Exclusion and Domination*, ed. Stephen Macedo and Melissa Williams (New York: New York University Press, 2005), 101.
60. Pettit, "The Domination Complaint," 102.
61. Pettit, *On the People's Terms*, 17; Skinner, "On the Slogans of Republican Political Theory," 98–100.
62. Pettit, "Republican Freedom," 110–111.
63. Pettit, "Republican Freedom," 111.
64. Pettit, "Republican Freedom," 113.
65. Kramer, "Liberty and Domination," 38; Kramer, *The Quality of Freedom*, 131–132.
66. Pettit, "Republican Freedom," 113.
67. Steiner, *An Essay on Rights*, 22–32.
68. Pettit, "Republican Freedom," 122.
69. Steiner, at least, has the intuition that "persons are free to do what they actually do." See Steiner, *An Essay on Rights*, 8.
70. Carter, *A Measure of Freedom*, 240.
71. Carter, "How Are Power and Unfreedom Related?," 63–64.
72. Carter, *A Measure of Freedom*, 233–245; Kramer, *The Quality of Freedom*, 174–178.
73. Kramer, *The Quality of Freedom*, 137.
74. Kramer, *The Quality of Freedom*, 129.
75. See especially Pettit, "The Instability of Freedom as Noninterference."
76. Pettit, "Republican Freedom," 113.
77. Pettit, "Freedom and Probability," 216–217; Pettit, *On the People's Terms*, 65; Pettit, "The Instability of Freedom as Noninterference," 704–705. List and Valentini also take this view in "Freedom as Independence," 1054.

176 NOTES

78. Pettit, "Freedom and Probability," 216.
79. Pettit, "The Instability of Freedom as Noninterference," 705.
80. E.g., Pettit, *On the People's Terms*, 59–61; Pettit, *Republicanism*, 22–23, 31–35.
81. Skinner, "Freedom as the Absence of Arbitrary Power," 90.
82. Skinner, "Freedom as the Absence of Arbitrary Power," 96–97.
83. Pettit, "Freedom and Probability," 217.
84. Kramer, "Liberty and Domination," 50–56; Kramer, *The Quality of Freedom*, 144–148.
85. Carter, *A Measure of Freedom*, 196–198. See also Steiner, "How Free," 77–78.
86. Kramer, "Why Freedoms Do Not Exist by Degrees," 234.
87. Kramer, "Liberty and Domination," 44.
88. Pettit, "The Instability of Freedom as Noninterference," 700, fn. 24.
89. List and Valentini, "Freedom as Independence," 1055.
90. Fabian Wendt, "Slaves, Prisoners, and Republican Freedom," *Res Publica* 17, no. 2 (2011): 179–182.
91. Lovett, *The Well-Ordered Republic*, 69, fn. 114.
92. List, "Republican Freedom and the Rule of Law," 218.
93. List, "Republican Freedom and the Rule of Law," 217.
94. Brennan and Hamlin, "Republican Liberty and Resilience"; Carter, *A Measure of Freedom*, 243.
95. Ferejohn, "Pettit's Republic," 85–86.
96. Kramer, *The Quality of Freedom*, 118.
97. Carter, "How Are Power and Unfreedom Related?"; Kramer, "Liberty and Domination," 46.

Chapter 4

1. Pettit, *Republicanism*, 55–57, 65.
2. Rawls, *Political Liberalism*, 476.
3. A person's "conception of the good," Rawls explains, consists of the ends and purposes the person considers worthy of her or his pursuit over a complete life. See Rawls, *Political Liberalism*, 104.
4. Rawls, *Political Liberalism*, lecture 3.
5. Rawls distinguishes conception-dependent desires from "object-dependent" and "principle-dependent" desires (*Political Liberalism*, 82–83). Object-dependent desires are satisfied by a state of affairs that can be described without moral terms. There are "[i]nfinitely many" kinds in this category, Rawls says, and mentions desires for sleep, food, power, and wealth as examples. Principle-dependent desires are held only by rational persons, as they are satisfied by acting according to some principle, such as adopting the most effective means to some end, selecting the most plausible alternative, and ordering options according to priority when they conflict. So, while we satisfy our conception-dependent desires by formulating principles for fair cooperation, we satisfy principle-dependent desires when we act on these principles.

NOTES 177

6. Rawls, *Political Liberalism*, 84.

7. T. M. Scanlon, "Contractualism and Utilitarianism," in *Utilitarianism and Beyond*, ed. Amartya Sen and Bernard Williams (Cambridge: Cambridge University Press, 1982), 119.

8. Scanlon, "Contractualism and Utilitarianism," 111–112. Scanlon calls his approach "contractualism" rather than "constructivism" because what he considers the relevant kind of agreement for producing moral reasons a hypothetical contract. Following Rawls, I shall treat Scanlon's "contractualism" as interchangeable with constructivism. See Rawls, *Political Liberalism*, 90–91, fn. 1.

9. Scanlon, "Contractualism and Utilitarianism," 110–111.

10. Rawls, *Political Liberalism*, 49.

11. Rawls, *Political Liberalism*, 49–50, fn. 2.

12. Rawls, *Political Liberalism*, 50, fn. 2.

13. Rawls, *Political Liberalism*, 50.

14. Rawls, *Political Liberalism*, 49, 54.

15. A comprehensive doctrine, Rawls explains, is a set of philosophical or religious convictions about how to live, which includes a conception of the good, how one ought to treat others and value social relationships, and, as Rawls says, "much else that is to inform our conduct." See Rawls, *Political Liberalism*, 13.

16. Rawls, *Political Liberalism*, 67, 386.

17. Rawls, *Political Liberalism*, 453.

18. Rawls, *Justice as Fairness*, 10.

19. Rawls, *Political Liberalism*, 36.

20. Rawls, *Political Liberalism*, 453.

21. Rawls, *Political Liberalism*, 137.

22. John Rawls, "Kantian Constructivism in Moral Theory," *Journal of Philosophy* 77, no. 9 (1980): 568.

23. Rawls, *Political Liberalism*, 83–86.

24. Rawls, *Political Liberalism*, 85, fn. 33.

25. Scanlon, "Contractualism and Utilitarianism," 112.

26. Rawls, *Political Liberalism*, 107–108.

27. Scanlon, "Contractualism and Utilitarianism," 112.

28. Rawls, *Political Liberalism*, 119.

29. Rawls, *Political Liberalism*, 54–58, 393–394, 488.

30. Scanlon, "Contractualism and Utilitarianism," 120–122.

31. Scanlon, "Contractualism and Utilitarianism," 123.

32. John Rawls, *A Theory of Justice*, rev. ed. (Cambridge, MA: Belknap Press of Harvard University Press, 1999), 297.

33. Rawls, *Political Liberalism*, 49.

34. Pettit, *On the People's Terms*, 124–125.

35. Pettit, *On the People's Terms*, 144.

36. Pettit, *On the People's Terms*, 144–145.

37. Pettit, *On the People's Terms*, 146.

38. Pettit, *Republicanism*, 201.

178 NOTES

39. Pettit, *On the People's Terms*, 146–153.

40. Pettit, *On the People's Terms*, 78.

41. Pettit, *Republicanism*, 187–188.

42. Pettit, "The Common Good," 165.

43. Viroli, *Republicanism*, 54. Skinner understands this idea of making decisions appealing to everyone's interests to be important in the republican tradition. See Quentin Skinner, *Reason and Rhetoric in the Philosophy of Hobbes* (Cambridge: Cambridge University Press, 1996), 15–16.

44. Viroli, *Republicanism*, 54.

45. Skinner, *Reason and Rhetoric in the Philosophy of Hobbes*, 15–16.

46. Pettit, *On the People's Terms*, 168–170.

47. Pettit, *On the People's Terms*, 78.

48. Pettit, *On the People's Terms*, 228.

49. Pettit, *On the People's Terms*, 203.

50. Pettit, *On the People's Terms*, 217. I explore Pettit's view of the basic liberties and their place in his theory in Section 4.7.

51. Pettit, *Republicanism*, 55–56, 290.

52. Pettit, *A Theory of Freedom*, 156.

53. Pettit, *On the People's Terms*, 245.

54. Christine M. Korsgaard, "The Reasons We Can Share: An Attack on the Distinction between Agent-Relative and Agent-Neutral Values," *Social Philosophy and Policy* 10, no. 1 (1993): 50, fn. 47.

55. Scanlon, "Contractualism and Utilitarianism," 119.

56. Pettit, *A Theory of Freedom*, 157, fn. 1. Pettit here uses the term "contractualist," but its referent is equivalent to that of "constructivist" as Rawls uses that term in his later works.

57. Pettit, *On the People's Terms*, 170–174.

58. Pettit, *On the People's Terms*, 170–171.

59. Pettit, *On the People's Terms*, 175.

60. Pettit, *Republicanism*, 185.

61. Pettit, *On the People's Terms*, 176.

62. Pettit, *On the People's Terms*, 175.

63. Pettit, *On the People's Terms*, 175.

64. Pettit, *On the People's Terms*, 177.

65. Pettit, *On the People's Terms*, 178.

66. Rawls, *Political Liberalism*, 48, lecture 4.

67. Other consensus theorists might require, more restrictively, that the reasons be shared. James Bohman and Henry S. Richardson, for example, defend the requirement that everyone must share, and not just can accept, the reasons because of the difficulty of formulating a workable interpretation of "can accept." See Bohman and Richardson, "Liberalism, Deliberative Democracy, and 'Reasons That All Can Accept,'" *Journal of Political Philosophy* 17, no. 3 (2009): 253–274.

68. Rawls, *Political Liberalism*, 137.

69. Pettit, *On the People's Terms*, 261.

NOTES 179

70. Gerald F. Gaus, *Justificatory Liberalism: An Essay on Epistemology and Political Theory* (New York: Oxford University Press, 1996); Kevin Vallier, "In Defence of Intelligible Reasons in Public Justification," *Philosophical Quarterly* 66, no. 264 (2016): 596–616.

71. Fred D'Agostino, *Free Public Reason: Making It Up as We Go* (Oxford: Oxford University Press, 1996), 30.

72. To be precise, a convergence model will also rely on idealization, albeit to a lesser extent than does a consensus model. It must at least assume that individuals are informed and meet standards of rational inference. See Kevin Vallier, "In Defense of Idealization in Public Reason," *Erkenntnis* 85, no. 5 (2020): 1109–1128.

73. Pettit, *Republicanism*, 187–188.

74. Pettit, *On the People's Terms*, 253–261.

75. Pettit, *On the People's Terms*, 260.

76. Pettit, *Republicanism*, 190. Consensus-theorists are usually more in favor of deliberation than are convergence theorists. For an example of a convergence theorist's defense of deliberation, see Rawls, *Political Liberalism*, 481; *Justice as Fairness*, 146. For an example of a convergence theorist opposing deliberation, see Kevin Vallier, "Public Justification versus Public Deliberation: The Case for Divorce," *Canadian Journal of Philosophy* 45, no. 2 (2015): 139–158.

77. Philip Pettit, "Political Realism Meets Civic Republicanism," *Critical Review of International Social and Political Philosophy* 20, no. 3 (2017): 343.

78. Pettit, *Republicanism*, 259.

79. Pettit, *On the People's Terms*, 260.

80. Pettit, *Republicanism*, 205.

81. Pettit, *On the People's Terms*, 259–261.

82. Pettit, *Republicanism*, 185.

83. Pettit, *Republicanism*, 246–247.

84. Pettit, *On the People's Terms*, 254, fn. 5.

85. Pettit, *On the People's Terms*, 254, fn. 5.

86. Rawls, "Kantian Constructivism in Moral Theory," 206.

87. Rawls, *Political Liberalism*, 450.

88. Rawls, *Political Liberalism*, 59.

89. Rawls, *A Theory of Justice*, 119.

90. Rawls, *Political Liberalism*, 450.

91. Rawls, *Political Liberalism*, 451.

92. Rawls, *Political Liberalism*, 59.

93. Rawls, *Political Liberalism*, 455, fn. 35.

94. Rawls, *Political Liberalism*, 452.

95. Rawls, *Political Liberalism*, 66.

96. Rawls, *A Theory of Justice*, 119.

97. Rawls, *Political Liberalism*, 454.

98. Rawls, *Political Liberalism*, 227.

99. Rawls, *Political Liberalism*, 228.

100. Rawls, *Political Liberalism*, 229.

180 NOTES

101. Jonathan Quong, *Liberalism without Perfection* (Oxford: Oxford University Press, 2011), 274. My emphasis.
102. Jonathan Quong, "The Scope of Public Reason," *Political Studies* 52, no. 2 (2004): 233–250; Quong, *Liberalism without Perfection*, ch. 9.
103. Pettit, *On the People's Terms*, 254, fn. 5.
104. Rawls, *Political Liberalism*, 450; John Rawls, *The Law of Peoples* (Cambridge, MA: Harvard University Press, 1999), 14.
105. Rawls, *A Theory of Justice*, xii.
106. Rawls, *Political Liberalism*, 104.
107. Rawls, *Political Liberalism*, 19, 72, 81.
108. Rawls, *Political Liberalism*, 302.
109. Rawls, *Political Liberalism*, 52.
110. Pettit, *On the People's Terms*, 8.
111. Pettit, *On the People's Terms*, 94.
112. Pettit, *On the People's Terms*, 95.
113. Pettit, *On the People's Terms*, 201–202.
114. Pettit, *On the People's Terms*, 94–95.
115. Pettit, *On the People's Terms*, 144, fn. 12. Pettit here cites the 1971 edition of *A Theory of Justice* at page 233. For the sake of consistency, I refer to the revised 1999 edition of *A Theory of Justice* in my discussion of Pettit's understanding of Rawls's view of the political liberties below. The relevant passages are identical in the two editions.
116. Rawls, *Political Liberalism*, 366.
117. Rawls, *A Theory of Justice*, 175.
118. Rawls, *A Theory of Justice*, 205.
119. Rawls, *A Theory of Justice*, 205.
120. Rawls, *A Theory of Justice*, 205.
121. Rawls, *A Theory of Justice*, 206.
122. Rawls, *A Theory of Justice*, 197–198.
123. Pettit, *On the People's Terms*, 11–18.
124. Rawls, *Political Liberalism*, 328.
125. Rawls, *A Theory of Justice*, 174–175.
126. Rawls, *Political Liberalism*, 357.
127. Rawls, *Political Liberalism*, 456.
128. Pettit, *On the People's Terms*, 234; Pettit, *Republicanism*, 194.
129. Philip Pettit, "The Basic Liberties," in *The Legacy of H. L. A. Hart: Legal, Political, and Moral Philosophy*, ed. Matthew H. Kramer, Claire Grant, Ben Colburn, and Antony Hatzistavrou (Oxford: Oxford University Press, 2008), 202.
130. Pettit, *On the People's Terms*, 92–107; Pettit, "The Basic Liberties."
131. Pettit, "The Basic Liberties," 218.
132. Pettit, *On the People's Terms*, 103; Pettit, "The Basic Liberties," 220.
133. Pettit, "The Basic Liberties," 215–216.
134. Rawls, *A Theory of Justice*, 53. For a similar but less specific list, see *Political Liberalism*, 291.
135. Pettit, *On the People's Terms*, 109.

NOTES 181

136. Rawls, *Political Liberalism*, 450; Rawls, *The Law of Peoples*, 14.
137. Pettit, *On the People's Terms*, 184.
138. Rawls, *A Theory of Justice*, 220.
139. Rawls, *A Theory of Justice*, 52–56.
140. Pettit, *On the People's Terms*, 184.
141. Pettit, *On the People's Terms*, 126.
142. Pettit, *On the People's Terms*, 126.
143. Rawls, *Political Liberalism*, 450; Rawls, *The Law of Peoples*, 14.
144. Andrés de Francisco also suggests the rational parties in Rawls's original position would choose the same two principles as in justice as fairness if they were motivated to minimize domination. See de Francisco, "A Republican Interpretation of the Late Rawls," 279.
145. Pettit, *On the People's Terms*, 90–91.
146. Pettit, *On the People's Terms*, 83.
147. Pettit, *On the People's Terms*, 88.
148. Pettit, *On the People's Terms*, 126.
149. Pettit, *Just Freedom*, 107.
150. Pettit, *On the People's Terms*, 126.
151. Pettit, *On the People's Terms*, 91.
152. Thomas, *Republic of Equals*, 375, n. 19
153. Samuel Freeman, *Rawls* (London: Routledge, 2007), 187.
154. Here I assume that overall freedom can be increased in a society. Against this view, Steiner's "law of conservation of liberty" holds that the amount of freedom in a society is fixed and only its distribution can change. Steiner therefore argues that "[a] universal quest for greater personal liberty is a zero-sum game." See Steiner, *An Essay on Rights*, 54. For a critique of Steiner's law of conservation of liberty, see Ian Carter, "Respect for Persons and the Interest in Freedom," in *Hillel Steiner and the Anatomy of Justice: Themes and Challenges*, ed. Stephen de Wijze, Matthew H. Kramer, and Ian Carter (London: Routledge, 2009), 167–184.
155. Carter, *A Measure of Freedom*, 265–267. See also Michael Taylor, *Community, Anarchy and Liberty* (Cambridge: Cambridge University Press, 1982), ch. 4.
156. This argument, of course, presupposes a rejection of Steiner's law of conservation of liberty. The case of the anarchical, cooperative community is actually a good case for showing why the law of conservation of liberty is false. As Carter and Kramer argue, the total amount of overall freedom is sensitive to people's preferences. See Carter and Kramer, "How Changes in One's Preferences Can Affect One's Freedom (and How They Cannot): A Reply to Dowding and van Hees," *Economics and Philosophy* 24, no. 1 (2008): 81–96.
157. Carter, *A Measure of Freedom*, sections 1.4–1.5.
158. See especially Ronald Dworkin, *Taking Rights Seriously* (London: Duckworth), 266–274.
159. Rawls, *A Theory of Justice*, 220.
160. Rawls, *Justice as Fairness*, 44–45; *Political Liberalism*, 291.
161. Pettit, "Political Realism Meets Civic Republicanism," 338.

182 NOTES

162. Pettit, *On the People's Terms*, 88.
163. Carter, *A Measure of Freedom*, 235–236; G. A. Cohen, "Freedom and Money," in *On the Currency of Egalitarian Justice, and Other Essays in Political Philosophy*, ed. Michael Otsuka (Princeton, NJ: Princeton University Press, 2011), 166–192.
164. Rawls, *Justice as Fairness*, 150.

Chapter 5

1. Pettit, *On the People's Terms*, 5.
2. Pettit, *On the People's Terms*, 5–6.
3. Pettit, *On the People's Terms*, 283.
4. Pettit, *On the People's Terms*, 232–233.
5. Pettit, *On the People's Terms*, 233–235.
6. Pettit, *On the People's Terms*, 235. Pettit might be right about strong party systems reducing special interest lobbying to some extent, but such lobbying still occurs in these systems, though it is directed more at the executive than at the legislature. To determine how resistant parliamentary systems are to the problem Pettit identifies, we must look at specific features, such as the number of parties represented and how large and cohesive the parties are. For some discussion of these matters, see John M. Carey, *Legislative Voting and Accountability* (Cambridge: Cambridge University Press, 2009).
7. Pettit, *On the People's Terms*, 235–238.
8. Ronald Dworkin, *Justice for Hedgehogs* (Cambridge, MA: Belknap Press of Harvard University Press, 2011), 395–399.
9. Pettit, *On the People's Terms*, 5.
10. Pettit, *On the People's Terms*, 279.
11. Pettit, *Republicanism*, 264.
12. Pettit, *On the People's Terms*, 226.
13. Pettit, *On the People's Terms*, 237; Pettit, *Republicanism*, 193.
14. Pettit, *Republicanism*, 186. My emphases.
15. Pettit, *On the People's Terms*, 228; Pettit, *Republicanism*, 39.
16. See especially Pettit, *Republicanism*, ch. 8.
17. List, "Republican Freedom and the Rule of Law," 206.
18. In a liberal society at least, I assume the set of actions the law permits but morality does not permit to be greater than the set of actions morality permits but the law does not permit.
19. List, "Republican Freedom and the Rule of Law."
20. List, "Republican Freedom and the Rule of Law," 211.
21. List, "Republican Freedom and the Rule of Law," 206.
22. List, "Republican Freedom and the Rule of Law," 209.
23. Pettit, *Republicanism*, 88.
24. Pettit, *Republicanism*, 73.
25. Pettit, *On the People's Terms*, 68–69.

NOTES 183

26. Raz, *The Authority of Law*, 214–218.
27. Raz, *The Authority of Law*, 219–220.
28. Raz, *The Authority of Law*, 211–214.
29. Leslie Green, "Legal Positivism," in *The Stanford Encyclopedia of Philosophy*, ed. Edward N. Zalta, last modified 8 March 2018, accessed 9 June 2018, URL: https://plato.stanford.edu/archives/spr2018/entries/legal-positivism.
30. Pettit, *Republicanism*, 5, 36–37, 55, 84, 122, 174, 184, 198.
31. Frank Lovett, *A General Theory of Domination and Justice* (Oxford: Oxford University Press, 2010), 111–119.
32. Pettit, *Republicanism*, 112.
33. Pettit, *Republicanism*, 84.
34. But as mentioned in Section 3.7, the slave will be interfered with at least by those enforcing the legal restrictions that come with being a slave, such as being denied political freedoms to vote and run for public office.
35. Kramer, "Liberty and Domination," 47–48; Kramer, *The Quality of Freedom*, 140–141.
36. Kramer, *The Quality of Freedom*, 141.
37. Kramer, "Liberty and Domination," 47.
38. Pettit, *On the People's Terms*, 62.
39. Skinner, "Freedom as the Absence of Arbitrary Power," 97.
40. Skinner, *Liberty before Liberalism*, 72.
41. Kramer, *The Quality of Freedom*, 140.
42. Kramer, "Liberty and Domination," 49.
43. Kramer, *The Quality of Freedom*, 142.
44. Lovett, *The Well-Ordered Republic*, 67–68.
45. Pettit, *On the People's Terms*, 8.
46. Dowding, "Republican Freedom, Rights, and the Coalition Problem," 312.
47. Pettit, *Republicanism*, 266. See also Lovett, *The Well-Ordered Republic*, 208.
48. Pettit, *Republicanism*, 246.
49. Pettit, "The Domination Complaint," 111.
50. Pettit, *On the People's Terms*, 173.
51. Pettit, *On the People's Terms*, 262.
52. Pettit, *Republicanism*, 246.
53. Pettit, "Freedom as Antipower," 592.
54. Pettit, *On the People's Terms*, 128.
55. Geoffrey Brennan, Lina Eriksson, Robert E. Goodin, and Nicholas Southwood, *Explaining Norms* (Oxford: Oxford University Press, 2013), 3, fn. 5.
56. David Lewis, *Philosophical Papers*, vol. 1 (Oxford: Oxford University Press, 1983), 181.
57. Pettit, *Republicanism*, 243.
58. Brennan et al., *Explaining Norms*, 10.
59. Brennan et al., *Explaining Norms*, 1.
60. Pettit, *Just Freedom*, 59–60; Pettit, *Republicanism*, 236. On the economy of esteem, see Geoffrey Brennan and Philip Pettit, *The Economy of Esteem: An Essay on Civil and Political Society* (New York: Oxford University Press, 2004).

184 NOTES

61. Pettit, *On the People's Terms*, 276–277.
62. Cristina Bicchieri, "Norms, Conventions, and the Power of Expectations," in *Philosophy of Social Science: A New Introduction*, ed. Nancy Cartwright and Eleonora Montuschi (New York: Oxford University Press, 2014), 224.
63. Pettit, *On the People's Terms*, 123–124.
64. Pettit, *Republicanism*, 246.
65. Pettit, *Republicanism*, 241.
66. Pettit, *On the People's Terms*, 128–129; Pettit, *Republicanism*, 242.
67. Niccolò Machiavelli, *Discourses on Livy*, ed. and trans. Julia Conway Bondanella and Peter Bondanella (New York: Oxford University Press, 2008), 68 (bk. 1, ch. 18).
68. Pettit, *Republicanism*, 246.
69. Pettit, *On the People's Terms*, 226.
70. Pettit, *Republicanism*, 250.
71. Pettit, *On the People's Terms*, 256.
72. Pettit, "Freedom as Antipower," 592.
73. Pettit, *Republicanism*, 138–140, 143–146.
74. Pettit, *Republicanism*, 232.
75. Pettit, *On the People's Terms*, 63.
76. Geoffrey Brennan and Philip Pettit, "Hands Invisible and Intangible," *Synthese* 94, no. 2 (1993): 191–225.
77. Pettit, *Republicanism*, 257.
78. Pettit, *Republicanism*, 245.
79. Pettit, *Republicanism*, 236. See also M. Victoria Costa, "Neo-Republicanism, Freedom as Non-Domination, and Citizen Virtue," *Politics, Philosophy & Economics* 8, no. 4 (2009): 410–411.
80. Pettit, *Republicanism*, 244.
81. It is for this reason that Rawls considers good norms necessary for giving reasonable persons an effective desire to support just institutions. See Rawls, *A Theory of Justice*, 128.
82. Frank Lovett and Philip Pettit, "Preserving Republican Freedom: A Reply to Simpson," *Philosophy and Public Affairs* 46, no. 4 (2019): 372.
83. Pettit, *On the People's Terms*, 183.
84. Pettit, *On the People's Terms*, 124.
85. Pettit, *On the People's Terms*, 63.
86. Pettit, *On the People's Terms*, 174.
87. Pettit, *Republicanism*, 154.
88. Pettit, *Republicanism*, 211.
89. Pettit, *Republicanism*, 254.
90. Costa, "Neo-Republicanism, Freedom as Non-Domination, and Citizen Virtue," 419, n. 31.
91. Costa, "Neo-Republicanism, Freedom as Non-Domination, and Citizen Virtue," 413.
92. Gerry Mackie, "Ending Footbinding and Infibulation: A Convention Account," *American Sociological Review* 61, no. 6 (1996): 999–1017.
93. Pettit, *On the People's Terms*, 174.

NOTES 185

94. Robert S. Baron, Sieg I. Hoppe, Chuan Feng Kao, Bethany Brunsman, Barbara Linneweh, and Diane Rogers, "Social Corroboration and Opinion Extremity," *Journal of Experimental Social Psychology* 32, no. 6 (1996): 537–560.
95. Pettit, *On the People's Terms*, 135.
96. Pettit, *On the People's Terms*, 181–184
97. Pettit, *On the People's Terms*, 183.
98. Joel Feinberg, "The Nature and Value of Rights," *Journal of Value Inquiry* 4, no. 4 (1970): 243–260.
99. Feinberg, "The Nature and Value of Rights," 243.
100. Feinberg, "The Nature and Value of Rights," 252.
101. Rawls, *A Theory of Justice*, 211.
102. On the burdens of judgment, see Rawls, *Political Liberalism*, 54–58.
103. Rawls, *A Theory of Justice*, 211.
104. In his defense of government even where people are perfectly virtuous, Gregory Kavka also bases his argument on the realistic assumption of pluralism. He also assumes that people will hold conflicting factual beliefs about the world. See Kavka, "Why Even Morally Perfect People Would Need Government," *Social Philosophy and Policy* 12, no. 1 (1995): 1–18.
105. Carter, *A Measure of Freedom*, 257.
106. Costa, "Neo-Republicanism, Freedom as Non-Domination, and Citizen Virtue," 407.

Chapter 6

1. Ingham and Lovett, "Republican Freedom, Popular Control, and Collective Action," 778–779.
2. As we saw in Section 3.2, a socially possible world is defined by a specific combinations of preference orderings across all individuals in a society.
3. Ingham and Lovett, "Republican Freedom, Popular Control, and Collective Action," 779.
4. Ingham and Lovett, "Republican Freedom, Popular Control, and Collective Action," 779.
5. Pettit, *On the People's Terms*, 47.
6. Pettit, *On the People's Terms*, 84.
7. List, "Republican Freedom and the Rule of Law," 209.
8. List, "Republican Freedom and the Rule of Law," 203–205.
9. Pettit, "Freedom and Probability," 207, fn. 3.
10. Ingham and Lovett, "Republican Freedom, Popular Control, and Collective Action," 778.
11. Ingham and Lovett, "Republican Freedom, Popular Control, and Collective Action," 775.
12. Pettit, *On the People's Terms*, 108–109.
13. Pettit, *On the People's Terms*, 109.

186   NOTES

14. Feinberg, "The Nature and Value of Rights," 252.
15. Rawls, *A Theory of Justice*, 386.
16. Rawls, *A Theory of Justice*, 155.
17. Pettit, *On the People's Terms*, 107.
18. Pettit, *On the People's Terms*, 107.
19. Pettit, *On the People's Terms*, 107.
20. Alan Patten makes the similar point against Skinner that his republicanism demands no more institutional protection than does the liberalism of Rawls and Dworkin. See Patten, "The Republican Critique of Liberalism," *British Journal of Political Science* 26, no. 1 (1996): 25–44. I show that the same holds with respect to Pettit's republicanism in Moen, "Republicanism as Critique of Liberalism," *Southern Journal of Philosophy* 61, no. 2 (2023): 308–324.
21. Rawls, *Justice as Fairness*, 144; Rawls, *Political Liberalism*, 205–206.
22. Rawls, *Justice as Fairness*, 142–145; Rawls, *Political Liberalism*, 205–206. Civic humanism has in recent decades been associated with writers such as Hannah Arendt and Michael Sandel.
23. Pettit, *On the People's Terms*, 11–18; Pettit, Republicanism, ch. 1; Pettit, "Two Republican Traditions." See also Skinner, "The Republican Ideal of Political Liberty."
24. Rawls, *Justice as Fairness*, 144.
25. Rawls, *Justice as Fairness*, 117–118; Rawls, *Political Liberalism*, 194–195.
26. Rawls, *Justice as Fairness*, 119.
27. Rawls, *Justice as Fairness*, 144. Rawls does not mention Pettit, but Pettit clearly also belongs to the republican tradition he refers to.
28. Pettit, *Republicanism*, 264.
29. Pettit, *On the People's Terms*, 226.
30. Pettit, *On the People's Terms*, 237; Pettit, *Republicanism*, 193.
31. Philip Pettit, "The Inescapability of Consequentialism," in *Luck, Value, and Commitment: Themes from the Ethics of Bernard Williams*, ed. Ulrike Heuer and Gerald Lang (Oxford: Oxford University Press, 2012), 45–46.
32. Pettit, *On the People's Terms*, 136, fn. 5.
33. Pettit, *On the People's Terms*, 174.
34. Pettit, *On the People's Terms*, 262.
35. List, "Republican Freedom and the Rule of Law," 218.
36. Goodin and Jackson, "Freedom from Fear."
37. List, "Republican Freedom and the Rule of Law," 217.
38. Lars J. K. Moen, "Republican Freedom and Liberal Neutrality," *Journal of Ethics and Social Philosophy* 26, no. 2 (2023): 325–348.
39. For a "liberal republicanism" in line with liberal perfectionism, see Richard Dagger, *Civic Virtues: Rights, Citizenship, and Republican Liberalism* (New York: Oxford University Press, 1997).
40. Cass R. Sunstein, "Republicanism and the Preference Problem," *Chicago-Kent Law Review* 66, no. 1 (1990): 181.
41. Machiavelli, *Discourses on Livy*.
42. Pettit, "The Determinacy of Republican Policy," 276.
43. Pettit, *Republicanism*, 8.

NOTES 187

44. Rawls, *Justice as Fairness*, 9.

45. Pettit, *Republicanism*, 146.

46. Pettit, *Republicanism*, 144.

47. Pettit, *Republicanism*, 96.

48. Pettit, *Republicanism*, 95.

49. Pettit, *Republicanism*, 90–92.

50. Pettit, *Republicanism*, 97.

51. Pettit, *Republicanism*, 96–97.

52. Pettit, "Political Realism Meets Civic Republicanism," 334.

53. Pettit, *Republicanism*, 120. Frank Lovett and Gregory Whitfield, however, argue that republicanism is incompatible with such neutral treatment, and that it cannot be impartial. They take impartiality to require that "public policies, institutions, and so forth be justifiable to all persons, regardless of their conception of the good, provided they are ready and willing to engage in social cooperation with others on fair terms." See Lovett and Whitfield, "Republicanism, Perfectionism, and Neutrality," *Journal of Political Philosophy* 24, no. 1 (2016): 129. Given the similarities between Pettit's republicanism and Rawls's political liberalism identified in this book, Lovett and Whitfield seems to implicitly also question the neutrality and impartiality of the latter. Kramer indeed denies that liberalism can be impartial. See Kramer, *Liberalism with Excellence* [Oxford: Oxford University Press, 2017], ch. 3.) On a strong interpretation, republicanism also fails Lovett and Whitfield's "principle of toleration," which they understand moderate republicanism to satisfy. On this principle, "[p]ublic policies, institutions, and so forth should impose no special disadvantages on any worthwhile conception of the good" (124). Lovett and Whitfield use the modifier "worthwhile" to exclude conceptions with "no possible benefit for those who hold them" (125). Promoting strong republican freedom will involve imposing "special disadvantages" on many "worthwhile conceptions of the good."

54. Ingham and Lovett, "Republican Freedom, Popular Control, and Collective Action," 775–776.

55. Lovett and Whitfield suggest a different reason for denying that non-domination is a primary good: Some reasonable persons, they argue, manage to pursue their conceptions of the good while being dominated, such as women who cannot pursue their conceptions of the good "unless subordinate to the unaccountable authority of a husband." But they only see this as an argument for republicanism not being impartial. See Lovett and Whitfield, "Republicanism, Perfectionism, and Neutrality," 131. Lovett also maintains that freedom from domination is a primary good because one cannot lead a fully flourishing life without it. See Lovett, *Domination and Justice*, 136; Lovett, *The Well-Ordered Republic*, 74–81.

56. Pettit, "Republican Freedom," 111.

57. Pettit, *Republicanism*, 96.

58. Pettit, *Republicanism*, 96.

59. John Rawls, "Social Unity and Primary Goods," in *Utilitarianism and beyond*, ed. Amartya Sen and Bernard Williams (Cambridge: Cambridge University Press, 1982), 160.

188 NOTES

60. Rawls, *Political Liberalism*, 269.
61. Rawls, *Political Liberalism*, 68.
62. Rawls, *A Theory of Justice*, 215.
63. Rawls, *Political Liberalism*, 205.
64. Frank Lovett and Philip Pettit, "Neorepublicanism: A Normative and Institutional Research Program," *Annual Review of Political Science* 12, no. 1 (2009): 23.
65. Rawls, *Political Liberalism*, 100.
66. Rawls, *Political Liberalism*, 49.
67. Rawls, *A Theory of Justice*, 399.
68. Pettit, "Political Realism Meets Civic Republicanism."
69. Pettit, *Republicanism*, 258.
70. Lovett also sees the same restrictions on institutional cultivation of civic virtue in liberalism and republicanism. See Lovett, *The Well-Ordered Republic*, 202–206.
71. Philip Pettit, "Institutions," in *Encyclopedia of Ethics*, ed. Lawrence C. Becker and Charlotte B. Becker (New York: Routledge, 2001), 859.
72. Geoffrey Brennan and Philip Pettit, "The Feasibility Issue," in *The Oxford Handbook of Contemporary Philosophy*, ed. Frank Jackson and Michael Smith (Oxford: Oxford University Press, 2005), 264.
73. Pettit, "Institutions," 859.
74. Brennan and Pettit, "The Feasibility Issue," 264.
75. Rawls, *Political Liberalism*, 142–143.
76. Pettit, "Political Realism Meets Civic Republicanism," 339–340.
77. Pettit, *On the People's Terms*, 228.
78. Pettit, "Political Realism Meets Civic Republicanism," 341–343; Pettit, "The Domination Complaint," 89.
79. Pettit, *Republicanism*, 242.
80. Rawls, *A Theory of Justice*, 398.
81. Rawls, *A Theory of Justice*, 293–294.
82. Rawls, *A Theory of Justice*, 296.
83. Pettit, *Republicanism*, 234.
84. Pettit, "Freedom and Probability," 218–219.
85. Pettit, *Republicanism*, 268–269.
86. Philip Pettit, "The Cunning of Trust," *Philosophy & Public Affairs* 24, no. 3 (1995): 202–225.
87. For empirical support for the view that distrust "crowds out" government officials' motivation to virtuously act for the best of their society, see Bruno S. Frey, *Not Just for the Money: An Economic Theory of Personal Motivation* (Cheltenham: Edward Elgar Publishing, 1997), ch. 6.
88. Pettit, *Republicanism*, 173.
89. Pettit, *Republicanism*, 256.
90. G. A. Cohen makes a similar point in his critique of Rawls. The principles of justice, he says, should not apply strictly to the basic structure; they should apply "where the action is." See Cohen, *Rescuing Justice and Equality* (Cambridge, MA: Harvard University Press, 2008), 142. However, we may say with Ronald Dworkin that the just basic structure will motivate citizens to make beneficial uncoerced choices.

NOTES 189

Dworkin made this response to Cohen in a seminar, and it is only referred to in writing in Cohen, *Rescuing Justice and Equality*, 127. In a later book, Cohen also notes that the challenge of creating the ethos justice requires is one of institutional design. See Cohen, *Why Not Socialism?* (Princeton, NJ: Princeton University Press, 2009), 57–58.

91. Viroli, *Republicanism*, 54.

92. A nudge is meant to serve the interests of the person who is nudged. See Richard H. Thaler and Cass R. Sunstein, *Nudge: Improving Decisions about Health, Wealth and Happiness* (London: Penguin, 2009). Here the nudge is meant to benefit society as a whole. However, republicans have traditionally thought of the individual's best interests and society's best interests as inseparable. Acting against society's best interests is the definition of "corruption" in the republican literature. "Corruption," as Skinner explains, "is simply a failure of rationality, an inability to recognize that our own liberty depends on committing ourselves to a life of virtue and public service." See Skinner, "The Republican Ideal of Political Liberty," 304. For a classic expression of this republican view, see Marcus Tullius Cicero, *On Obligations*, ed. and trans. P. G. Walsh. (Oxford: Oxford University Press, 2008), esp. 7–8.

93. Rawls, *Justice as Fairness*, 156.

94. Quoted in Gordon Wood, *The Creation of the American Republic, 1776–1787* (Chapel Hill: University of North Carolina Press, 1998), 427.

95. Pettit, *Republicanism*, 253.

96. Lovett, *The Well-Ordered Republic*, 215–219.

97. Costa, "Neo-Republicanism, Freedom as Non-Domination, and Citizen Virtue," 412.

98. Costa, "Neo-Republicanism, Freedom as Non-Domination, and Citizen Virtue," 412.

99. Brennan and Lomasky, "Against Reviving Republicanism," 233.

100. List, "Republican Freedom and the Rule of Law," 217.

101. Brennan and Lomasky, "Against Reviving Republicanism," 234.

102. Brennan and Lomasky, "Against Reviving Republicanism," 247.

103. Pettit, *On the People's Terms*, 12.

104. Pettit, *Republicanism*, 8.

105. Brennan and Lomasky, "Against Reviving Republicanism," 233.

106. Pettit, *On the People's Terms*, 200.

107. Costa, "Neo-Republicanism, Freedom as Non-Domination, and Citizen Virtue," 403.

108. M. Victoria Costa, "Rawls on Liberty and Domination," *Res Publica* 15, no. 4 (2009): 397–413.

Chapter 7

1. G. A. Cohen, "How to Do Political Philosophy?," in *On the Currency of Egalitarian Justice and Other Essays in Political Philosophy*, ed. Michael Otsuka (Princeton, NJ: Princeton University Press, 2011), 227.

2. Cohen, "How to Do Political Philosophy?," 227.

3. Cohen explicitly also rejects constructivism in *Rescuing Justice and Equality*, ch. 7.

190 NOTES

4. Rawls, *A Theory of Justice*, 3.
5. Ingham and Lovett, "Republican Freedom, Popular Control, and Collective Action," 775.
6. Cohen, *Rescuing Justice and Equality*, 4.
7. Cohen, *Rescuing Justice and Equality*, ch. 6.
8. Pettit, *On the People's Terms*, 74.
9. Pettit, "Political Realism Meets Civic Republicanism," 341–343; Pettit, "The Domination Complaint," 89.
10. Rawls, *Justice as Fairness*, 4.
11. Pettit, "Political Realism Meets Civic Republicanism," 339.
12. Pettit, "Political Realism Meets Civic Republicanism," 340.
13. Pettit, *Republicanism*, 234.
14. Cohen, *Rescuing Justice and Equality*, 263–272.
15. Cohen, *Rescuing Justice and Equality*, 266.
16. Cohen, *Rescuing*, 285.
17. Cohen, *Rescuing Justice and Equality*, 330; Rawls, *A Theory of Justice*, 398.
18. Cohen, *Rescuing Justice and Equality*, 367.
19. Cohen, *Rescuing*, 302.
20. Pablo Gilabert, "Feasibility and Socialism," *Journal of Political Philosophy* 19, no. 1 (2011): 56.
21. Gilabert, "Feasibility and Socialism," 56.
22. Rawls, *A Theory of Justice*, 3.
23. Cohen, *Rescuing Justice and Equality*, 303–304
24. Cohen, *Rescuing Justice and Equality*, 327. Emphasis in the original.
25. Rawls, *The Law of Peoples*, 89.
26. David Estlund, "Liberalism, Equality, and Fraternity in Cohen's Critique of Rawls," *Journal of Political Philosophy* 6, no. 1 (1998): 99–112; Michael G. Titelbaum, "What Would a Rawlsian Ethos of Justice Look Like?," *Philosophy & Public Affairs* 36, no. 3 (2008): 289–322; Andrew Williams, "Incentives, Inequality, and Publicity," *Philosophy & Public Affairs* 27, no. 3 (1998): 225–247.
27. Samuel Scheffler, *The Rejection of Consequentialism: A Philosophical Investigation of the Considerations Underlying Rival Moral Conceptions*, rev. ed. (Oxford: Clarendon Press, 1994).
28. Rawls, *A Theory of Justice*, 153–160.
29. Rawls, *A Theory of Justice*, 495.
30. Rawls, *Justice as Fairness*, 128.
31. Pettit, *Republicanism*, 173. See also Section 6.7 above.
32. Ingham and Lovett, "Republican Freedom, Popular Control, and Collective Action," 775.
33. Rawls, *A Theory of Justice*, 125–126.
34. Samuel Scheffler, "Prerogatives without Restrictions," *Philosophical Perspectives* 6, no. 3 (1992): 378.
35. Joshua Cohen also takes this view of Rawls's methodology in "Taking People as They Are?," *Philosophy & Public Affairs* 30, no. 4 (2002): 377.

NOTES   191

36. Cohen, *Rescuing Justice and Equality*, 10. Larmore mistakenly uses this quote to claim that Cohen attributes the personal prerogative to the nature of justice. See Charles Larmore, "What Is Political Philosophy?," *Journal of Moral Philosophy* 10 (2013): 300–301.

37. Cohen, *Rescuing Justice and Equality*, 10–11, 71, 391.

38. Philip Pettit, "The Consequentialist Can Recognise Rights," *Philosophical Quarterly* 38, no. 150 (1988): 52.

39. Pettit, "The Consequentialist Can Recognise Rights," 52.

40. Williams, "Incentives, Inequality, and Publicity," 233.

41. Williams, "Incentives, Inequality, and Publicity," 246.

42. Rawls, *A Theory of Justice*, 115.

43. Rawls, *A Theory of Justice*, 159.

44. Rawls, *A Theory of Justice*, 211.

45. Rawls, *A Theory of Justice*, 154–155.

46. Rawls, *A Theory of Justice*, 115.

47. Rawls, *Political Liberalism*, 68.

48. Pettit, *On the People's Terms*, 236–237.

49. Pettit, *On the People's Terms*, 177–179.

50. Pettit, *On the People's Terms*, 177–179.

51. Rawls, *A Theory of Justice*, 155.

52. Rawls, *A Theory of Justice*, 156.

53. Cohen, *Rescuing Justice and Equality*, 356.

54. Rawls, *A Theory of Justice*, 115.

55. Philip Pettit, "A Consequentialist Perspective on Contractualism," *Theoria* 66, no. 3 (2000): 228–236; Philip Pettit, "Non-Consequentialism and Political Philosophy," in *Robert Nozick*, ed. David Schmidtz (Cambridge: Cambridge University Press, 2002), 83–104; Philip Pettit, "Non-Consequentialism and Universalizability," *Philosophical Quarterly* 50, no. 199 (2000): 175–190; Philip Pettit, "The Consequentialist Perspective," in *Three Methods of Ethics: A Debate*, ed. Marcia W. Baron, Philip Pettit, and Michael A. Slote (Oxford: Blackwell, 1997), 92–174.

56. Pettit, *On the People's Terms*, 74, 123–125; Pettit, *Republicanism*, 97–109.

57. Scheffler, *The Rejection of Consequentialism*, 2–3.

58. Scheffler, *The Rejection of Consequentialism*, 81.

59. Scheffler, *The Rejection of Consequentialism*, 23–25.

60. Rawls, *A Theory of Justice*, 26.

61. Rawls, *A Theory of Justice*, 24, 160–168.

62. Scheffler, *The Rejection of Consequentialism*, 17.

63. For an account and defense of sophisticated consequentialism, see Peter Railton, "Alienation, Consequentialism, and the Demands of Morality," *Philosophy & Public Affairs* 13, no. 2 (1984): 134–171.

64. Railton, "Alienation, Consequentialism, and the Demands of Morality," 163.

65. Pettit, *Republicanism*, 97–109.

66. Pettit, *Republicanism*, 102.

67. Rawls, *A Theory of Justice*, 26–27.

192 NOTES

68. Philip Pettit and Geoffrey Brennan, "Restrictive Consequentialism," *Australasian Journal of Philosophy* 64, no. 4 (1986): 451; Pettit, "The Consequentialist Can Recognise Rights," 53–54.
69. Pettit and Brennan, "Restrictive Consequentialism"; Pettit, "The Inescapability of Consequentialism," 46–50.
70. Pettit, "The Inescapability of Consequentialism," 43–47. See also Railton, "Alienation, Consequentialism, and the Demands of Morality," 152.
71. Pettit, "The Inescapability of Consequentialism," 46.
72. Pettit, "A Consequentialist Perspective on Contractualism," 232; Rawls, *A Theory of Justice*, 156.
73. Rawls, *A Theory of Justice*, 158.
74. Christman, "Review of Pettit, *Republicanism*," 206.
75. Railton, "Alienation, Consequentialism, and the Demands of Morality," 155.
76. David O. Brink, "Utilitarian Morality and the Personal Point of View," *Journal of Philosophy* 83, no. 8 (1986): 428.
77. Gilabert, "Feasibility and Socialism," 58.
78. Rawls, *A Theory of Justice*, 37.
79. William A. Galston, "Realism in Political Theory," *European Journal of Political Theory* 9, no. 4 (2010): 406.
80. Brennan and Pettit, "The Feasibility Issue," 261.
81. Gerald F. Gaus, *The Tyranny of the Ideal: Justice in a Diverse Society* (Princeton, NJ: Princeton University Press), 16.
82. David Miller, *Justice for Earthlings: Essays in Political Philosophy* (New York: Cambridge University Press, 2013), 232.
83. Miller, *Justice for Earthlings*, 237–238.
84. Miller, *Justice for Earthlings*, 233.
85. Miller, *Justice for Earthlings*, ch. 10.
86. Cohen, *Rescuing Justice and Equality*, 268.
87. Holly Lawford-Smith, "Ideal Theory—A Reply to Valentini," *Journal of Political Philosophy* 18, no. 3 (2010): 360. See also Gilabert, "Feasibility and Socialism," 58; Adam Swift, "The Value of Philosophy in Nonideal Circumstances," *Social Theory and Practice* 34, no. 3 (2008): 364.
88. Patrick Tomlin, "Should We Be Utopophobes about Democracy in Particular?," *Political Studies Review* 10, no. 1 (2012): 42.
89. Cohen, *Rescuing Justice and Equality*, 269.
90. Pettit, "Political Realism Meets Civic Republicanism," 335.
91. Isaiah Berlin gets this right in his view that "[w]e are doomed to choose [between values], and every choice may entail an irreparable loss." See Berlin, "The Pursuit of the Ideal," in *The Crooked Timber of Humanity: Chapters in the History of Ideas*, ed. Henry Hardy (New York: Alfred A. Knopf, 1991), 14.
92. Alan Hamlin and Zofia Stemplowska, "Theory, Ideal Theory and the Theory of Ideals," *Political Studies Review* 10, no. 1 (2012): 52–58.
93. Cohen, *Rescuing Justice and Equality*, ch. 5.
94. Cohen, *Rescuing Justice and Equality*, 189–195.

NOTES 193

95. Cohen, *Rescuing Justice and Equality*, 193.

96. Samuel Bowles, *The Moral Economy: Why Good Incentives Are No Substitute for Good Citizens* (New Haven, CT: Yale University Press, 2016), 165–171.

97. Pettit, *Republicanism*, 210.

98. Pettit, *Republicanism*, 207.

99. Moen, "Republicanism as Critique of Liberalism."

100. Cohen, *Rescuing*, 353–361. Others have also made this point. David Estlund says, "[t]he fact that people will not live up to [a theory's standards] even though they could is, evidently, a defect of people, not of the theory." See Estlund, "Utopophobia," *Philosophy & Public Affairs* 42, no. 2 (2014): 118. And David Copp writes that "if justice by the lights of a theory is unachievable or unsustainable because of the motivations of those who benefit from something the theory would view as unjust, this may be no objection to the theory. . . . A theory's failure to satisfy the constraint is not sufficient to show it to be unjustified." See Copp, "Pluralism and Stability in Liberal Theory," *Journal of Political Philosophy* 4, no. 3 (1996): 205–206.

101. Pettit, "Political Realism Meets Civic Republicanism," 331.

102. Anca Gheaus also uses this disease metaphor in her "The Feasibility Constraint on the Concept of Justice," *Philosophical Quarterly* 63, no. 252 (2013): 456, 463.

103. Cécile Laborde, *Critical Republicanism: The Hijab Controversy and Political Philosophy* (Oxford: Oxford University Press, 2008), 231.

104. Laborde, *Critical Republicanism*, 10.

Chapter 8

1. Pettit, *On the People's Terms*, 20.

2. Brennan and Lomasky, "Against Reviving Republicanism," 241.

3. Pettit, *On the People's Terms*, 107.

4. Pettit, *On the People's Terms*, 107.

5. Pettit, *On the People's Terms*, 107.

6. Brennan and Lomasky, "Against Reviving Republicanism," 222.

7. Viroli, *Republicanism*, 17–19.

8. Viroli, *Republicanism*, 18.

9. Viroli, *Republicanism*, 18.

10. Viroli, *Republicanism*, 19.

11. Viroli, *Republicanism*, 18.

12. Viroli, *Republicanism*, 19.

13. Ronald Dworkin, "What Is Equality? Part 3: The Place of Liberty," *Iowa Law Review* 73, no. 1 (1987): 5.

14. Viroli, *Republicanism*, 55.

Bibliography

Bader, Ralf M. "Moralizing Liberty." In *Oxford Studies in Political Philosophy*, Vol. 4, edited by Peter Vallentyne, David Sobel, and Steven Wall, 141–166. Oxford: Oxford University Press, 2018.

Baron, Robert S., Sieg I. Hoppe, Chuan Feng Kao, Bethany Brunsman, Barbara Linneweh, and Diane Rogers. "Social Corroboration and Opinion Extremity." *Journal of Experimental Social Psychology* 32, no. 6 (1996): 537–560.

Bentham, Jeremy. "Anarchical Fallacies: An Examination of the Declaration of Rights Issued during the French Revolution." In *The Works of Jeremy Bentham*, Vol. 2, edited by John Bowring, 489–534. Edinburgh: William Tait, 1843.

Bentham, Jeremy. *The Theory of Legislation*. Edited by C. K. Ogden. Translated (from French) by Richard Hildreth. London: Kegan Paul, Trench, Trubner & Co., 1931.

Berlin, Isaiah. *Liberty*. Edited by Henry Hardy. Oxford: Oxford University Press, 2002.

Berlin, Isaiah. "The Pursuit of the Ideal." In *The Crooked Timber of Humanity: Chapters in the History of Ideas*, edited by Henry Hardy, 1–20. New York: Alfred A. Knopf, 1991.

Bicchieri, Cristina. "Norms, Conventions, and the Power of Expectations." In *Philosophy of Social Science: A New Introduction*, edited by Nancy Cartwright and Eleonora Montuschi, 208–229. New York: Oxford University Press, 2014.

Boesche, Roger. "Thinking about Freedom." *Political Theory* 26, no. 6 (1998): 855–873.

Bohman, James, and Henry S. Richardson. "Liberalism, Deliberative Democracy, and 'Reasons That All Can Accept.'" *Journal of Political Philosophy* 17, no. 3 (2009): 253–274.

Bowles, Samuel. *The Moral Economy: Why Good Incentives Are No Substitute for Good Citizens*. New Haven, CT: Yale University Press, 2016.

Bramhall, John. "Selections from Bramhall, *A Defence of True Liberty*." In *Hobbes and Bramhall on Liberty and Necessity*, edited by Vere Chappell, 43–68. Cambridge: Cambridge University Press, 1999.

Brennan, Geoffrey, and Alan Hamlin. "Republican Liberty and Resilience." *The Monist* 84, no. 1 (2001): 45–59.

Brennan, Geoffrey, and Loren Lomasky. "Against Reviving Republicanism." *Politics, Philosophy & Economics* 5, no. 2 (2006): 221–252.

Brennan, Geoffrey, and Philip Pettit. *The Economy of Esteem: An Essay on Civil and Political Society*. New York: Oxford University Press, 2004.

Brennan, Geoffrey, and Philip Pettit. "The Feasibility Issue." In *The Oxford Handbook of Contemporary Philosophy*, edited by Frank Jackson and Michael Smith, 258–279. Oxford: Oxford University Press, 2005.

Brennan, Geoffrey, and Philip Pettit. "Hands Invisible and Intangible." *Synthese* 94, no. 2 (1993): 191–225.

Brennan, Geoffrey, Lina Eriksson, Robert E. Goodin, and Nicholas Southwood. *Explaining Norms*. Oxford: Oxford University Press, 2013.

Brink, David O. "Utilitarian Morality and the Personal Point of View." *Journal of Philosophy* 83, no. 8 (1986): 417–438.

196 BIBLIOGRAPHY

Carey, John M. *Legislative Voting and Accountability*. Cambridge: Cambridge University Press, 2009.

Carter, Ian. "A Critique of Freedom as Non-Domination." *The Good Society* 9, no. 3 (2000): 43–46.

Carter, Ian. *A Measure of Freedom*. Oxford: Oxford University Press, 1999.

Carter, Ian. "How Are Power and Unfreedom Related?" In *Republicanism and Political Theory*, edited by Cécile Laborde and John Maynor, 58–82. Oxford: Blackwell, 2008.

Carter, Ian. "Respect for Persons and the Interest in Freedom." In *Hillel Steiner and the Anatomy of Justice: Themes and Challenges*, edited by Stephen de Wijze, Matthew H. Kramer, and Ian Carter, 167–184. London: Routledge, 2009.

Carter, Ian, and Matthew H. Kramer. "How Changes in One's Preferences Can Affect One's Freedom (and How They Cannot): A Reply to Dowding and van Hees." *Economics and Philosophy* 24, no. 1 (2008): 81–96.

Carter, Ian, and Ronen Shnayderman. "The Impossibility of 'Freedom as Independence.'" *Political Studies Review* 17, no. 2 (2019): 136–146.

Carter, Ian, and Hillel Steiner. "Freedom without Trimmings: The Perils of Trivalence." In *Without Trimmings: The Legal, Moral, and Political Philosophy of Matthew Kramer*, edited by Mack McBride and Visa A. J. Kurki, 239–267. Oxford: Oxford University Press, 2022.

Christman, John. "Review of Pettit's Republicanism." *Ethics* 109, no. 1 (1998): 202–206.

Cicero, Marcus Tullius. *On Obligations*. Edited and translated by P. G. Walsh. Oxford: Oxford University Press, 2008.

Cohen, G. A. "Capitalism, Freedom and the Proletariat." In *The Idea of Freedom: Essays in Honour of Isaiah Berlin*, edited by Alan Ryan, 9–25. Oxford: Oxford University Press, 1979.

Cohen, G. A. "Freedom and Money." In *On the Currency of Egalitarian Justice, and Other Essays in Political Philosophy*, edited by Michael Otsuka, 166–192. Princeton, NJ: Princeton University Press, 2011.

Cohen, G. A. "Freedom, Justice and Capitalism." *New Left Review* 126 (1981): 3–16.

Cohen, G. A. *History, Labour, and Freedom: Themes from Marx*. Oxford: Oxford University Press, 1988.

Cohen, G. A. "How to Do Political Philosophy?" In *On the Currency of Egalitarian Justice and Other Essays in Political Philosophy*, edited by Michael Otsuka, 225–235. Princeton, NJ: Princeton University Press, 2011.

Cohen, G. A. *Rescuing Justice and Equality*. Cambridge, MA: Harvard University Press, 2008.

Cohen, Joshua. "Taking People as They Are?" *Philosophy & Public Affairs* 30, no. 4 (2002): 363–386.

Copp, David. "Pluralism and Stability in Liberal Theory." *Journal of Political Philosophy* 4, no. 3 (1996): 191–206.

Costa, M. Victoria. "Neo-Republicanism, Freedom as Non-Domination, and Citizen Virtue." *Politics, Philosophy & Economics* 8, no. 4 (2009): 401–419.

Costa, M. Victoria. "Rawls on Liberty and Domination." *Res Publica* 15, no. 4 (2009): 397–413.

Dagger, Richard. *Civic Virtues: Rights, Citizenship, and Republican Liberalism*. New York: Oxford University Press, 1997.

D'Agostino, Fred. *Free Public Reason: Making It Up as We Go*. Oxford: Oxford University Press, 1996.

BIBLIOGRAPHY 197

Day, J. P. "On Liberty and the Real Will." *Philosophy* 45, no. 173 (1970): 177–192.

De Dijn, Annelien. *Freedom: An Unruly History.* Cambridge: Cambridge University Press, 2020.

De Francisco, Andrés. "A Republican Interpretation of the Late Rawls." *Journal of Political Philosophy* 14, no. 3 (2006): 270–288.

Dowding, Keith. "Republican Freedom, Rights, and the Coalition Problem." *Politics, Philosophy & Economics* 10, no. 3 (2011): 301–322.

Dworkin, Ronald. *Justice for Hedgehogs.* Cambridge, MA: Belknap Press of Harvard University Press, 2011.

Dworkin, Ronald. *A Matter of Principle.* Cambridge, MA: Harvard University Press, 1985.

Dworkin, Ronald. "What Is Equality? Part 3: The Place of Liberty." *Iowa Law Review* 73, no. 1 (1987): 1–54.

Estlund, David. "Liberalism, Equality, and Fraternity in Cohen's Critique of Rawls." *Journal of Political Philosophy* 6, no. 1 (1998): 99–112.

Estlund, David. "Review of *On the People's Terms: A Republican Theory and Model of Democracy,* by Philip Pettit." *Australasian Journal of Philosophy* 92, no. 4 (2014): 799–802.

Estlund, David. "Utopophobia." *Philosophy & Public Affairs* 42, no. 2 (2014): 113–134.

Feinberg, Joel. "The Nature and Value of Rights." *Journal of Value Inquiry* 4, no. 4 (1970): 243–260.

Ferejohn, John. "Pettit's Republic." *The Monist* 84, no. 1 (2001): 77–97.

Freeman, Samuel. *Rawls.* London: Routledge, 2007.

Frey, Bruno S. *Not Just for the Money: An Economic Theory of Personal Motivation.* Cheltenham: Edward Elgar Publishing, 1997.

Galston, William A. "Realism in Political Theory." *European Journal of Political Theory* 9, no. 4 (2010): 385–411.

Gaus, Gerald F. "Backwards into the Future: Neorepublicanism as a Postsocialist Critique of Market Society." *Social Philosophy and Policy* 20, no. 1 (2003): 59–91.

Gaus, Gerald F. *Justificatory Liberalism: An Essay on Epistemology and Political Theory.* New York: Oxford University Press, 1996.

Gaus, Gerald F. *The Tyranny of the Ideal: Justice in a Diverse Society.* Princeton, NJ: Princeton University Press, 2016.

Gheaus, Anca. "The Feasibility Constraint on the Concept of Justice." *Philosophical Quarterly* 63, no. 252 (2013): 445–464.

Gilabert, Pablo. "Feasibility and Socialism." *Journal of Political Philosophy* 19, no. 1 (2011): 52–63.

Goodin, Robert E., and Frank Jackson. "Freedom from Fear." *Philosophy & Public Affairs* 35, no. 3 (2007): 249–265.

Green, Leslie. "Legal Positivism." In *The Stanford Encyclopedia of Philosophy,* edited by Edward N. Zalta. Last modified 8 March 2018, accessed 9 June 2018. https://plato.stanford.edu/archives/spr2018/entries/legal-positivism.

Hamlin, Alan, and Zofia Stemplowska. "Theory, Ideal Theory and the Theory of Ideals." *Political Studies Review* 10, no. 1 (2012): 48–62.

Hart, H. L. A. "Rawls on Liberty and Its Priority." In *Reading Rawls: Critical Studies on Rawls' "A Theory of Justice,"* edited by Norman Daniels, 230–252. New York: Basic Books, 1975.

Hobbes, Thomas. *Leviathan.* Edited by J. C. A. Gaskin. Oxford: Oxford University Press, 2008.

198 BIBLIOGRAPHY

Hobbes, Thomas. "Selections from Hobbes, *The Questions Concerning Liberty, Necessity, and Chance*." In *Hobbes and Bramhall on Liberty and Necessity*, edited by Vere Chappell, 69–90. Cambridge: Cambridge University Press, 1999.

Ingham, Sean, and Frank Lovett. "Republican Freedom, Popular Control, and Collective Action." *American Journal of Political Science* 63, no. 4 (2019): 774–787.

Kavka, Gregory. "Why Even Morally Perfect People Would Need Government." *Social Philosophy and Policy* 12, no. 1 (1995): 1–18.

Korsgaard, Christine M. "The Reasons We Can Share: An Attack on the Distinction between Agent-Relative and Agent-Neutral Values." *Social Philosophy and Policy*, 10, no. 1 (1993): 24–51.

Kramer, Matthew H. "Freedom and the Rule of Law." *Alabama Law Review* 61, no. 4 (2010): 827–845.

Kramer, Matthew H. "Liberty and Domination." In *Republicanism and Political Theory*, edited by Cécile Laborde and John Maynor, 31–57. Oxford: Blackwell, 2008.

Kramer, Matthew H. "Looking Back and Looking Ahead: Replies to the Contributors." In *Without Trimmings: The Legal, Moral, and Political Philosophy of Matthew Kramer*, edited by Mack McBride and Visa A. J. Kurki, 363–552. Oxford: Oxford University Press, 2022.

Kramer, Matthew H. *The Quality of Freedom*. Oxford: Oxford University Press, 2003.

Kramer, Matthew H. "Why Freedoms Do Not Exist by Degrees." *Political Studies* 50, no. 2 (2002): 230–243.

Kristjánsson, Kristjan. *Social Freedom: The Responsibility View*. Cambridge: Cambridge University Press, 1996.

Laborde, Cécile. *Critical Republicanism: The Hijab Controversy and Political Philosophy*. Oxford: Oxford University Press, 2008.

Laden, Anthony Simon. "Republican Moments in Political Liberalism." *Revue Internationale de Philosophie* 3, no. 237 (2006): 341–367.

Larmore, Charles. "A Critique of Philip Pettit's Republicanism." *Philosophical Issues* 11, no. 1 (2001): 229–243.

Larmore, Charles. "Liberal and Republican Conceptions of Freedom." *Critical Review of International Social and Political Philosophy* 6, no. 1 (2003): 96–119.

Larmore, Charles. "What Is Political Philosophy?" *Journal of Moral Philosophy* 10, no. 3 (2013): 276–306.

Lawford-Smith, Holly. "Ideal Theory—A Reply to Valentini." *Journal of Political Philosophy* 18, no. 3 (2010): 357–368.

Lewis, David. *Philosophical Papers*. Vol. 1. Oxford: Oxford University Press, 1983.

List, Christian. "The Impossibility of a Paretian Republican? Some Comments on Pettit and Sen." *Economics and Philosophy* 20, no. 1 (2004): 65–87.

List, Christian. "Republican Freedom and the Rule of Law." *Politics, Philosophy & Economics* 5, no. 2 (2006): 201–220.

List, Christian, and Laura Valentini. "Freedom as Independence." *Ethics* 126, no. 4 (2016): 1043–1074.

Locke, John. *Two Treatises of Government*. Edited by Peter Laslett. Cambridge: Cambridge University Press, 1988.

Lovett, Frank. *A General Theory of Domination and Justice*. Oxford: Oxford University Press, 2010.

Lovett, Frank. *The Well-Ordered Republic*. Oxford: Oxford University Press, 2022.

Lovett, Frank, and Philip Pettit. "Neorepublicanism: A Normative and Institutional Research Program." *Annual Review of Political Science* 12, no. 1 (2009): 11–29.

BIBLIOGRAPHY 199

Lovett, Frank, and Philip Pettit. "Preserving Republican Freedom: A Reply to Simpson." *Philosophy & Public Affairs* 46, no. 4 (2019): 363–383.

Lovett, Frank, and Gregory Whitfield. "Republicanism, Perfectionism, and Neutrality." *Journal of Political Philosophy* 24, no. 1 (2016): 120–134.

MacCallum, Gerald C. "Negative and Positive Freedom." *Philosophical Review* 76, no. 3 (1967): 312–334.

Machiavelli, Niccolò. *Discourses on Livy*. Edited and translated by Julia Conway Bondanella and Peter Bondanella. New York: Oxford University Press, 2008.

Mackie, Gerry. "Ending Footbinding and Infibulation: A Convention Account." *American Sociological Review* 61, no. 6 (1996): 999–1017.

McMahon, Christopher. "The Indeterminacy of Republican Policy." *Philosophy & Public Affairs* 33, no. 1 (2005): 67–93.

Miller, David. *Justice for Earthlings: Essays in Political Philosophy*. New York: Cambridge University Press, 2013.

Moen, Lars J. K. "Eliminating Terms of Confusion: Resolving the Liberal–Republican Dispute." *Journal of Ethics* 26, no. 2 (2022): 247–271.

Moen, Lars J. K. "Freedom and Its Unavoidable Trade-Off." *Analytic Philosophy*. Published online (2023). DOI: 10.1111/phib.12301.

Moen, Lars J. K. "Republican Freedom and Liberal Neutrality." *Journal of Ethics and Social Philosophy* 26, no. 2 (2023): 325–348.

Moen, Lars J. K. "Republicanism and Moralised Freedom." *Politics, Philosophy & Economics* 22, no. 4 (2023): 423–440.

Moen, Lars J. K. "Republicanism as Critique of Liberalism." *Southern Journal of Philosophy* 61, no. 2 (2023): 308–324.

Montesquieu. *The Spirit of the Laws*. Edited and translated by Anne M. Cohler, Basia C. Miller, and Harold S. Stone. Cambridge: Cambridge University Press, 1989.

Nozick, Robert. *Anarchy, State and Utopia*. New York: Basic Books, 1974.

Oppenheim, Felix E. *Political Concepts: A Reconstruction*. Chicago: University of Chicago Press, 1981.

Oppenheim, Felix E. "Social Freedom and Its Parameters." *Journal of Theoretical Politics* 7, no. 4 (1995): 5–37.

Patten, Alan. "The Republican Critique of Liberalism." *British Journal of Political Science* 26, no. 1 (1996): 25–44.

Pettit, Philip. "The Basic Liberties." In *The Legacy of H. L. A. Hart: Legal, Political, and Moral Philosophy*, edited by Claire Grant, Matthew H. Kramer, Ben Colburn, and Antony Hatzistavrou, 201–221. Oxford: Oxford University Press, 2008.

Pettit, Philip. "Capability and Freedom: A Defence of Sen." *Economics and Philosophy* 17, no. 1 (2001): 1–20.

Pettit, Philip. "The Common Good." In *Justice and Democracy: Essays for Brian Barry*, edited by Robert E. Goodin, Keith Dowding, and Carole Pateman, 150–169. Cambridge: Cambridge University Press, 2004.

Pettit, Philip. "The Consequentialist Can Recognise Rights." *Philosophical Quarterly* 38, no. 150 (1988): 42–55.

Pettit, Philip. "The Consequentialist Perspective." In *Three Methods of Ethics: A Debate*, edited by Marcia W. Baron, Philip Pettit, and Michael A. Slote, 92–174. Oxford: Blackwell, 1997.

Pettit, Philip. "A Consequentialist Perspective on Contractualism." *Theoria* 66, no. 3 (2000): 228–236.

Pettit, Philip. "The Cunning of Trust." *Philosophy & Public Affairs* 24, no. 3 (1995): 202–225.

200   BIBLIOGRAPHY

Pettit, Philip. "The Determinacy of Republican Policy: A Reply to McMahon." *Philosophy & Public Affairs* 34, no. 3 (2006): 275–283.

Pettit, Philip. "The Domination Complaint." In *Nomos 46: Political Exclusion and Domination*, edited by Melissa Williams and Stephen Macedo, 87–117. New York: New York University Press, 2005.

Pettit, Philip. "Free Persons and Free Choices." *History of Political Thought* 28, no. 4 (2007): 709–718.

Pettit, Philip. "Freedom and Probability: A Comment on Goodin and Jackson." *Philosophy & Public Affairs* 36, no. 2 (2008): 206–220.

Pettit, Philip. "Freedom as Antipower." *Ethics* 106, no. 3 (1996): 576–604.

Pettit, Philip. "The Inescapability of Consequentialism." In *Luck, Value, and Commitment: Themes from the Ethics of Bernard Williams*, edited by Ulrike Heuer and Gerald Lang, 41–70. Oxford: Oxford University Press, 2012.

Pettit, Philip. "The Instability of Freedom as Noninterference: The Case of Isaiah Berlin." *Ethics* 121, no. 4 (2011): 693–716.

Pettit, Philip. "Institutions." In *Encyclopedia of Ethics*, edited by Lawrence C. Becker and Charlotte B. Becker, 858–863. New York: Routledge, 2001.

Pettit, Philip. *Just Freedom: A Moral Compass for a Complex World*. London: W. W. Norton, 2014.

Pettit, Philip. "Keeping Republican Freedom Simple: On a Difference with Quentin Skinner." *Political Theory* 30, no. 3 (2002): 339–356.

Pettit, Philip. "Neo-Liberalism and Neo-Republicanism." *Korea Observer* 50, no. 2 (2019): 191–206.

Pettit, Philip. "Non-Consequentialism and Political Philosophy." In *Robert Nozick*, edited by David Schmidtz, 83–104. Cambridge: Cambridge University Press, 2002.

Pettit, Philip. "Non-Consequentialism and Universalizability." *Philosophical Quarterly* 50, no. 199 (2000): 175–190.

Pettit, Philip. *On the People's Terms: A Republican Theory and Model of Democracy*. Cambridge: Cambridge University Press, 2012.

Pettit, Philip. "Political Realism Meets Civic Republicanism." *Critical Review of International Social and Political Philosophy* 20, no. 3 (2017): 331–347.

Pettit, Philip. "Republican Freedom: Three Axioms, Four Theorems." In *Republicanism and Political Theory*, edited by Cécile Laborde and John Maynor, 102–130. Oxford: Blackwell, 2008.

Pettit, Philip. *Republicanism: A Theory of Freedom and Government*. Oxford: Oxford University Press, 1997.

Pettit, Philip. "Reworking Sandel's Republicanism." *Journal of Philosophy* 95, no. 2 (1998): 73–96.

Pettit, Philip. *A Theory of Freedom: From the Psychology to the Politics of Agency*. Oxford: Oxford University Press, 2001.

Pettit, Philip. "Two Republican Traditions." In *Republican Democracy: Liberty, Law and Politics*, edited by Andreas Niederberger and Philipp Schink, 169–204. Edinburgh: Edinburgh University Press, 2013.

Pettit, Philip, and Geoffrey Brennan. "Restrictive Consequentialism." *Australasian Journal of Philosophy* 64, no. 4 (1986): 438–455.

Quong, Jonathan. *Liberalism without Perfection*. Oxford: Oxford University Press, 2011.

Quong, Jonathan. "The Scope of Public Reason." *Political Studies* 52, no. 2 (2004): 233–250.

BIBLIOGRAPHY 201

Railton, Peter. "Alienation, Consequentialism, and the Demands of Morality." *Philosophy & Public Affairs* 13, no. 2 (1984): 134–171.

Rawls, John. *Justice as Fairness: A Restatement.* Cambridge, MA: Belknap Press of Harvard University Press, 2001.

Rawls, John. "Kantian Constructivism in Moral Theory." *Journal of Philosophy* 77, no. 9 (1980): 515–572.

Rawls, John. *The Law of Peoples.* Cambridge, MA: Harvard University Press, 1999.

Rawls, John. *Political Liberalism.* Expanded ed. New York: Columbia University Press, 2005.

Rawls, John. "Social Unity and Primary Goods." In *Utilitarianism and Beyond*, edited by Amartya Sen and Bernard Williams, 159–185. Cambridge: Cambridge University Press, 1982.

Rawls, John. *A Theory of Justice.* Rev. ed. Cambridge, MA: Belknap Press of Harvard University Press, 1999.

Raz, Joseph. *The Authority of Law: Essays on Law and Morality.* Oxford: Oxford University Press, 1979.

Scanlon, T. M. "Contractualism and Utilitarianism." In *Utilitarianism and Beyond*, edited by Amartya Sen and Bernard Williams, 103–128. Cambridge: Cambridge University Press, 1982.

Scheffler, Samuel. "Prerogatives without Restrictions." *Philosophical Perspectives* 6, no. 3 (1992): 377–397.

Scheffler, Samuel. *The Rejection of Consequentialism: A Philosophical Investigation of the Considerations Underlying Rival Moral Conceptions.* Rev. ed. Oxford: Clarendon Press, 1994.

Sen, Amartya. *Collective Choice and Social Welfare.* Expanded ed. London: Penguin, 2017.

Sen, Amartya. *Development as Freedom.* Oxford: Oxford University Press, 1999.

Sen, Amartya. "The Impossibility of a Paretian Liberal." *Journal of Political Economy* 78, no. 1 (1970): 152–157.

Sharon, Assaf. "Domination and the Rule of Law." In *Oxford Studies in Political Philosophy*, edited by Peter Vallentyne, David Sobel, and Steven Wall, 128–155. Oxford: Oxford University Press, 2016.

Simpson, Thomas W. "The Impossibility of Republican Freedom." *Philosophy & Public Affairs* 45, no. 1 (2017): 27–53.

Skinner, Quentin. "Freedom as the Absence of Arbitrary Power." In *Republicanism and Political Theory*, edited by Cécile Laborde and John Maynor, 83–101. Oxford: Blackwell, 2008.

Skinner, Quentin. "The Idea of Negative Liberty." In *Philosophy in History*, edited by Richard Rorty, J. B. Schneewind, and Quentin Skinner, 193–221. Cambridge: Cambridge University Press, 1984.

Skinner, Quentin. *Liberty before Liberalism.* Cambridge: Cambridge University Press, 1998.

Skinner, Quentin. "On the Slogans of Republican Political Theory." *European Journal of Political Theory* 9, no. 1 (2010): 95–102.

Skinner, Quentin. *Reason and Rhetoric in the Philosophy of Hobbes.* Cambridge: Cambridge University Press, 1996.

Skinner, Quentin. "The Republican Ideal of Political Liberty." In *Machiavelli and Republicanism*, edited by Quentin Skinner, Gisela Bock, Maurizio Viroli, 293–309. Cambridge: Cambridge University Press, 1990.

202 BIBLIOGRAPHY

Steiner, Hillel. *An Essay on Rights*. Oxford: Blackwell, 1994.

Steiner, Hillel. "How Free: Computing Personal Liberty." *Royal Institute of Philosophy Supplement* 15 (1983): 73–89.

Sunstein, Cass R. "Republicanism and the Preference Problem." *Chicago-Kent Law Review* 66, no. 1 (1990): 181–203.

Swift, Adam. "The Value of Philosophy in Nonideal Circumstances." *Social Theory and Practice* 34, no. 3 (2008): 363–387.

Taylor, Michael. *Community, Anarchy and Liberty*. Cambridge: Cambridge University Press, 1982.

Thaler, Richard H., and Cass R. Sunstein. *Nudge: Improving Decisions about Health, Wealth and Happiness*. London: Penguin, 2009.

Thomas, Alan. *Republic of Equals: Predistribution and Property-Owning Democracy*. Oxford: Oxford University Press, 2017.

Titelbaum, Michael G. "What Would a Rawlsian Ethos of Justice Look Like?" *Philosophy & Public Affairs* 36, no. 3 (2008): 289–322.

Tomlin, Patrick. "Should We Be Utopophobes about Democracy in Particular?" *Political Studies Review* 10, no. 1 (2012): 36–47.

Vallier, Kevin. "In Defence of Intelligible Reasons in Public Justification." *Philosophical Quarterly* 66, no. 264 (2016): 596–616.

Vallier, Kevin. "In Defense of Idealization in Public Reason." *Erkenntnis* 85, no. 5 (2020): 1109–1128.

Vallier, Kevin. "Public Justification versus Public Deliberation: The Case for Divorce." *Canadian Journal of Philosophy* 45, no. 2 (2015): 139–158.

Viroli, Maurizio. *Republicanism*. Translated by Antony Shugaar. New York: Hill & Wang, 2002.

Waldron, Jeremy. "Pettit's Molecule." In *Common Minds: Themes from the Philosophy of Philip Pettit*, edited by Robert Goodin, Geoffrey Brennan, Frank Jackson, and Michael Smith, 143–160. Oxford: Clarendon Press, 2007.

Wendt, Fabian. "Slaves, Prisoners, and Republican Freedom." *Res Publica* 17, no. 2 (2011): 175–192.

Williams, Andrew. "Incentives, Inequality, and Publicity." *Philosophy & Public Affairs* 27, no. 3 (1998): 225–247.

Wood, Gordon S. *The Creation of the American Republic, 1776-1787*. Chapel Hill: University of North Carolina Press, 1998.

Index

For the benefit of digital users, indexed terms that span two pages (e.g., 52–53) may, on occasion, appear on only one of those pages.

anarchy, 9, 82–83, 95, 109
Arendt, Hannah, 10
Aristotle, 10

basic liberties, 8, 75–79
Bentham, Jeremy, 167–68n.37
Berlin, Isaiah, 16–18, 192n.91
Boesche, Roger, 167n.31
Bohman, James, 178n.67
Bowles, Samuel, 152–53, 155
Brennan, Geoffrey
  and feasibility, 150
  and norms, 100–1, 102–3
  and republicanism, 8, 11, 131–32, 160, 161, 173n.8

Carey, John M. 182n.6
Carter, Ian
  and act-trees, 54, 83
  and bivalence, 166n.17
  and the equivalent-judgments thesis, 4–5
  and freedom as independence, 173n.7
  and measurement of freedom, 51, 165n.9
  and moralized freedom, 26, 31, 34
  and prevention, 22
  and republican freedom, 2, 51
  and the specific- and overall-freedom theses, 83
Christman, John, 149
Cicero, Marcus Tullius, 189n.92
claims, evaluative and prescriptive, 139, 150
Cohen, G. A.
  and the basic structure objection, 188–89n.90
  and constructivism, 137, 140

  and facts and principles, 138–39
  and libertarianism, 9, 25
  and moralized freedom, 34–35, 171n.46
  and the possibility of freedom, efficiency, and equality, 152–53
  and publicity, 145–46
  and radical pluralism, 137, 138–40, 142
  and three kinds of question, 136–37
Cohen, Joshua, 190n.35
consequentialism, 146–49
  sophisticated, 147–48
constraint
  deontic, 140
  external and internal, 103–6
constructivism, 62–65
  political, 62–65, 69–70, 135–36, 137–39, 141–42
control
  active, 118–19, 127–29
  popular, 21, 25–26, 66–70, 88–91, 99, 105, 106–7, 110
  virtual, 118, 123
Copp, David, 193n.100
Costa, M. Victoria, 105, 110–11, 130, 133–34

Dagger, Richard, 186n.39
Day, J. P. 17
de Dijn, Annelien, 168n.46
de Francisco, Andrés, 181n.144
difference principle, 80–82
Dowding, Keith, 32, 46, 98
Dworkin, Ronald, 89, 162, 188–89n.90

economy of esteem, 100–1, 102–3, 160
education, 129–30
Estlund, David, 193n.100

204 INDEX

eyeball test, 47–48, 58, 59, 97, 113–14, 115

fact-sensitivity, 136, 137, 138–39, 143–44, 150–52
Feinberg, Joel, 107–8
Ferejohn, John, 31
freedom
  measurement of, 3–4, 42, 51–52, 165n.9
  moralized, 25–29, 31, 34–35, 162–63, 171n.46
  as non-frustration, 16–17
  pure negative, 3–4, 18–19, 22–24, 41–43
  republican, 1, 3, 20–22, 43–48
  value of, 23–24, 83
Freeman, Samuel, 82
Frey, Bruno S. 188n.87

Galston, William, 150
Gaus, Gerald, 150
Gheaus, Anca, 193n.102
Green, Leslie, 94

Hamlin, Alan, 152, 173n.8
Harrington, James, 10
Hart, H. L. A. 167–68n.37
Hobbes, Thomas, 16

Ingham, Sean, 46–47, 113–14, 122, 137, 141, 158–59
institution, formal and informal, 13–14

Kant, Immanuel, 107
Kavka, Gregory, 185n.104
Korsgaard, Christine, 68
Kramer, Matthew
  and the Barry and Ernest example, 53–54
  and the gentle giant example, 95–96, 109
  and impartiality, 187n.53
  and the Mark and Molly example, 22–23
  and measurement of freedom, 51–52, 165n.9, 170n.36
  and prevention, 41
  and republican freedom, 2, 45, 50, 51–52, 54, 58
  and trivalence, 166n.17

Laborde, Cécile, 156
Larmore, Charles, 167n.31, 191n.36

Lawford-Smith, Holly, 150–51
liberation by ingratiation, 19–20, 43, 52–54
libertarianism, 8–9
liberty. See freedom
List, Christian
  and the dimensions of freedom, 5, 42–43, 57, 169n.2
  and freedom as independence, 173n.7
  and the republican paradox, 37–38, 39, 57
  and strong republicanism, 114, 119–20, 131
  and three kinds of normative law, 91–92
lobbyism, 88–89, 182n.6
Lomasky, Loren, 8, 11, 131–32, 160, 161
lottery, 31
Lovett, Frank
  and the gentle giant example, 97
  and neutrality, 129–30, 187n.53, 187n.55, 188n.70
  and political conception of freedom, 137, 141
  and the slave example, 56
  and strong and moderate republicanism, 46–47, 113–14, 122, 158–59
  and substantive and procedural domination, 94
  and welfarist understanding of republicanism, 172n.86

MacCallum, Gerald, 5–6, 15
Machiavelli, Niccolò, 10, 101–2, 120–21, 161
Mackie, Gerry, 105
manipulation, 18
Miller, David, 150
Milton, John, 10
mixed constitution, 88, 160
Montesquieu, 175n.51

neutrality, 120–24, 160
Nozick, Robert, 9, 24–25, 162–63
nudging, 189n.92

Oppenheim, Felix, 170n.43

Patten, Alan, 186n.20

INDEX   205

perfectionism, 120–21
Pettit, Philip
  and acceptance and acceptability
    games, 71–72
  and active control, 127–29
  and "arbitrary" 166n.12
  and the basic liberties, 8, 76–77, 79
  and common interests, 61–62, 67–68
  and consequentialism, 146, 148–49
  and contestation, 30, 89–90, 118
  and contractualism, 65, 66, 68
  and dignity and respect, 143,
    145, 148–49
  and external constraint, 104
  and feasibility, 125–26, 137–38, 150
  and interference, 18
  and the Kingdom of Ends, 107
  and liberal republicanism, 8
  and libertarianism, 8–9, 25
  and moralized freedom, 25–29
  and neutrality, 121–22
  and norms, 99, 101–3, 107
  and persistent majorities, 31
  and political ideals, 125–26, 137–38
  and political liberties, 77, 78–79
  and Rawls, 73–75, 77–82,
    115–16, 160
  and reasonableness, 65–66, 67, 142
  and trust, 127
pluralistic ignorance, 105, 106
power-sharing equilibrium, 88
prerogative, personal/agent-
    centered, 141–44
prevention, 3, 22
  subjunctive, 3, 23, 41, 49–50, 92
publicity, 144–46
public justification
  consensus model of, 70–72
  convergence model of, 71

Quong, Jonathan, 75

Railton, Peter, 191n.63
Rawls, John
  and the basic liberties, 76, 79
  and the basic structure, 63
  and the burdens of judgment, 108
  and comprehensive doctrine, 177n.15

and conception of the good, 176n.3
and consequentialism, 147, 148, 149
and the curse of money, 78–79
and impartiality, 65
and justice as the first virtue,
    137, 139–40
and moral powers, 76
and natural duties, 126
and overlapping consensus, 70
and political conception of justice, 63,
    73, 75–76, 81, 125–26, 144–45, 150
and political liberties, 77–79
and political possibility, 137–38
and political virtue, 124
and publicity, 144, 145
and public reason, 61–62, 74–75
and reasonableness, 62–63, 64, 65, 142
and republicanism, 11, 85, 116
and self-respect, 115
and strains of commitment, 141
Raz, Joseph, 94, 173n.94
republican ethos, 101
republicanism
  comprehensive, 99–101, 112
  critical, 153–56
  formal, 92–95, 97, 98–99, 112
  liberal, 8, 135–36, 159–60
  moderate, 46–47, 113–15, 122, 126–27,
    133, 158–59
  as an ideal, 143, 157
  and virtual control, 118, 123, 131–32
  neo-Athenian/Continental/Franco-
    German, 10, 131–32
  neo-Roman/Italian-Atlantic, 10
  strong, 14, 46, 113–15, 116–17, 120–21,
    123–24, 126–27, 133, 158–59
  and active control, 118–20, 122–23
  and education, 130
  as an ideal, 136, 143, 150, 153–57, 159
  three core ideas of, 88–90
restriction, agent-centered, 147
rhetoric, 161–63
Richardson, Henry S. 178n.67
Rousseau, Jean-Jacques, 10
rule of law, 46, 92–94, 173n.94
Rush, Benjamin, 129

Sandel, Michael, 10

206 INDEX

Scanlon, T. M. 62–63, 64–65
Scheffler, Samuel, 142, 147
Sen, Amartya, 38–39, 166n.15
Sharon, Assaf, 172n.74
Shnayderman, Ronen, 173n.7
Skinner, Quentin
  and common interests, 66
  and consent, 172n.75
  and corruption, 189n.92
  and the gentle giant example, 95–96
  and the neo-Roman tradition, 10
  and the slave example, 53, 94–95
slave example, 19, 44–45, 47–48, 50, 53–54, 55–56, 94–95, 96–97
social norms, 99–101
  legal, 101
  moral, 101–3
Steiner, Hillel
  and bivalence, 166n.17

and compossibility, 41
and conservation of liberty, 181n.154, 181n.156
and measurement of freedom, 165n.9
and moralized freedom, 34–35
Stemplowska, Zofia, 152
Stoicism, 16
Sunstein, Cass, 120–21

Taylor, Charles, 10
Thomas, Alan, 82
threat, 42, 50–52
trust, 127

Valentini, Laura, 173n.7
Viroli, Maurizio, 66, 129, 161, 163

Wendt, Fabian, 55–56
Whitfield, Gregory, 187n.53, 187n.55